Dorothy in a Man's World

Dorothy aged twenty-one

Dorothy in a Man's World

A VICTORIAN WOMAN PHYSICIAN'S TRIALS AND TRIUMPHS

Peter Dawson

ISBN-13: 9781523749034
ISBN-10: 1523749032
Library of Congress Control Number: 2016901664
CreateSpace Independent Publishing Platform
North Charleston, South Carolina

Whatever may befall thee, it was preordained from everlasting.

—MARCUS AURELIUS

Contents

Preface

MY GOAL IN WRITING THIS book has been to provide a dynamic portrait of an extraordinary, intrepid and indomitable woman doctor, set against the social background of the last quarter of the nineteenth and the first half of the twentieth centuries. It highlights the problems all women physicians faced in the male-dominated medical profession, and the abysmal health care physicians generally provided to mothers and their children.

When I was a resident in pathology, I developed a special interest in Hodgkin's disease and its history. Fifteen years ago I published a paper, "The Original Illustrations of Hodgkin's Disease," which included one of Dorothy Reed's drawings of the giant cells that characterize the condition. At the time I wondered why she had not followed up on this important work and what had happened to her. Inquiries among a number of the leading pathologists led nowhere. Eventually I discovered Jill Ker Conway's book *Written by Herself*, which includes a truncated version of Dorothy Reed Mendenhall's handwritten autobiography. It turned out that the people in the field of public health knew about Dorothy's work on maternal and child health. But nobody had a complete picture of her struggles in the male-dominated medical profession, the tragedies in her own life, and her formidable personality.

Fortunately, the Sophia Smith Collection at Smith College possessed her autobiography and a great many of her papers. In addition,

Dorothy's younger son, Dr. John T. Mendenhall, and her daughter-in-law Cornelia (Nellie) Mendenhall generously invited me into their homes, shared their recollections of Dorothy, and gave me access to their personal files and photographs.

My own memory extends back into the 1930s. Because I began medical school just after the end of World War II, I have a unique perspective on the practice of medicine in Dorothy's time. I have tried to convey a feeling for the period in the language and physical appearance of the pages that follow.

Acknowledgments

I WISH TO ACKNOWLEDGE THE many kindnesses and the immense amount of information provided by Dorothy's younger son, Dr. John T. Mendenhall, and her daughter-in-law Cornelia (Nellie) Mendenhall. Dorothy's grandchildren, Nealie Small and Dory Blobner, have made available their parents' collections of papers and photographs. The staff of the Sophia Smith Collection at Smith College in Northampton, Massachusetts, have always been most kind and helpful, particularly Nanci Young, Amy Hague, and the late Susan Barker. I am deeply indebted to medical librarians Danny O'Neal and Laurie Barnet for their indefatigable help with references. Henry Miller of the Wisconsin Historical Society and Gerard Shorb of the Alan Chesney Medical Archives at Johns Hopkins Medical Institutions courteously answered my many questions. Doctors Risa Mann and Grover Hutchins of the pathology department of Johns Hopkins Medical School showed me the original microscopic slides of some of Dorothy's original cases of Hodgkin's disease as well as her autopsy reports. The staff of the National Archives in College Park, Maryland, were most kind and helpful. Ms. Emily Early gave me the history of the Walrus Club. Mrs. Mary Hearn kindly showed me over the Old Stone House in Talcottville, and Dr. Harvey Barrach allowed me to see Dorothy's house on Prospect Avenue in Madison. Susan Nordstrom kindly typed the first draft of my book. I received friendly and courteous help from Rima D. Apple and Micaela Sullivan-Fowler in Madison, the staff of innumerable libraries and other institutions Baltimore and New York, and a host of individuals in many places.

Finally, I wish to thank Ann, my wife, for her endless patience during my many research trips and innumerable hours in my library.

List of Illustrations and Credits

Frontispiece. Dorothy aged twenty-one.

Photograph Patch Bros., New York, 1895. Courtesy of The Alan Mason Chesney Archives of The Johns Hopkins Medical Institutions and Sophia Smith Collection, Smith College.

Dorothy on horseback.

Photograph 1888. Courtesy of Sophia Smith Collection, Smith College and Mrs. T.C. Mendenhall and family.

Old Stone House, Talcottville, New York.

Photograph by the author, 2001.

Grace Reed and Miss Gunning.

Photograph undated. Courtesy of Mrs. T.C. Mendenhall and family.

Mary Elizabeth Garrett with the Friday Evening group.

Photograph N.H. Busey, circa 1878. Courtesy of The Alan Mason Chesney Archives of The Johns Hopkins Medical Institutions.

Dorothy and friends as nurses.

Photograph Alva Pearsall, Brooklyn, New York, 1898. Courtesy of Sophia Smith Collection, Smith College.

Doctor William Osler.

Portrait of William Osler by Seymour Thomas, 1908. Courtesy of The Alan Mason Chesney Archives of The Johns Hopkins Medical Institutions.

Doctor Henry Mills Hurd.

Photographer unknown, circa 1908. Courtesy of The Alan Mason Chesney Archives of The Johns Hopkins Medical Institutions.

Doctor William H. Welch.

Photograph David Bachrach, 1893. Courtesy of The Alan Mason Chesney Archives of The Johns Hopkins Medical Institutions.

Dorothy Reed's drawings of the giant cells in Hodgkin's disease.

"The Pathological Changes in Hodgkin's Disease, with Especial Reference to its Relation to Tuberculosis." *Johns Hopkins Hospital Reports* 10 (1902): 133-196. Courtesy of The Alan Mason Chesney Archives of The Johns Hopkins Medical Institutions.

Dorothy in her Baby Clinic.

Photograph 1926. Courtesy of University of Wisconsin, Madison, Wisconsin.

Dorothy with baby John.

Photograph 1913. Courtesy of Dr. John T. Mendenhall and family.

Mendenhall family group.

Photograph circa 1919. Courtesy of Sophia Smith Collection, Smith College.

The Mendenhalls' twenty-fifth wedding anniversary.

Photograph 1931. Courtesy of Mrs. T.C. Mendenhall and family.

Dorothy's personal photograph of Dr. William G. MacCallum.

Photograph Elmer Chickening, Boston, Massachusetts, 1901. Courtesy of Sophia Smith Collection, Smith College.

Dorothy's notation on the death of William MacCallum on page 25 of her copy of *The Meditations of Marcus Aurelius*. Courtesy of Mrs. T.C. Mendenhall and family.

Fleuron: Bust of Dorothy Reed aged fourteen.

Sculpture by Orazio Andreoni, Rome, Italy, 1887. Courtesy of Sophia Smith Collection, Smith College.

Note: Dorothy aged twenty-one; Dorothy on horseback; Dorothy Reed's drawings of the giant cells in Hodgkin's disease; the Mendenhalls' twenty-fifth wedding anniversary; Dorothy's personal photograph of Dr. William G. MacCallum and Dorothy's notation on the death of William MacCallum all first appeared in the author's articles: "The Original Illustrations of Hodgkin's Disease," *Annals of Diagnostic Pathology* 3 (1999): 386–393, or "Whatever Happened to Dorothy Reed?" *Annals of Diagnostic Pathology* 7 (2003): 195–203, and are reproduced with permission of Elsevier Inc.

Prologue

Imperative: Go Home!

IN THE FALL OF 1896, a dark-haired, fashionably dressed young woman stepped out of the sleeping car in Baltimore, Maryland. A horse-drawn cab carried her to 812 South Paul Street, where Miss Conway, a pre-war southern belle, answered the door. Yes—she had just one vacancy, a tiny room under the eaves, barely big enough for her prospective tenant and her box of books. The young woman took it. As soon as she had freshened up, she boarded a horse-drawn tram headed for Johns Hopkins Hospital.

The trolley bumped east, clanging its bell, presenting along the way a kaleidoscopic view of this new and strange southern town. Suddenly the woman realized that the only other passenger—a middle-aged, sallow-skinned man with a rat-tail mustache—was eyeing her intently. Although he *looked* like a gentleman in his gray morning coat, striped trousers, and silk hat, his unwavering gaze frightened her. She felt alone and very vulnerable. The instant the streetcar stopped at Broadway, she jumped off and hurried toward the hospital. To her horror, the stranger followed and quickly drew abreast.

"Are you entering the medical school?" he asked in a very matter-of-fact way.[*1]

---

* All dialogue in quotations is taken directly from Dorothy's memoirs and letters or other historical documents as cited.

Caught off guard, she nodded.

"Don't—go home."[1]

Without another word, her inquisitor strode ahead into the building, leaving the young woman to puzzle over the encounter.

Who was this man? How did he know she was about to enter medical school? Why had he warned against it? Almost certainly she considered his remarks impertinent and resented his intrusion into what she had conceived of as a private expedition to spy out her new venue. His unsought advice—coming after her prolonged effort to qualify for medical school and a long summer listening to her Victorian mother's nonstop diatribe over her decision to follow the then socially unacceptable career of a physician—was the last thing she needed.

Although she did not realize it at the time, her encounter exemplified the overbearing, insensitive attitude of nineteenth-century medical men toward their female colleagues—one that would eventually compromise her whole professional life. He, on the other hand, could hardly have anticipated that the young woman he had encountered was one of the very few who would never let a male physician push her around.

After some reflection, the young woman's customary decisiveness and determination reasserted themselves. She decided to ignore the incident. No man was going to interfere with her plans to escape from her mother's frivolous and pointless existence and become independent.

The next morning, she again took the streetcar to Johns Hopkins University, this time without incident. She described her experiences there:

I found the floor with no difficulty and a dozen or more men waiting in an anteroom. I remember no women being there… At last, my name, Dorothy Reed, was called and with my heart-thumping until I thought it would break my chest, I entered a long, impressive room…Around an enormous table sat a distinguished gathering of men, representing, I presumed, the faculty of the new medical school…I was too scared to do more than take the chair offered me. The chairman, or at least the man sitting at the head and next to whom my chair was placed, was the Dean, Dr. Welch…He asked questions of me, referring to the credentials I had sent to him. Then he said, "I think Miss Reed has fulfilled all our requirements." One man I cannot place, possibly Remsen [the professor of chemistry] asked me about the number of chemistry laboratory hours I had taken. When I looked up to answer him, to my amazement, next to him was the man of [the] streetcar incident. I mumbled a reply. Dr. Welch rose and bowed and intimated that the interview was over, telling me to be at the medical school the next morning at 9 o'clock. I got up and, not knowing what to do, *backed out* of the room until I reached the door, feeling that this group represented to me, royalty.[2]

On her return to the waiting room, she asked the name of the man sitting on Welch's left. Someone said he was Dr. Osler, the chief of medicine at Hopkins. The name meant nothing to the young woman.

Her acceptance into medical school thrilled Dorothy, although she had no conception of what life would be like in her new profession. Despite her encounter with the stranger, she had no notion of the way arrogant, domineering, and sexist men would try to control her professional life and ultimately ruin her career.

CHAPTER 1

Foundations

Ancestors and an Unencumbered Childhood

DOROTHY MABEL REED WAS BORN on September 22, 1874, at a time when tumultuous change engulfed the nation. The steam engine had revolutionized both transportation and manufacturing. Electricity was starting to light homes and produce labor-saving inventions. Exciting discoveries poured from laboratories and dramatically changed our understanding of science. Darwin questioned the very origins of humankind. In medicine, anesthesia dramatically changed the scope and practice of surgery. The microscope opened the eyes of physicians to disease at the cellular level, and the discovery of bacteria produced an understanding of infectious illnesses—then the most common cause of death. Social change followed. Basic education became universal, and many new colleges opened their doors. Democracy took hold, and universal voting rights would soon become the norm—for men. Women, too, were starting to make their voices heard. Dorothy's parents could have had no conception of how these changes would affect their daughter's life.

Dorothy traced her ancestors on both sides of the family to the earliest colonial times. They included two governors of the Massachusetts Bay Colony, the poet Anne Bradstreet, and, regrettably, the perpetrator of the Talcott Massacre of the Narragansett Indians. On her father's side, Sir William Reade arrived from Brockett Hall in Hertfordshire on board *Defense*, landing in Boston on October 6, 1635.[3] His great-great-great-great-grandson, Dorothy's grandfather Jonathan Reed, and his wife, Elizabeth (Temple), owned a farm near Shrewsbury, Massachusetts. William Pratt Reed, the second youngest of their eight children, attended school in nearby Worcester and then entered the boot and shoe trade. At age seventeen, with the restless energy that would characterize his life, Will headed west to Rockford, Illinois. For four years he roamed the West, reappearing in Columbus, Ohio, then a bustling city of over fifteen thousand people with many fine homes. There he found work in Hannibal H. Kimball's shoe store.

Reed's intelligence, ingenuity, and industry quickly impressed his new employer, who soon made him his partner. In 1865 Will cemented this business relationship by marrying his employer's only daughter, Adeline Grace. Six years his junior, she was a refined, poised beauty with an open heart and generous nature who brought to the marriage connections and social skills attractive to the hard-driving young businessman. Contrary to the expectations of cynics, the couple's letters reveal their deep affection for each other and make it clear that their marriage was much more than a business arrangement.[4]

The firm of Kimball and Reed prospered, but the ambitious Will Reed soon struck out on his own. He started, in partnership with E. O. Jones, a boot and shoe manufacturing business with $15,000 capital. Reed, Jones and Company grew dramatically and eventually employed 120 people in Columbus. They opened branches in Mansfield, Ohio; Omaha, Nebraska; and Baltimore, Maryland, where for a time Will personally supervised the 210 prisoners who labored for the firm. Profits grew along with the firm, and its assets would be valued at over $600,000.[5] The dynamic, gregarious, and shrewd Will Reed traveled widely on business, accumulating real estate from Tennessee to Minnesota.[6] He enjoyed his home and family as well as his fortune. He could now afford a coach, and after work he regularly rode his horses.

Will, his wife, Grace as she was always called, and their two other children, William Kimball and Elizabeth Adaline, respectively five and three years older than Dorothy, lived in a house on Town Street in Columbus, Ohio. On the morning of November 11, 1880—a day Dorothy, aged six, would never forget—she awoke to find her home strangely quiet, her mother and the servants speaking in hushed tones as they glided through darkened rooms. Her father, William Pratt Reed, who suffered from diabetes and tuberculosis, had died in his sleep. Those who knew him well thought his excessive zeal for business contributed to his demise at the early age of forty-five.[7] Highly principled although not particularly religious, he had lived by a moral code of behavior given him by his father—a code he passed on to his daughter.[8]

Dorothy adored her father—a sandy-haired man with a high forehead, aquiline nose, deep-set gray eyes, a reddish Van Dyke beard, and a warm smile. She recalled him coughing bright-red blood into a silk handkerchief as he lay in bed beside her, teaching her to read. Her fondest memory was of her father pinning bunches of lilies of the valley to her favorite white lace dress with the blue slip and giving her a big kiss as she and her brother headed the procession at a grand ball.

Years later, she wrote about him:

> [My father] was the one I turned to for a standard of conduct in those years when there seemed to be nothing else to hold on to but his memory. I even prayed to my father because... there was no one else to turn to for help...He became [my] ideal almost hidden companion, and my touchstone for conduct and important decisions.[9]

Dorothy followed his precepts all her life and even arranged her wedding on the anniversary of his birth.

Unfortunately, widowhood exposed irremediable flaws in Grace Reed's character that ultimately led to role reversal with her youngest daughter. Will Reed left his wife over $200,000, a very substantial sum in those days (probably more than $18 million in today's money).[10] Grace was an attractive, stylish young widow who carried herself with the air of a grand dame. Dominated in childhood by an assertive father and later by her driven husband, she was ill-equipped to handle her new fortune, although she relished the freedom and power it gave her. After her husband's death, she never willingly mentioned his name and assuaged any guilt she may have felt over his demise by erecting a seven-foot-high granite monument atop his grave at a cost of $1,500. In later life, Dorothy described her mother as "a woman of refinement but no culture," of great generosity but superficial values, and "the kindest woman I have ever known [but with] the poorest judgment."[11] Heedless of expense, she would buy things by the dozen to give to her friends. Her total lack of self-discipline would be her undoing.

After her husband's death, Grace was unwilling to accept the responsibilities of running a large household and moved with her three children into the home of her step-grandmother, Eliza. Hannibal H. Kimball, Eliza's second husband, had died eight years earlier, leaving her well provided for. The Kimballs were a well-established colonial family. The first of the family, Richard, had arrived in Boston on the *Elizabeth* in 1634 from the hamlet of Rattlesden, near Bury Saint Edmunds in Suffolk, and settled in Ipswich, Massachusetts.[12] Eventually the family moved to Columbus, Ohio, where they grew rich and socially prominent. There Hannibal built a substantial Italianate mansion on a forty-acre parcel of land bequeathed to him by his father. Four large, square rooms filled with heavy Victorian furniture opened off a wide central hall that led to a grand staircase. The kitchen contained the only cold-water faucet in the house, and the entire family used the outdoor privy. Grandma Eliza, a big woman with blue eyes and silver hair braided around her head, possessed a dignity and simplicity of character that children found reassuring. Forgoing the usual rigid, restrictive Victorian approach to parenting, she accorded her grandchildren almost total freedom, treating them like real people and effortlessly incorporating them into her activities. Her first husband, a portrait painter, had taught her to paint, and every day she worked in her studio. There, she showed Dorothy how to draw and later sent her to art school in Columbus. Although Grace did not approve of her stepmother's laissez-faire approach to life or to her children growing up "in a household where everybody did what they liked when they liked," she lacked the strength of character to change it.[13]

Grace, as might be expected from her unwillingness to stand up for anything or to anybody, badly spoiled her two older children. Her son, Will, in the absence of firm fatherly guidance, grew up fun-loving and totally irresponsible. He immediately spent any money he might have and was frequently in trouble—a pattern that would persist throughout his life.

Grace's two daughters possessed quite different personalities. Bess—or Bessie, as the older sister was called—drew most of her mother's attention. A typical genteel Victorian girl, she enjoyed indoor games and playing with her dollhouse. At an early age, she displayed a remarkable musical talent. As she grew into adolescence, she shared her mother's social interests and developed into a beautiful, charming, and cultivated young woman of whom her mother was justifiably proud. Dorothy, in contrast, hated to be confined in any way. She loved to lark about "like an unbroken colt" on the mansion's extensive grounds.[14] The family groom taught her to ride, and she became an enthusiastic and intrepid horsewoman. As the youngest child, she lived in her own private world: "[My] pleasantest companions," she asserted, "have always been imaginary."[15] Her mother seemed rather to have despaired over her independent—not to say difficult—younger daughter who refused to accede to her wishes. Grace Reed shared the conventional goals of all well-to-do

Victorian matrons and hoped to marry both her daughters to well-bred and wealthy young men. The possibility that Dorothy might develop other ideas never crossed her mind.

In one important regard, Grace Reed was ahead of her time. Ever mindful of her own embarrassment when one day at school she suddenly began to menstruate, she taught her daughters everything she knew about bodily functions and reproduction and did her best to answer their questions about where babies came from. She led them to realize that womanhood and the changes that came with it were normal and natural and nothing to feel ashamed of. Dorothy always appreciated her mother's openness, which gave her an unusually modern approach to sex and reproduction, although the young woman's moral values always remained Victorian.

Death all too frequently punctuated the lives of nineteenth-century families. Just one year after Dorothy's father's demise, her mother's youngest half-brother, Richard, a freshman at the University of Michigan, became ill and returned home to die of typhoid fever. Once again the shades were drawn; distant relatives appeared and spoke in hushed tones. The flower-covered casket was placed in a hearse drawn by black-plumed horses. Dorothy's mother and grandmother, their faces hidden by black veils that reached the hems of their black dresses, climbed into one of the many carriages, and the cortege began the long, slow journey through dusty lanes to Green Lawn Cemetery. Since her uncle was a member of the National Guard, his young friends in their uniforms gave a martial air to the ceremony. At the graveside, Dorothy jumped at the volley of gunfire as the flag-draped casket disappeared into the ground. At the mournful sound of "Taps," she wept.

Both girls subsequently succumbed to the same dreaded disease. Dorothy suffered a particularly severe attack, marked by frequent bouts of delirium, and was ill for almost six months (in those days in the absence of specific remedies, recovery was frequently protracted). Grace Reed hired a superstitious old nurse who frightened the girls into submission with threats of the "bug-a-boos." Dorothy would lie awake for hours on guard against these fearsome creatures; as a result she developed a lifelong fear of the dark. Tragedy struck this small family again when Bessie developed tuberculosis of the spine, which necessitated multiple visits to expensive specialists in New York City and resulted in a prominent lateral curvature of the spine. Years later, an x-ray revealed at the apex of Dorothy's right lung an old calcified tuberculous lesion. Both girls probably contracted the infection from their father, whose mother, two brothers, and younger sister—for whom Dorothy was named—had all died from consumption, as it was then called. Dorothy's strong constitution coupled with her love of the outdoors undoubtedly saved her from developing a more progressive disease.

The strain of widowhood and the girls' serious illnesses took its toll on Grace, who, for the first time, bore responsibility for the family. Feeling in need of a vacation, she set off in 1887 for Europe, accompanied by her cousins Will and Emma Kimball and her youngest daughter (both Will and Bessie were away at school). At their first stop, Paris, Dorothy spent hours on their balcony, fascinated by the ever-changing street scene; she'd seen nothing like it in Columbus. She worshipped Cousin Will, following him around like a puppy and insisting he eat all his meals with her. By the time they reached the Riviera, Dorothy, as a result of too much time in adult company, had become self-centered, opinionated, and bossy. Will and Emma, in need of a day on their own, hired a gendarme to watch over her. The twelve-going-on-sixteen-year-old girl considered this demeaning and devoted most of the day to giving him the slip. For the cousins, this was the last straw. Undoubtedly, they told Grace that her younger daughter, who had never attended school, was in serious need of both discipline and a formal education—a conversation that was to change the course of Dorothy's life.

The group journeyed leisurely on to Rome, where Mrs. Reed commissioned Orazio Andreoni, a fashionable Roman sculptor, to do a bust of her daughter. Now at Smith College, it depicts the full, rounded features of an attractive adolescent girl. Dorothy always hated it, probably because the dress with shoulder bows, which her mother made her wear, failed to project the image of the cosmopolitan young woman she thought she was. They continued south to Naples, Sorrento, and the still-unspoiled Capri, where a fisherman rowed Dorothy under the low grotto opening so she could marvel at the famously blue water. After visiting Herculaneum and Pompeii, they returned to Rome so that the cousins could watch an Easter candlelight procession. Grace, contrary to her usual practice, let her daughter remain alone in their hotel, an old palace with immensely thick stone walls and rooms so high that false canvas ceilings had been installed. Because of the exceptional heat and Dorothy's fear of the dark, a lamp was left burning on a table between two open windows. The young girl soon fell asleep. Later she awoke to find the curtains in flames and the room full of smoke. "This must be hell," she thought.[16] Quickly coming to her senses, she got up, groped her way to the door, and, shutting it behind her, left the room. Befuddled from the smoke and only half-awake, she wandered down corridors and up stairways until through an open door she spied a turned-down bed, into which she clambered and promptly fell asleep.

When the adults returned and saw smoke and flames pouring from the windows of Dorothy's room, her mother fainted right away. After the fire was extinguished, they searched the ashes, but of Dorothy they could find no trace. Distraught, the family finally went to bed, if not to sleep. Past midnight, the hotel cook returned to her room, where to her amazement she found Dorothy asleep in her bed—unharmed. Sweeping the young girl up in her arms, she triumphantly restored her to her ecstatic mother. The local populace thought Dorothy's escape a miracle and pointed her out as she went about town; the hotel took a more secular view and billed Mrs. Reed for the damages.

Their European trip climaxed with a visit to London for Queen Victoria's Golden Jubilee Parade. On the great day, June 21, 1887, crowds packed the guardsman-lined streets. Dorothy thrilled at the sight of an open landau drawn by six cream Hanoverian horses escorted by the royal sons, grandsons, sons-in-law, and grandsons-in-law mounted on their chargers, followed by a sovereign's guard of Indian cavalry. In an era of gorgeous uniforms and glittering decorations, the carriage's solitary occupant chose to wear a plain black dress, as she had every day since dear Albert's death twenty-five years earlier. In honor of the very special occasion, she'd added the pale-blue ribbon of the Garter, the glistening Star of India, and a diamond-studded white lace bonnet. The overwhelming joy and enthusiasm of her subjects surprised even the Queen-Empress. Dorothy, her heart pounding with excitement, could scarcely believe her eyes and her own good fortune. Not far away in the crowd was a boy her own age who shared her romanticism and the thrill of the occasion and, after a lifetime of cataclysmic change, would remain like Dorothy a Victorian at heart—Winston Churchill.

CHAPTER 2

Salvation

A Governess to the Rescue

For Grace Reed her European trip had at least one important benefit: it forced her to recognize her younger daughter's outrageous behavior. To everybody's surprise, she decided to act on her cousin's advice. She hired a governess for Dorothy—an action that would change her daughter's life forever.

On their return from Europe, the family, as was their custom, spent the summer at Talcottville in upstate New York. There Grace Reed for many years had leased the family's ancestral home—an imposing eighteenth-century manor house situated in the small bucolic community founded by her forebears. When Dorothy went there as a child, the black-and-white Holstein cattle that stippled the rolling pastures supplied milk to five cheese factories. These, in turn, supported a prosperous village of 120 people with a general store, a blacksmith's forge, and a wagon shop. As a child Dorothy adored the place, and as she grew older, it assumed a special significance—it became her spiritual refuge. Her female ancestors provided the model and inspiration for her life.

The Talcotts came from an old English family with aristocratic connections. Lieutenant Colonel John Talcott with his wife, Dorothy Mott, arrived in Boston on board the *Lion* in 1632. Talcott, a man of

14

substance with several servants, settled in Newtown and later moved to Hartford, Connecticut. After the Revolutionary War, his Tory great-grandson, Hezekiah (Dorothy's great-great-grandfather), moved his family by oxcart to 1,600 acres of raw land on the edge of Tug Hill Plateau. There, on the banks of the beautiful Sugar River Falls, he built a log cabin and a sawmill and began to clear his property. Later, after the original cabin burned down, Hezekiah replaced it with an elegant manor house. Following the death of his two sons, the property passed to his granddaughter, Saphronia Talcott, who at age forty-four married Thomas Baker, a widower with nine children.[17] Baker had none of the pretentiousness of the Talcotts and shocked the village by turning the house into a tavern, which at that time was a resting place for travelers rather than a bar. Baker subsequently added a ballroom over the stables and operated the village post office out of a closet in the dining room.

By the time Dorothy began summering there, the farm and mill had been sold, and the house had reverted to a private residence. The Old Stone House, as it is now called, was built to last, with two-foot-thick limestone walls and rough-hewn timbers secured by handmade eighteen-inch nails. A wide two-story covered porch shades the dark-green front door framed by lattice side windows and a sunburst fanlight. Four rooms, each with a unique white fireplace, connect to a spacious central hall; the two on the north side com-municate through a wide arch to accommodate large gatherings. In Dorothy's girlhood, water came from a well, and everybody used the outside privy. In the winter, all activities, including bathing in a tin tub, took place in the kitchen, with its large fireplace flanked by two bake ovens. Dorothy's mother remembered undressing by the fire and running upstairs wrapped in a shawl to snuggle between the toasty sheets as soon as her aunt moved the ember-filled warming pan to the next bed. Dorothy calculated that fifty kinfolk had died in the old house.[18] On pitch-black, moonless nights, when the wind howled, the house creaked, and the lamplight flickered, she claimed she could sense "shadows of [her] own blood" filling every room.[19]

The Old Stone House occupied a special place in Dorothy's heart. Like her grandmother and sister, she would be married there. While the Talcott women excited her imagination, she had no time for her male ancestors, who possessed neither cultural nor social aspirations and were content to let drink take over their lives. "You feel," her cousin Edmund Wilson wrote in his book *Upstate*, "the struggle of the settlers to make themselves a place in the wilderness, the will to found a society, and the spirit of adventure, their thirst for freedom, the need to make a new life for themselves that carried them further and further west."[20] Dorothy, as she grew older, strongly identified with the struggles of these pioneer women. She shared their sense of adventure and their physical and moral courage, and like them she strove to build a new life for herself—on the intellectual frontier of the twentieth century.

In 1887, as the autumn chill sharpened the air, the family returned to Columbus. There an incredulous, shocked, and speechless Dorothy found Miss Anna C. Gunning—her new governess—awaiting her. How could a cosmopolitan young woman fresh from Europe be subject to such an indignity? The idea that she was in need of a governess and schooling was frankly absurd. The more she thought about it, the angrier she became. She would show them! But she had met her match in this quiet, self-effacing, but tough former high-school teacher. Miss Gunning had encountered many rebellious adolescents and knew just how to handle them.

Miss Anna's first task was to get her spoiled, impetuous, and headstrong charge to sit still and pay attention. After every twenty-five-minute lesson, Miss Gunning allowed her pupil a break to stretch and "bounce" around. In good weather, the family groom carried a table and chairs into the garden so the two could work outdoors. Dorothy hated math. "Why do I have to learn this stuff?" she demanded. "What does it have to do with my life?"[21] She liked to read but spelled phonetically. She had never heard of history, geography, or geometry; of grammar, she knew nothing. Miss Gunning began with basic arithmetic and English; later she added French, algebra, and plane geometry. By allowing Dorothy to choose the books and poems they read together, she turned her pupil into an avid reader.

During those first few months, Miss Gunning almost despaired of taming her obstreperous pupil. Grace Reed's insistence on placing social obligations ahead of schoolwork undercut her authority, and many arguments ensued before lesson time became inviolate. The poised and fashionably dressed Grace Reed, with her superficial approach to life, contrasted sharply with the governess, whose frail, mouse like appearance masked a strong character, a formidable intellect, and an implacable purpose. Gradually the two women came to respect each other, and Miss Gunning stayed on for over three years. That is not to say that Miss Gunning won every battle.

Dorothy loved to ride and insisted that her mother give her governess an old riding habit and that their groom teach her to ride. Every afternoon they all went out riding together. One day Miss Gunning's horse threw her. Dorothy, after quickly checking that her governess was unharmed, galloped off in pursuit, eventually returning, triumphant, with the runaway. This is an early example of Dorothy's ability to make rapid judgments and act on them—a skill that would be invaluable in her chosen profession.

Grace Reed lavished care and attention on her beautiful and talented older daughter, Bessie, who shared her mother's social values. This made Dorothy feel like an ugly duckling and hide those feminine characteristics her mother valued most. In the spring of 1888, Grace decided to take Bessie, already an accomplished pianist, to Berlin, Germany, to continue her musical education. On the way, the pair stopped in Paris, where, feeling guilty, they sent Dorothy her first formal gown, complete with a train—a dress the fourteen-year-old never forgot.

That September, Dorothy and Miss Gunning followed them to Europe. Before they embarked, Will treated his sister to a farewell dinner in a fancy New York restaurant, where, to her great consternation and embarrassment, he got drunk. Spoiled and liberally supplied with money by his mother, he had done nothing with his life and was already becoming something of a problem.

Dorothy found Berlin much more exciting than stuffy old Columbus. Mornings, Miss Gunning continued her lessons, which now included German classes that they took together; afternoons they went sightseeing, shopping, and gallery viewing. Dorothy became an enthusiastic Berliner. She delighted in the vibrant street scene with its ever-present oompah band. She was thrilled by the grand military parades with their stirring music, the plumed cavalry jangling by, and the long ranks of marching soldiers. Walking along the Unter den Linden or in the Tiergarten presented its own problems. Arrogant Prussian officers in tightly fitting blue uniforms strutted down the sidewalks, giving way to nobody. Whenever Grace Reed saw a group approaching, she would move aside, saying, "I prefer to step off [the sidewalk] than to be pushed off."[22] Dorothy, made of sterner stuff, would stand up to them, as she did to other bullies all her life. The family regularly attended recitals and orchestral concerts, which put Dorothy to sleep. Opera was different. As the great pageant unfurled, she would sit enthralled, identifying with the heroine and sharing her dreams and perils. Wagner's music stirred her soul.

The family traveled widely throughout Germany. They saw the passion play at Oberammergau and summered on the beautiful Baltic island of Rügen. Dorothy loved the enchanting medieval towns and villages, particularly the beautiful baroque city of Dresden (unfortunately totally destroyed by British air raids toward the end of World War II). The group also visited Denmark and Sweden. Despite these diversions, Miss Gunning's lessons continued.

Bessie, meanwhile, had become the fairy queen of the family. Her enormous, deep-set dark eyes and her translucent olive skin accentuated by her silky black hair produced an ethereal look. Always beautifully attired, she enchanted everyone. To Dorothy's continued amazement, her sister welcomed the attentions of Willard M. I. Furbish, the son of a highly successful paper manufacturer, whose principal interests were music and society. They made a stunning couple as he stood singing at the piano beside her. Bessie, who always liked to be the center of attention, chose Dorothy's sixteenth birthday to announce her engagement to Willard, which did nothing for her sister's self-image. Dorothy, envious of the attention her gorgeous, poised, and talented older sister received, reacted with surly, spiteful, and obstructive behavior. Besides, she felt, in the fashion of teenagers, that her own features were irretrievably marred by an almost imperceptible kink in her nose she'd acquired when her sister, years earlier, had pushed her down the front steps of Hannibal Kimball's Columbus mansion. Dorothy chose to ignore the fact that with her well-developed figure, dark hair, and fine features, she too was becoming an attractive young woman. Under her mother's influence, she was remarkably sophisticated and socially poised, although, like other girls her age, she remained in some ways quite immature. At sixteen, Dorothy's lively intellect, her common-sense, direct approach to problems, her physical courage, and her great strength of character distinguished her sharply from the rest of the family.

The following summer, Grace Reed and Bessie returned to the United States, leaving Dorothy and Miss Gunning behind in a nearby pension. There they met Murat Halstead, editor of the *Cincinnati Inquirer*, and his four daughters and, through them, the daughters of the president of Smith College.[23] These contacts, together with some subtle prodding by Miss Gunning, started Dorothy thinking about college. Her mother wanted her to attend embroidery school in Paris and improve her French, but Dorothy could think of nothing worse. Miss Gunning, sensing an opportunity, urged her pupil to apply to Smith College and arranged for her to take the college boards in Berlin. This was Dorothy's first examination. She found it a terrible ordeal. Afterward she feared she had done poorly.

Miss Gunning scanned her papers and confirmed her fears. When the results arrived, she found, to everybody's surprise, that she had passed every subject except geography.

Dorothy, looking back over that last year in Berlin, thought it one of the hardest yet happiest years of her life. The undemonstrative Miss Gunning had taught her pupil self-discipline (so lacking in her mother and brother) and the importance of meeting deadlines. Dorothy later wrote,

> Thinking over this period in my life, I cannot be grateful enough to this quiet, austere, unattractive woman who came into my life at the crucial moment...She literally set my feet solidly on the paths of higher learning and inspired me with her real love of knowledge and respect for mental attainment.[24]

The two women stayed in touch for years.

Leaving Miss Gunning in Germany, Dorothy, accompanied by the inevitable chaperone, crossed the Atlantic by steamship and returned to Talcottville. There, with the aid of a tutor ostensibly hired to get her brother Will reinstated at MIT, she spent the summer cramming for her geography exam.

CHAPTER 3

Transformation

A Victorian Women's College

AT THE END OF THE nineteenth century, only a handful of well-to-do young women attended college; the majority followed their mothers around the social circuit until a suitable husband could be found. Grace Reed certainly expected her daughters to follow the prescribed route. She never understood why Dorothy wanted to attend Smith College and had absolutely no understanding of how the experience might change her daughter's life.

Fearful of the unknown and unspeakable moral dangers to which Dorothy might be exposed, Grace insisted her sister Bessie accompany her on her first visit to Northampton. The moment they stepped off the train, Bessie—ever prim and proper—was horrified. The contrast to Berlin, with its fashionable crowds, stately buildings, and broad avenues full of splendid carriages, was just too much. How could anybody want to live in this small, rural town with its narrow, dusty and squalid streets full of farm wagons and shabbily dressed countryfolk? The very idea overwhelmed her. As it was the start of the academic year, the streets were full of groups of hatless and gloveless young women laughing and shouting to one another—behavior their mother would never have countenanced. Against this backdrop, the demure Reed girls in their hats and gloves and low-cut fashionable dresses looked and felt desperately out of place. (Mrs. Reed always insisted on décolletage, as she thought it strengthened the lungs, although it seems unlikely that other aspects of this type of dress escaped her.) Bessie, who had attended a fashionable private girls school, immediately wrote their mother, confirming her worst fears about this depressing, disgusting, and, in all probability, morally corrupting community. She urged her to order her sister home.

But Dorothy, once she had decided on a course of action, was not easily deterred. As soon as she had settled into her assigned lodgings, she went to the college office. After a long wait in a room packed with chattering young women who all seemed acquainted, the registrar called her name. Dorothy said she was there for a makeup examination. Unable to find Dorothy's name on any of her numerous lists, the registrar asked, "What subject?"

Dorothy replied, "Geography," whereupon everyone began to giggle, as *nobody* flunked geography. The registrar gave a smile of recognition.

"Oh, you are the girl who took her examinations in Germany. They had a faculty meeting about you, and, as no one felt ready to give an examination in geography, they waived it—you are allowed to enter the freshman class."[25]

Dorothy, embarrassed and humiliated, slunk from the room.

Sophia Smith established the college that bears her name in 1875 to provide young women with educations "equal to those afforded young men in their colleges." By 1891 it was the largest women's school in the United States, with about 550 students.[26] At that time, the value of higher education for women remained highly controversial. Opponents argued that it placed too great a strain on young female minds and bodies and, in all probability, would deprive them of their sexuality. To guard against this possibility, as well as the disturbingly intimate relationships rumored to develop between some students in the monolithic buildings of certain of Smith's sister colleges, the trustees housed the students in a series of freestanding "cottages." These dwellings, with their gables and wide porches, added an air of Victorian domesticity to the beautiful, well-treed riparian campus and accommodated about half the students. Ready access to the neighboring community and its amenities formed an important part of the founder's plan, so for this reason the red brick main academic building with its neo-Gothic crenellated clock tower faced outward over the town.

Dorothy thought the college president, the Reverend Lauranus Clark Seelye, DD, came straight out of the seventeenth century. A tall, handsome, and dignified Amherst graduate, he was a father figure to his "young ladies," as he invariably referred to his students, bowing politely to them on campus and raising his hat when he met them in town. Prexy, as the students called him, felt it important that everyone should understand that "it is neither the aim nor the tendency of higher education to make women less feminine or less attractive in those graces peculiar to her sex."[27] Under his leadership, the college offered a surprisingly broad scientific program that included chemistry, physics, biology, and astronomy. Almost all his "young ladies" came from good families, and he expected them to behave like sensible, well-bred young gentlewomen.

Dorothy's choice of Smith College was fortuitous because its open, less regulated environment eased her transition from the drawing rooms of Berlin. Even so, strict Victorian rules of etiquette prevailed. For example, young men could not be received in a cottage parlor without a chaperone present. Students were free to walk or ride wherever young women could do so safely, including about town, but no student was permitted to leave Northampton unless accompanied by an older woman. Attendance at dances or football games at Amherst, some eight miles distant, required written parental consent.[28] Such restrictions sound draconian today; a century ago they represented an unbelievable degree of freedom, and Dr. Seelye's young ladies found them easy to live with.

Grace Reed, as might be expected, provided her daughter with an ample, stylish, and expensive wardrobe—including elaborate evening gowns and smart day dresses, some with short trains—all of which were totally unsuited to a New England women's college. Dorothy immediately went out and bought the "regulation" wardrobe of tailored shirtwaist blouses with leg-of-mutton sleeves and high, stiff collars, which she wore with a golf skirt shortened several inches from the floor. For much of the day, an informal gym costume consisting of a blouse and a short navy woolen skirt or bloomers, black woolen stockings, and low-heeled shoes sufficed.

Some of her fellow classmates initially overawed Dorothy. She particularly envied a tall, gorgeous creature in a "lavender gingham dress and red sailor hat, [who] looked like a princess."[29] Ethelyn McKinney, the daughter of a Standard Oil man, belonged to the "swells," the fast set at Smith, composed of good-looking girls from well-to-do families intent on having a good time. Initially Dorothy saw herself as one of them, but soon she realized that they represented the frivolous, purposeless life from which she was trying to escape. Neither a "grinch" nor a "freak," as the overly studious or more eccentric students were called, Dorothy found her true place among the "all-rounders," who shared her sense of mission and strove to balance the many competing facets of college life. She took "literary studies"—Latin, English, French, mathematics, and history—together with Dr. Seelye's mandatory Bible course. Her time in Berlin stood her in good stead, and after she had brushed up on grammar, Frau Kopp allowed her to take advanced German. Classes stopped at one o'clock in the afternoon, although there remained assignments to complete, themes to write, and, if one took a science course, experiments to finish.

Dorothy was initially assigned to lodgings in town, but partway through the year, she moved into the newly opened Wallace House, where she enjoyed afternoon teas and, after ten o'clock lights-out, daring impromptu feasts. Every evening, the students changed into silk dresses for a formal dinner presided over by the resident faculty member, who ensured that good manners prevailed and the conversation remained suitably elevated. Dorothy participated enthusiastically in numerous social activities, including theatricals, but she avoided concerts. With her outgoing personality and her well-honed social skills, she soon made many friends. Among the earliest was Kate Deane, a shy, exquisitely beautiful young woman who had grown up in Amherst. Through Kate, she acquired a series of boyfriends, several of whom proposed marriage. She was not interested.

The description of prim, decorous Victorian young ladies would hardly apply to the Smithies. As a group they possessed strong emotions, fertile imaginations, and an exuberant zeal for life. They enjoyed their freedom and lived life to the fullest. President Seelye believed in regular exercise and did all he could to encourage it.[30] Basketball, then a new sport, was played with great energy and enthusiasm. At interclass games, Dorothy wore her class colors and, in a decidedly unladylike manner, supported her team vociferously.

The students loved to dance and often polkaed and did the schottische in the cottages for half an hour after dinner. On Saturday evenings, Dr. Seelye allowed them to use the gymnasium, but only until sundown, as he refused to pay for the gas lighting. Gentlemen were invited only to the grand formal balls, or promenades, as they were called. These proms involved more walking than dancing, as only marches and square dances were allowed. During one such event, in Dorothy's sophomore year, the tempo suddenly changed, and everyone began to waltz. President Seelye, horrified at the sight of his students dancing in the arms of young men to this new and seductive beat, left immediately. His protest was to no avail; his young ladies continued waltzing for the rest of their lives.

Dorothy's freshman year passed quickly and happily. She returned to Talcottville anxious to hear all the news and revisit her old haunts. She spent many blissful hours on the front porch, reading. In the evenings, as the northern twilight slowly deepened, she would join her aunts Lan and Lin on the screened back porch and reminisce about her Talcott ancestors and the old days. At Smith she had "sensed the excitement and potential power of the new educated American women."[31] Now on the brink of the twentieth century, she saw herself setting out on a new endeavor in much the same way as her ancestor Hezekiah had when he trekked into the wilderness of upstate New York.

At the beginning of her sophomore year, Dorothy, unhappy with both her English and French teachers, registered for a general biology course offered by a new pint-sized redheaded professor named Harris Hawthorne Wilder. An ambidextrous young man, he fascinated the class by drawing both sides of a skeleton simultaneously. For Dorothy, his first lecture was an absolute revelation. When it ended, she found herself breathless with excitement. "This is it," she said to herself. "This makes sense; this is what I have been waiting for all these years."[32] Biology became her passion. She pronounced Wilder the "first great teacher [she] had ever had" and counted him together with her father and Miss Gunning as the three most influential people in her life.

Dorothy became part of a set—the Seven—that included Ethelyn McKinney (the apparition who so impressed her as a freshman) and Margaret Long (who was in the class behind her). The group stayed in touch all their lives. Pat, or Patsy, Long was a very special, unbridled person with little time for feminine niceties. The first intimation of her idiosyncrasies came when she was about to return home for Thanksgiving. Dorothy asked if she could help her pack. "I have nothing to get ready," replied Pat.[33] The trunk she'd brought to Smith at the beginning of the semester remained unopened; she simply shipped it back. Patsy disdained social occasions. She habitually dressed in a well-worn corduroy suit and shirtwaist blouse and rarely wore a hat. Physically strong and quite fearless, she once rescued a student who while skating (against the rules) on Paradise Pond had fallen through the ice. The two women became close friends, exchanging flowers and notes, and after college they planned to travel around the world and live together. Contrary to what might have been imagined, their surviving correspondence suggests a normal friendship.[34]

President Seelye decided to celebrate the four hundredth anniversary of Christopher Columbus's landing on San Salvador Island. Since the exact hour was at two o'clock in the morning, he decided to mark the event at a more convenient time. Dorothy disagreed with his decision, and she organized a student rally to mark the hour. That summer night, everyone—dressed mostly in their nightgowns—gathered on the darkened campus armed with every kind of musical instrument and noisemaker. The college clock struck two. The lights flashed on in the student houses, and a thunderous, discordant roar shattered the night. The housemothers were horror-struck. With the aid of the night watchmen, everybody was herded back to bed. Dorothy recalled it as "one of the most hilarious nights of [her] life." Prexy was not amused. At chapel the next morning, the tired and testy doctor preached on the disappearance from the English language of the word *gentlewoman*.[35]

Family problems troubled Dorothy throughout her college career and for a long time afterward. In her sophomore year, she had returned to Talcottville for the wedding of her sister to Willard M. I. Furbish. The groom's father, Henry H. Furbish, personified Grace's ideal man—rich, handsome, jovial, and socially prominent. He had perfected the soda process for making paper and owned the largest mill in the United States, located in Berlin, New Hampshire, where he lived in a huge granite mansion. To Bessie's ecstatic mother, the obvious material advantages outweighed any consideration of her daughter's feelings. Dorothy had disliked Willard from the outset; she thought him mean, selfish, and devoid of both character and moral scruples. She feared that if her sister's tuberculosis relapsed, he would fail to take proper care of her. Besides, she felt certain that Bessie's heart still belonged to the Kimball cousin to whom she had been previously engaged. Dorothy, torn between loyalty to her mother and concern for her sister's happiness, anguished over the marriage—to no avail.

Grace Reed gave her favorite daughter a lavish society wedding. An orchestra played for the guests who thronged the chrysanthemum-bedecked Old Stone House.[36] The handsome couple exchanged vows on the same spot between the two windows in the north parlor where Grandma Adaline Talcott had married Hannibal H. Kimball. The bride, attended by Dorothy as maid of honor and four bridesmaids, looked with her frail figure, pale complexion, and deep-set eyes quite ravishing. The groom was good looking and upstanding with perhaps a slight weakness to the jaw. Dorothy described the affair as "pretentious enough to rejoice my mother's heart." Privately she thought, "No more unhappy bride has ever been known."[37] Fourteen years later, Dorothy would be married on the same spot under circumstances that, in many ways, paralleled those of her sister.

Willard soon took over the management of his father's paper mill on the banks of the Androscoggin River in Berlin, in the northernmost part of New Hampshire, over one hundred miles from the nearest big city. There could be no comparison between this remote and rough mill town and its namesake city in Germany with its concerts, operas, and galleries that the newlyweds had enjoyed so much together. It must have broken their hearts. Unfortunately there was an even bigger problem: Bessie's husband was quite unsuited for a business career and had absolutely no interest in papermaking. Inevitably, financial disaster ensued.

The following summer, when Dorothy returned to Talcottville, she found Walter Martin, an old family friend and her father's executor, staying there. He explained that her mother's extravagance was bankrupting them. The situation was desperate. Unless somebody else took charge of the family finances, they all would be ruined. The natural choice was Brother Will. Unfortunately, he spent money faster than even his mother. After flunking out of Phillips Exeter Academy and being dismissed from MIT, he had moved from one unsuccessful business venture to another. By this time he had spent his share of their father's estate and was constantly trying to wheedle more money out of his mother—not exactly the man to trust with the residue of the family fortune. The crisis was not easily resolved. But after many long discussions and heated arguments, Grace and Bessie agreed to sign over their shares in the estate to the practical, determined, and hard-nosed Dorothy. At nineteen, she knew nothing of finance, but under Walter's tutelage, she soon learned, and for the rest of her life, she managed the family money, as it turned out, with considerable success.

After Grace lost control of the family fortune and could no longer help Will, he tried to beg money from Bessie:

Palmer House, Chicago.
May 11, 1893.
Dear Sis, I am going to confide in you and unless you will never say a word to any one about what I say please tear this letter up and not read any further. I am in an awful scrape and I would not have mother know it for anything in the world and you are the only one I know that can get me out of it...I must have twelve hundred dollars by the seventeenth of this month. I think I can pay you back within a year but cannot promise. I have lost this money and involved other people in it. It was not entirely my fault but I have to stand all of the blame...I can't say any more but for God's sake help me out and trust me to do

what is right. Telegraph me care of Palmer House if you help me send money by express, as a draft will delay too long.
Yours, Will
Don't ever let Mother know.[38]

Bessie's response has not survived, so we don't know whether she sent him the money. But it was not long before Will was in trouble again. According to Dorothy, in the fall of 1894, he demanded $500 from Bessie.[39] When she refused him, he fired off a terrible letter, cursing her and her unborn child. Terrified and horrified, Bessie forwarded it to her sister. When no money was forthcoming, Will sent his elder sister another demand letter in which he threatened suicide. When Dorothy heard this, she was furious over his abuse of her frail, sick sister and telegraphed back that his death would solve everyone's problem. Immediately afterward she regretted her words and spent an angry, sleepless night. She need not have worried; Will had no intention of carrying out his threat. He left his sister alone— for the time being.

Dorothy, worried and depressed by family problems that would continue to plague her for many years to come, returned to Smith. There she acquired a copy of *The Meditations of Marcus Aurelius*. This slim volume, subdivided into twelve books with numbered paragraphs, offered guidance on many of life's problems. Dorothy began reading a section every day, using the margins to record significant dates such as birthdays and anniversaries and storing between the pages clippings of prayers and poems—a practice she continued for over fifty years.[40]

Every year, the college chose two of the prettiest juniors to usher at commencement. When Dorothy was picked, she claimed it was the first time she realized she was beautiful. "Good looks," she wrote, "are something that are mighty hard to get along without, but since you yourself have nothing to do with making them, I never could see why you should take any credit to yourself for having them."[41] This superior moral attitude never stopped her from taking advantage of her own particular charms. Grace, thrilled by her daughter's selection, bought her a new wardrobe for the occasion. The two ushers, dressed in their white brocade frocks at the dramatics and their long organdy gowns at commencement, looked absolutely stunning. And they knew it: "We thought ourselves the handsomest tigers in the jungle—it was our night to howl."[42]

Dorothy's decision to go to college represented a rejection of her mother's hollow social values and extravagant, purposeless existence. Her initial goal was to be "freed from having to live with mother, and do the sort of thing she felt would be likely to make me a good marriage."[43] Now she needed to find a worthwhile occupation that would give her financial independence. Of all the subjects at Smith, biology interested her the most. She recounted how the reigning college tennis champion, Bertha Bardeen, had asked her to look after her brother Charles, who was coming from Harvard to watch her play. Dorothy described the encounter:

> He was an agreeable young man, who, like all the very young, was most easily entertained by talking of himself. So during a long afternoon, he told me in detail of a remarkable school of medicine being started in Baltimore where every student accepted would be a graduate of an accredited college with special preparation in science and a reading knowledge of French and German. My friend's brother had been accepted and was to enter in the fall. My interest was aroused enough to ask if women were to be admitted and how information concerning Johns Hopkins Medical School could be obtained.[44]

Medicine clearly fulfilled Dorothy's quest for a career that combined biology with the potential to achieve independence from her mother. That night she addressed a query letter to William H. Welch, MD, who was the dean at Johns Hopkins Medical School. This small action—taken without apparent reflection and certainly without consultation with her family or her professors—changed her life. It also illustrates Dorothy's continued ability to rapidly size up a situation, make a decision, and act.

She remembered very little of her senior year, except the Yale-Harvard football game in which Yale's infamous flying wedge inflicted such horrendous casualties among the unpadded Harvard players that a rematch did not occur for two years. She found commencement a harrowing experience: "Mother came for the weekend—but I remember very little except roaming around, saying goodbyes to old friends, and doing last things with them and revisiting favorite haunts. My girlhood had ended."[45]

In retrospect, she thought her contact with people her own age and the making of a few close friends were the two most valuable things to come out of her time at Smith. She seems to have forgotten the recruitment of Harris Wilder to Smith and Charles Bardeen's visit to the tennis match. When these events are added to her father's premature death, her journey to Europe accompanied by her cousins, the hiring of Miss Gunning, and her contact with Murat Halstead and President Seelye's daughters, the path to Hopkins is clearly laid out. But was this the hand of Providence or just plain chance? Years later, Dorothy was convinced it was the former.

Dorothy had hoped to begin medical school that fall, but Dr. Welch decided she needed extra physics and chemistry. Radcliffe refused her application to take them there, but a friend told her that MIT was now admitting women. The next day, she went to Cambridge, where she learned that with approval of the professor, she could take General Physics and Acoustics in one year, but "heat" (thermodynamics) was a third-year subject. An enthusiastic recommendation from Smith assured her physics professor that she could handle the math, although privately she had her doubts. With trepidation, both on her part and that of the professor of acoustics, who feared what the men might do, she began classes in the fall of 1895.

These were early days for coeducation on the East Coast. Only one other woman attended her classes. Dorothy soon discovered that the male students were conflicted between their respect for the "frailty" of women and good manners and their deep resentment over women's attempt to enter what they perceived as their world and their birthright. Dorothy quickly learned to arrive early for lectures, for if she appeared after the professor had begun to speak an embarrassing pause ensued while the men all rose and remained standing until she had sat down. This display of customary good manners did not prevent the chemistry students from taking her laboratory equipment and interfering with her experiments. She worked hard, and although the lectures were dull, she enjoyed the practical work. Two female seniors, embittered by their long struggle against sexual antagonism, told her she could avoid a second year at MIT by doing the laboratory work in "heat" and taking the exam at the end of the year. Borrowing their notes, she set to work to master this notoriously difficult subject.

Outside the classroom, Dorothy passed a dull and tedious year living in a boardinghouse on Saint James Place populated by highbrow Bostonians. She "read a lot and dreamed a lot," but had few friends and no romantic attachments.[46] After passing all her courses, many with credit, the highest mark then given, she immediately wrote to Dr. Welch. He replied in his own hand, telling her that she had fully met "all the requirements for admission and [could] enter the first year of [the] Medical Department next October without examination and without condition."[47]

Happy, excited, and twenty-five pounds lighter, she returned to the rural charms of the Old Stone House to rest and recuperate before beginning her medical education. Not that anybody in Talcottville cared. Her mother refused to believe that a daughter of hers could contemplate entering a profession that, unlike today, commanded so little respect and involved close contact with the socially unacceptable and frequently unwashed. Dorothy's great-aunts Lin and Lan were aghast at the very idea. During the time she spent in Baltimore, they never told a soul she was attending medical school. They explained her absence by saying she had gone "south for the winter."[48]

Dorothy on horseback on her way to her first horse show.
The house in the background is the home of Hannibal H.
Kimball where she spent much of her adolescence.

The Old Stone House in Talcottville in upstate New York. The ancestral
home of the Talcotts where the Reed family spent their summers.

Grace Reed and Miss Gunning (seated), the governess
who single handedly redirected Dorothy's life

CHAPTER 4

Feminist Triumph

A Medical School Capitulates

THE MORNING AFTER DOROTHY REED's admission interview, she joined the thirty men and twelve women who made up the class of 1900, the fourth at the recently opened Johns Hopkins Medical School. Today such an event would pass unnoticed. Back then it was an extraordinary achievement. The entry of women into mainstream American medicine did not happen by chance or simply through public-spirited philanthropy. It resulted from a brilliant campaign waged by a small group of exceptionally intelligent, progressive, and well-educated young Baltimore women imbued with modern suffragette ambitions. Anxious to escape the suffocating confines of Victorian morality, they challenged the authority of their fathers as well as the established order of things in their bid to reshape their world. Their unaided actions resulted in two interrelated events—the opening of Johns Hopkins Medical School and the first admission of women to a major eastern university medical school.

Social change followed the industrial revolution and the great scientific discoveries of the nineteenth century. Basic education became universal, and many new colleges opened their doors. Authoritarian governments were giving way to democracies, elected by the people—specifically the men. Throughout the nineteenth century, women remained second-class citizens, their lives encircled by the insufferable constrictions placed on them by men in the name of respect for their femininity. Most were denied an education. Husbands controlled their wives' lives and frequently treated them as little more than chattel. By law, a married woman's money and property belonged to her spouse, who also had undisputed control of her children.[49] She had no vote.

Women were determined to change all this. They demanded an education and opened colleges for their own sex. These, in turn, produced a generation of liberated, confident, well-informed young ladies, typified by the Smithies, who refused to accept the passive, decorative role assigned them by their brothers and husbands. Interested, energetic and progressive, they were determined to redress the wrongs to which they had been subjected for so long. Suffragettes chained themselves to trees and campaigned for the vote. Mothers bristled over the brusque, callous, and insensitive treatment they and their children received at the hands of overbearing male doctors. Determined to improve health care for themselves and their children, women resolved to become physicians.

Progress in health care came first to nursing. Women have always been regarded as compassionate caregivers. In ancient times they functioned as physicians, but by the beginning of the nineteenth century, men had almost exclusively subsumed this function, and women were reduced to the role of nurses. Even the best of these had little education or training, like the "nurse" who cared for the Reed girls when they had typhoid; many were aging prostitutes who were often unclean, untrained, and invariably ignorant.

Florence Nightingale revolutionized nursing. Born into a wealthy and socially prominent family, she wanted to be a nurse from an early age, a notion her family equated with becoming a scullery maid. Uninterested in the social whirl, Florence moped about until, when the family was taking the waters at a German spa, she was able to take three months of nurse's training in Kaiserswerth. At age thirty-one, she became superintendent of a charitable nursing home in London. When word reached the British capital of the terrible fate of the sick and wounded during the Crimean War, Nightingale's life and the nursing profession changed forever. Four thousand sick and wounded men were crammed into a hospital designed for one-quarter that number. Conditions were unspeakable. The patients lay in filthy beds without ventilation or sanitation. Nursing care was minimal and the food scanty. Amputations were performed daily on the wards in full view of the sick and dying.

Nightingale, with the approval of the head of the War Office (an old friend) and enthusiastic public support, collected a heterogeneous group of thirty-eight nurses and set out for Crimea. When she arrived she found the situation at the British military hospital at Scutari even worse than she'd imagined and the bewhiskered military establishment unconcerned. Unimpressed by either rank or facial hair and confident of the support of the minister of war, she challenged the authorities directly and refused to back down. It turned out the famous Lady with the Lamp was much more than a humanitarian; she was a highly skilled administrator and a tough negotiator. Eventually she became responsible for all army medical supplies, largely paid for by public subscription and her own money, as well as for food and clothing. She saved thousands of lives. On her return to London, she was received by the queen and given a jeweled pin. With money donated by a grateful public, Nightingale opened the first school of nursing at Saint Thomas's Hospital, London, and introduced the characteristic uniform of cap and starched apron. She published a book on hospital design and management and became the authority on health care. Contemporaneously, Clara Barton was working on the battlefields of the American Civil War and later the Franco-Prussian War, attempting to alleviate the terrible suffering of the wounded and reinforce the almost nonexistent army medical services. She went on to found and become chief executive officer of the American Red Cross. The work of these two individuals ultimately revolutionized and regularized the profession so that by the end of the nineteenth century, young women from respectable families could choose between *two* possible careers—teaching and nursing—in addition to the age-old options of marriage or spinsterhood.

Change came much later to the medical profession. When Dorothy entered Hopkins, some 102,000 physicians practiced in the United States, of whom only about 7,000 were women. Generally men denied women entry into mainstream medicine, and they were forced to practice such minor specialties as herbal medicine or hydrotherapy. The liberation of women at the beginning of the twentieth century might have been expected to increase their numbers, but progress in medicine came slowly, and parity between men and women was not attained in Dorothy's lifetime.[50]

At the close of the nineteenth century, aspiring male physicians entered the profession either through university medical schools or the numerous proprietary medical schools that then existed. Since women at that time were denied admission to almost all major universities and their associated medical schools, the only avenue open to them was through private schools.[51] These were generally owned by one or more local practitioners and operated strictly for financial gain. They usually consisted of one or two classrooms, often located over a local pharmacy. While access to a mortuary was possible, none of these schools included a laboratory or a library. The National Medical Convention of 1846 recommended three months of anatomic dissection and two terms of courses, taught by at least seven different "professors." In practice, the second term was often merely a repeat of the first. Following a year's apprenticeship (which was frequently waived), the student was free to apply for membership in the local medical society and hang up his or her shingle. Obviously, these establishments produced physicians with rudimentary clinical skills. Aspiring doctors from university-associated schools were not much better, as these schools too had no meaningful entry standards and offered neither scientific laboratory training nor hands-on clinical experience.

The first major breakthrough in medical education for women occurred in Baltimore, Maryland, where amid southern gentility and savage prejudices, the actions of a handful of extraordinary men and women brought about epoch-making changes both in the education of physicians and the status of women in medicine. The cascade of events was unwittingly initiated by Johns Hopkins himself, a member of the Society of Friends, whose unusual first name was the family name of his paternal great-grandmother, Margaret Johns. Hopkins began his career in the dry goods and provisioning business, selling whiskey under the label Hopkins Best. As his fortune grew, he moved into banking and railroads, particularly the Baltimore and Ohio Railroad, where he became a director and chairman of the finance committee. His Quaker virtues of industry and thrift made him the richest man in town. Unmarried, he long agonized over how best to dispose of his great fortune after his death. Hopkins eventually concluded that education and health care were ever-present needs in all communities and decided to use his vast financial resources to found the university and medical school that today bear his name. Anxious that the associated hospital rank among the very best, he instructed his trustees to employ "surgeons of the highest character" and emphasized that "in all your arrangements in relation to the hospital, you will bear constantly in mind that it is my wish and purpose that the institution should form part of the medical school of that university for which I have made ample provision by my will."[52] It is doubtful that Hopkins realized that the institution he envisioned would revolutionize medical education and open the door for women to enter mainstream medicine.

Hopkins died on Christmas Eve in 1873, leaving the then enormous fortune of $7 million. He directed that the hospital receive his stock in the Baltimore and Ohio Railroad and that his other assets should pass to the university—a division of funds that was to have far-reaching consequences. The trustees of the new university moved swiftly and appointed as president Daniel Coit Gilman, a tall, courteous, genial, and well-dressed Yale man. Behind his high forehead and impressive sideburns was a skilled administrator with a progressive educational approach but a conservative Victorian outlook. Within three years, Gilman recruited six professors, and Johns Hopkins University admitted its first students.

The gestation of the hospital and medical school took infinitely longer and was followed by a painful and complicated labor and delivery. The hospital trustees chose John Shaw Billings, a distinguished medical administrator and planner, to realize Hopkins's dream. Billings, far in advance of his time, laid down the credo for the twentieth-century research medical school:

> The hospital should advance our knowledge of the causes, symptoms and pathology of disease, and methods of treatment...Its work shall in part consist in furnishing more knowledge of disease and more power to control it, for the benefit of the sick and afflicted of all countries and all future time.[53]

Billings believed medical knowledge was "not to be mainly acquired from textbooks or lectures, but from observation, experiment and personal investigation," and he developed his plans for the hospital and medical school accordingly.[54] He designed a hospital composed of freestanding buildings, or pavilions, to help control the spread of infection, then a major problem. Covered breezeways interconnected the pavilions and the operating rooms and pharmacy. A separate two-story pathology building housed the autopsy room, laboratories, pathology museum, and photographic room; later two floors of student laboratories were added.[55] Billings made no separate provision for black patients, whom, he thought, could share pavilions with whites. Here he was way ahead of his time. The dominant, if not most numerous, section of the population immediately objected to this heretical arrangement, and he was forced to provide separate accommodations for the two races. (Baltimore would not accept racial integration for another seventy years.) Billings sent his plans to Florence Nightingale, who by now was an international authority on hospitals and health care. Her reply ran to twelve pages. The hospital received its first patient in 1889, and the trustees turned their attention to the establishment of the medical school.

President Gilman believed that people, not buildings, made a university, and he convinced the trustees that preclinical professors in the medical school should be full-time salaried men (no qualified women existed then) and that each clinical service should operate under the direction of a permanent chief. This novel approach became one of the main reasons for Hopkins's preeminence in the years to come. In 1885, before either the hospital or the medical school was completed, Gilman named William H. Welch, MD, professor of pathology. Welch was an inspired choice. His obsession with laboratory work, honed by his training in Germany, made him the only man in America capable of transforming Gilman's and Billings's ideas of a medical school based on science into reality. Four years later, when the clinical facilities opened, he appointed William Osler, MD, chief of medicine; William S. Halsted, MD, chief of surgery; and Howard A. Kelly, MD, chief of obstetrics and gynecology. These three and Welch were subsequently immortalized in John Singer Sargent's painting *The Four Doctors*. Henry Mills Hurd, MD, was recruited as hospital superintendent. This remarkable group of young men (Hurd, at forty-six, was the oldest) arrived full of enthusiasm to start teaching. Unfortunately, the school appeared in danger of stillbirth from lack of funds. Its $1 million endowment, invested in B&O stock, had regularly paid a dividend of 8 to 10 percent; then suddenly in 1887 the company halved its payment and, in the two subsequent years, omitted it entirely. President Gilman was forced to launch an emergency appeal for operating funds. The professors became restless. Drawn to Baltimore by the promise of a new school in which to implement their own ideas, they began to doubt it would ever materialize. Other institutions sensed a problem and tried to lure them away. Harvard tried to recruit both Welch and Osler, and McGill offered the latter, who had trained there, $1 million to build up his department if he would return. The situation was critical. Failure of the trustees to raise the necessary funds would cause the faculty to leave and abort Hopkins's dream.

At this point a group of young women intervened. They all came from the wealthy families of university and hospital trustees and happened to learn of the financial crisis facing the medical school from discussions among their parents in the parlor or at the dinner table. Led by Martha Carey Thomas, a remarkably forceful individual of great intellect, they saw a unique opportunity to advance the feminist cause. Carey, as she was always called, had tried to obtain a PhD from Johns Hopkins University, but the authorities refused her access to the requisite courses and forced her to complete her degree in Zurich, Switzerland—a rebuff she never forgave. She vowed to open higher education at Hopkins to women.

Although Carey Thomas led the group, Mary Elizabeth Garrett provided the financing and negotiating skills. Her portrait by John Singer Sargent, which still hangs at Hopkins, shows a prim, round-faced, bespectacled gentlewoman, whom Carey Thomas's biographer, Edith Finch, described as a "combination of elegance and primness."[56] Her benign appearance masked a tough and determined character. Despite an ankle injury that immobilized her as a child, she rode horses fearlessly as a girl; as a young woman, she acted as secretary to her father, John W. Garrett, when he presided over the board of the B&O and actively ran the railroad. She undoubtedly received many put-downs from her father's self-important business associates and became well versed in their shenanigans. Mary actually enjoyed studying financial reports and balance sheets and kept meticulous accounts of her personal expenditures all her life. She learned the art of negotiation from her father, who thought she possessed one of the best business brains he had ever encountered. On his death, Garrett left a fortune of over

$17 million; the residue, after various bequests, was divided equally among his daughter and his two sons.[57] Mary, a close friend of Susan B. Anthony, became a dedicated suffragette and used her money to further the cause of women. Arguably the richest woman in America, she lived in regal splendor in an imposing Baltimore mansion complete with a two-story art gallery at 101 West Monument Street, then the most fashionable part of the city. Two other women played important roles in the opening of Johns Hopkins Medical School: Mary (Mamie) Gwinn, daughter of Charles J. M. Gwinn, a prominent lawyer (later attorney general for the state of Maryland) who served as counsel for the B&O and executor for Johns Hopkins's estate, and Elizabeth King, daughter of Francis T. King, chairman of the hospital board of trustees. Close personal friendships bound the group; Carey and Mamie had an intense lesbian affair, although Mamie later married, and much later Mary Garrett moved to live with Carey after she became president of the newly founded Bryn Mawr College.

Carey Thomas first met with President Gilman in 1889 and volunteered to raise the $100,000 the trustees deemed necessary to open the medical school. Her offer did not please Gilman, who sensed her hidden agenda—the admission of women. He would have liked to refuse her offer outright, but because of her powerful family connections, he dared not. Both he and the trustees found it inconceivable that a small group of young ladies would dare to challenge their authority and the established order of things. Besides, they doubted the women could raise the very large sum of money required. The men, who had no intention of surrendering the keys to the castle they had controlled for so long, resorted to delaying tactics. Gilman explained to Carey that they were in the middle of an emergency campaign to raise operating funds for the hospital, and it would be better to wait until that was completed before tackling the issue of funding for the school.

A year later, encouraged by promises of support from friends in Boston, the women reopened their campaign. As President Gilman was away in Europe, Carey Thomas and Elizabeth King met with some of the trustees, one of whom wrote Gilman explaining that they agreed to the conference only to please Miss King's father. He continued:

> We listened patiently to what they said (and they stated their case with great eloquence) and we told them in reply that with whatever favor we might look upon their enterprise in the future, the University was not now in a condition to commence the school, especially in your absence, and that we could not even talk about it at present.[58]

Undeterred, the women organized a meeting at Elizabeth King's home, where they formed the Women's Fund Committee and elected Mrs. Nancy Morris Davis, the socially prominent widow of a Maryland congressman, as chair. The group set up chapters in several major cities where other groups were having similar ideas, and the First Lady, Mrs. Benjamin Harrison, accepted the national chairmanship. The wives of the hospital superintendent and the professor of chemistry as well as Dr. Osler's niece, Georgette, all joined the cause.

In the hope of avoiding public rancor and private unpleasantness at the dinner table, the trustees paid lip service to the idea, though, in truth, the last thing they wanted was women in their medical school. When the scholarly, grave-faced, and ever-courteous President Gilman returned home, he dissembled and wrote Mrs. Davis a letter that appeared to support the project:

> I am sure your efforts will result in great good[;] most, if not all, of the difficulties which have been suggested appear to have vanished under the wise and conciliatory measures suggested by your committee.[59]

The group organized a national convention in Baltimore, chaired by Mrs. Benjamin Harrison. The trustees, anxious to appear in a favorable light, invited the Women's Committee to visit the hospital. The lunchtime speaker was Mary Putnam Jacobi, MD, one of the most distinguished female physicians of the time, who like Carey Thomas, had been forced to obtain her medical degree abroad. Medical education, she explained, belonged in a university. She urged the audience to "participate to the full in this intellectual aspect of medicine and to follow it to the highest plane of intellectual development to which it [could] be carried."[60]

That evening, Mary Garrett hosted a magnificent reception in her palatial home. Roses, chrysanthemums, and tropical plants decorated the elaborate paneled hallway and ornately carved curved twin staircases. An orchestra played while footmen served champagne in her two-story art gallery. As the guests were announced, Mary, dressed in a blue crepe gown decorated with lace and pearls and a superb gold and diamond necklace, presented them to the First Lady, who was gowned in seal-brown velvet, also trimmed with lace and pearls.[61] Cardinal Gibbons, the head of the Roman Catholic Church in America, resplendent in his scarlet skullcap and cassock, graced the proceedings and later opined, "There is no obstacle in ecclesiastical or canon law to the education of women for the medical profession." [62] In addition to the out-of-town ladies in all their finery, the guest list included a general and several colonels, President Gilman, the trustees and faculty, as well as civic dignitaries and Baltimore society. Besides the social and financial success of the occasion, this display of feminine power produced the desired effect on the men. Welch wrote to Mull, the first professor of anatomy:

> Pres. Gilman and some of the Trustees do not want (sub rosa) the women to succeed, for they do not like the idea of co-sexual medical education. I do not myself hanker after it, but I do not see how they can refuse such a large sum of money.[63]

Hurd, the hospital superintendent, wrote a forceful memorandum to the board of trustees: "Every year renders it more and more evident that the Hospital must continue to be hampered in its work until the Medical School of the University is established."[64] He pointed out that the hospital was paying the professors' salaries and the cost of the pathological laboratory and that, after three years, the school had still not opened. The medical staff (Doctors Osler, Halsted, and Kelly) also wrote a strong letter of support, although privately Osler had reservations about women in medicine. Welch, ever the medical politician, avoided committing himself and hid behind the questionable technicality that, as the pathologist, he did not belong to the medical staff. A lifelong bachelor, he dreaded the moment when he would have to explain intimate details of the human body to a mixed audience.

The women's success greatly exceeded the men's expectations. By the spring of 1891, they had raised $111,300, and by fall the total had reached $193,023. But the board had second thoughts and responded to the women's offer by raising the ante to half a million dollars, a sum they now deemed "sufficient for the establishment and maintenance of a Medical School worthy of the reputation of [the] University."[65] Only then, they added, could women be admitted equally with men. The trustees, wishing to appear conciliatory, continued:

> This Board is satisfied that in hospital practice among women in penal institutions in which women are prisoners, in charitable institutions in which women are cared for, and in private life when women are to be attended, there is a need and a place for learned and capable women physicians.[66]

This put-down did nothing to assuage the feelings of the women but instead understandably inflamed them. President Gilman tried to repel the womanly onslaught with courtly evasions, but they insisted on discussing the matter "man-to-man." His churlish behavior infuriated Carey Thomas:

> Mr. Gilman[,] although he had approved of our attempting to raise the money when we had consulted him beforehand, used every unfair device—and he had many in his bag of tricks—to persuade the Trustees to refuse this $100,000 and would finally have defeated us had it not been that two of our fathers, mine and Mamie's, were on the University Board and another father, Francis T. King, was President of the Hospital Board.[67]

On Christmas Eve 1892, the nineteenth anniversary of Johns Hopkins's death, Mr. Gwinn called the university trustees to his home to review a long and detailed letter from Mary Garrett that clearly displayed her wisdom and business acumen.[68] To ensure the opening of the medical school, she proposed to make up the difference between the money in hand and the board's target of half a million dollars with an additional donation of $306,977.00 which brought her total gift to the munificent sum of $354,764.50.[69] She added the caveat that this money would revert to her if the university should cease to offer medical education to men and women or if proper legal proceedings proved that women did not enjoy its advantages on the same terms as men or were not eligible on an equal basis for all prizes and honors. She also stipulated that only college graduates who had taken chemistry, physics, and biology and who were able to read French and German could be admitted and that not more than fifty thousand dollars could be spent on a building.

It is doubtful that President Gilman (never a fan of "co-sexual" education) had ever received a letter that on the one hand offered him such a large sum of money and on the other told him quite clearly what he must do to retain it, but he kept his thoughts to himself, glossing over the affair in his memoirs in a single sentence.[70] It may be conjectured that he accepted neither the money nor the conditions with unalloyed joy.

The trustees were also unhappy. In retrospect, they regretted their refusal of the women's initial offer, as it had come without the present onerous conditions. More importantly, they wished they had been able to find a rich *male* benefactor, which would have obviated, in their minds, the whole disagreeable business of dealing with the women.

After all these years, the trustees and faculty were anxious to see the medical school open and complied with all of Mary Garrett's conditions. In 1922, Welch, in a letter to Harvey Cushing, disingenuously tried to claim credit for the draconian terms of admission imposed by the women.[71] In fact Huxley had suggested them in his inaugural address in 1876, Billings laid them out in his lecture at the university in 1877, and Dr. Gilman included them in his special report to the trustees in 1878.[72]

The medical school accepted its first class of fourteen men and three women in the fall of 1893. The university itself did not admit women to its graduate school until 1907 and, incredibly, not as undergraduates until 1970. William T. Councilman, MD, associate in pathology, the only faculty member who refused to work with female medical students, moved to Harvard Medical School, where as Shattuck Professor of Pathology, he would not have encountered a female medical student until fifty-two years later (1945).

The women did not relax their vigilance. The trustees decided to use the fifty thousand dollars for an anatomy building, which they were required to call the Women's Fund Building. Subsequently, the professor of anatomy and Dean Welch tried to get Mary Garrett's approval to move the plaque from the outside to the inside of the building. She refused. A little later she wrote President Gilman. She had looked at the university directory for 1894–95 and was surprised to find that the new building on the medical-school lot did not appear under its proper name but was instead listed as the Anatomical Laboratory. She demanded that a new and corrected edition of the directory be issued forthwith.[73] President Gilman promptly replied that the omission was an oversight and that they would be more careful in the future. Mary Garrett, not about to let him off the hook, responded, "I judge that I am correct in inferring from your note that you will at once have a new issue of the Directory printed and sent out and destroy what remains of the present one."[74] From this exchange, it is clear that Miss Garrett intended to keep her side of the bargain and was determined to hold the men to theirs.

The words "Supported by the Women's Fund" appear in the Johns Hopkins Medical School catalogue to this day.

CHAPTER 5

Initiation

Preclinical Years at Hopkins

AT LONG LAST, DOROTHY WAS about to start her medical education proper. With her entry interview behind her and the encounter
with the stranger on the tram only a memory, she was eager to start
classes. At Hopkins, the medical-school curriculum was vastly different from that of any other school. It consisted of two years of
the basic sciences followed by two more of hands-on experience in
the wards and clinics. Students began with anatomy and physiology followed in the second year by pharmacology, pathology, and
bacteriology. Actual training in the art and science of medicine and
surgery—the real stuff—did not begin until the third year.

At registration, the liberated and independent Dorothy took
care of something that had bothered her for years, namely her middle name—Mabel. She hated it. She probably considered it common and undistinguished. The name appears in her father's will
and on her college transcript. At Hopkins she used only the initial
M. A short time later, she began using the distinctive Mott—the
family name of the wife of her first Talcott ancestor to arrive in the
New World. In the family Bible, the name Mott has been written
over an obvious erasure. Dorothy Mott Reed is the name on her
marriage certificate, and that is how her grandchildren have always
known her.

Dorothy joined Johns Hopkins Medical School's fourth class, the largest to date. It was composed of twenty-nine men and fourteen women. In 1896 it excited comment because of its size and composition. The increase in the total number of students from twenty in the first class—fifteen of whom graduated—to forty-three came as a gratifying surprise to the faculty, who feared the draconian admission standards insisted upon by Carey Thomas would prove a serious barrier to recruitment. As Welch told Osler when they were first proposed, "It is lucky that we get in as professors; we could never make it as students."[75] Now, contrary to expectations, the school was attracting not only some of the brightest of its own university graduates but others from as far away as Canada.

The number of female students in Dorothy's year also astounded the faculty. Women made up nearly one-third of the class—a percentage that would not be exceeded for more than eighty years. All the females had graduated from established women's colleges; none came from Johns Hopkins university as female students would not be admitted for another seventy years. It is highly doubtful that any of them knew that only five percent of all physicians at that time were women and that most practiced on the fringes of mainstream medicine. The activities of Clara Barton in the United States and Florence Nightingale in Great Britain had drawn widespread attention to nursing and made it an acceptable profession for well-brought-up young ladies. The logical extension of this interest in medical care was for forward-looking graduates from the new women's colleges with an interest in science and an urge to improve the world to view medicine as an attractive career. While almost all university-associated medical schools sought to keep them out, Hopkins, under its agreement with the Women's Fund, legally could not deny places to qualified female applicants. While much has been made of the passive attitudes of women in the nineteenth century, the majority of women graduating from women's colleges were capable and energetic and, by the standards of the time, uninhibited and adventurous. They were prepared to tackle whatever took their fancy. Importantly, the girls at Hopkins thought of themselves as medical students, not *women* medical students. Certainly there were things that they did not do and a few parts of the medical curriculum (such as the male genitourinary clinic) from which they were excluded, but they accepted these and did not waste time fretting about them.

The medical-school campus included the administrative building with its imposing tower and its network of common wards interconnected by interminably long corridors, to which the surgery building and operating rooms, dispensary, and pathology building were subsequently joined. The Women's Fund Building, where anatomy was taught, was situated on the medical-school lot at the corner of Monument and Wolfe. Hopkins offered, uniquely among its peers, a curriculum focused on the new scientific advances that were changing the practice of medicine.

Much has been made of the Germanic influence at Hopkins; certainly all of Welch's scientific training took place there. In reality, Hopkins's four-year course more closely resembled that found in the United Kingdom and contrasted sharply with the two-year course offered in other American medical schools, where attendance at class was largely optional and laboratory work and meaningful clinical experience were absent.

The state of medical education before Hopkins's dream became a reality is well exemplified by the experiences of William H. Welch, the founding dean and professor of pathology. Born at the midpoint of the nineteenth century, Welch's early life was not unusual for the period. His mother died when he was six, and his older sister was sent to live with relatives, leaving him alone with a busy physician father who, in addition to his practice, found time to serve in the state legislature and to start various commercial enterprises. His father's big love was horse trading, and it seems he provided more emotional support to his horses than he did to his son. Welch's life was not as bleak as it sounds, as he spent most of his time next door with his uncle's large, bustling, and happy family. As a young teenager, he suffered a severe emotional shock brought about by his father's second marriage. He hated his stepmother intensely; the two never bonded. After boarding school, he entered Yale, where he excelled in the classics and graduated third in his class. During college, his character traits of self-sufficiency and self-control and his ability to charm people without revealing his own inner thoughts became apparent. A member of Skull and Bones, he made many acquaintances but had no confidants. As a youth, Welch showed little interest in a career in medicine and hoped to become a professor of Greek. As no faculty vacancy existed at Yale, he was forced to spend a year teaching school; afterward, with no position in sight, he joined his father's practice as an apprentice. This was not a particularly happy time. His gregarious father spent most of the day gossiping with the townsfolk and practicing medicine the old-fashioned way, eschewing objective measurements of temperature and blood pressure and mixing his prescriptions by taste. Amazingly, the old doctor was aware of the new scientific concepts of the day, including the tenet of the great German pathologist Rudolph Virchow that the cell was the fundamental building block of the body. For reasons that are unclear, this experience fired up Welch's interest in medical school, and, stimulated by his father's interest in science, he returned to New Haven to study chemistry at the Sheffield Scientific School, where the curriculum was all laboratory work—a decision that would have far-reaching consequences for both Welch and Dorothy.

Welch began his medical training at the College of Physicians and Surgeons in New York in the fall of 1872. In his first year, he signed up for Anatomy, Physiology, Materia Medica (the study of drugs), and Theory and Practice of Medicine. He soon found he preferred the hard realities of the dissecting room to the vagaries of clinical practice. He became fascinated by the autopsies that took place in what were then called deadhouses and made arrangements to attend them at other institutions. Pathological anatomy (the changes of disease visible to the naked eye) was the only scientific element in the curriculum at Physicians and Surgeons, as there was no lab work. He attended hospital clinics at the school and Bellevue Hospital, an activity that the majority of students disdained. He would later describe the final examination for his medical degree as the easiest he had taken since leaving school.

Pathological anatomy was first widely practiced in Paris and formed the underpinnings of clinical medicine. In the United States, that was as far as medical science had advanced. In Germany, new techniques for handling and processing tissue specimens as well as improved optics for the microscope had opened up the enormously exciting field of cellular pathology. Unfortunately, these breathtaking scientific discoveries had yet to reach American shores. Although Welch won a microscope in a contest and several of his professors owned one, he did not then know how to use it. After graduation, Welch performed autopsies with Dr. Francis Delafield, the most distinguished pathologist in New York City and one of the first American physicians to practice microscopy. Welch, still intent on a clinical career, realized that the center of medical research lay in Germany and Austria. Borrowing money from relatives, he crossed the Atlantic and studied among the European greats, notably Julius Cohnheim in Breslau (now Wroclaw in Poland) and Carl Ludwig in Leipzig. On his return from Germany, he set up the first pathology laboratory at Bellevue Hospital. John Shaw Billings, who had met Welch in Germany, would later mention his name to Coit Gilman, president of Johns Hopkins University. Gilman, in large part because of his own experiences in the great German laboratories, recruited him to Hopkins nine years before his new medical school admitted its first student as the medical school's first professor and subsequently its first dean.

Medical training similar to Welch's would remain the national norm for decades. The new, innovative, and highly practical training that Welch and William Osler, professor of medicine, introduced at Hopkins was largely responsible for the school's subsequent preeminence. Twenty years later it would become the model for the Flexner

Report, the standard by which American medical education would be judged for decades.

Medical school began for Dorothy, as it does for everyone, with anatomy and continued with physiology, the study of how the body works. By the end of the nineteenth century, human anatomy was relatively well known, whereas knowledge of bodily functions remained rudimentary. Her first hurdle was osteology—the study of the bones of the skeleton. Like every other student, she had her own box of bones and began to learn their names and those of the joints between them, as well as the attachment sites of surrounding muscles. She found this as dry as the bones themselves and "the greatest bore."[76] Even so, it was easier than gross anatomy (as distinct from microscopic anatomy or histology), in which, in addition to memorizing the name and course of, say, an artery, her instructors expected her to name all the surrounding structures. Accurate and detailed anatomical knowledge was of crucial importance in those days of early and decidedly risky anesthesia, when the patient's chances of survival depended in large measure on the surgeon's operative speed.

Since the dissecting room lacked air conditioning, gross anatomy did not begin until the cool weather set in. Dorothy and the other young Victorian gentlewomen were totally unprepared for the rows of naked corpses stretched out before them in that holy of holies. They were shocked. Even the men found the thought of cutting up one of their fellows deeply disturbing. But everybody had worked hard to get into Hopkins, and nobody was going to be put off by the sight of a few corpses—or the characteristic and pervasive odor that clung to their hands, clothes, and books, persisting on the pages of the latter for many years. Dorothy soon became accustomed to her macabre surroundings. Every morning, she took up "her arm," unwrapped the gauze from around it, and with energetic determination began work. The students dissected the body by regions (head and neck, thorax and abdomen, and limbs), each of which was subdivided into stages roughly corresponding to a week's work. Before proceeding from one stage to the next, Dorothy had to pass an oral quiz. For the first of these, she "crammed to the gunnels." To her everlasting annoyance, her instructor, Dr. Lewellys Barker, whom she remembered as "an industrious and extremely ambitious Canadian with devil-may-care good looks" and great personal charm, who would later succeed Osler as professor of medicine, pointed to a yellow stain on his finger and asked, "What is that?"

"A cigarette stain, probably," she replied.

"That is all, Miss Reed."[77]

Dorothy never forgave him for this affront.

The professor of anatomy, Franklin P. Mall, probably the most distinguished laboratory researcher on the faculty, never gave lectures, as he thought the students, given a cadaver and a book—not *Gray's Anatomy*, which he loathed—would learn best by themselves. He would just wander gloomily around the dissecting room, asking irrelevant questions. As a consequence, the students learned very little, and their lack of anatomical knowledge became a standing joke in the hospital.[78]

A major change since Welch's student years was the use of the microscope. Now every student owned one. Perched on tall stools in a well-lit laboratory, Dorothy and her classmates squinted into their monocular instruments, trying to make out the cellular structure of the human body. Dorothy also began to study physiology. As in all courses at Hopkins, laboratory work and practical demonstrations formed an important part of the curriculum. She learned how signals from the brain were transmitted by tiny electrical currents that could be measured with the recently invented galvanometer. The resulting muscular contraction could be studied with the latest research tool—a kymograph, which traced by means of a mechanically linked needle the pattern of the muscular response on carbon-blackened paper fastened to a clockwork-driven rotating drum. She learned how oxygen and carbon dioxide were carried by the hemoglobin in the red cells and to recognize through her microscope the different types of white cells and the tiny "blood-plates," as they were called. In Professor William H. Howell's textbook (one of the earliest multiauthored works), she read about carbohydrates, fats, and "proteids," as proteins were then called, as well as the actions of the few enzymes then known.[79] Even at Hopkins, the most advanced school in the United States, the level of understanding of bodily functions remained unbelievably elementary.

In the nineteenth century, prescribing was a definite art, although few prescriptions had any real therapeutic effect. Students learned about drugs and their effects long before they encountered any patients—a standard practice in medical schools for decades. They were shown how to prepare extracts, tinctures, infusions, powders, and pills. Most physicians had their own special medicines and tonics that an apothecary would concoct from the doctor's handwritten and frequently illegible prescriptions, using an arcane system of weights and measures with its grains and minims, drams and scruples. For centuries, physicians had employed Latin to cover their ignorance. For example, no doctor could tell a patient he was having difficulty in walking (which the patient already knew) and expect to collect a fee. But if he told the patient he had locomotor ataxia, the sufferer would readily part with his money and happily relate the details of his impressive-sounding illness to his relatives and friends.

Dorothy was lonely boarding at Miss Conway's. "It never occurred to me," she later wrote, "that you could know a man you had not met socially [i.e., been formally introduced to], so for over a year I never spoke to any of my class on the street."[80] Soon after she arrived in Baltimore, she encountered a childhood friend from Columbus, Charles Mendenhall, a graduate student in physics. She gave him her address, but he never contacted her.

Partway through the year, Mabel Austin from the Woman's Medical College of Pennsylvania joined the class because she felt the teaching was better at Hopkins. She and Dorothy quickly became friends. The pair shared rooms near the hospital and ate their meals at the home of one of the librarians. Poised, good looking, well dressed, and outgoing, they stood out among their plainer, dowdier, and less confident classmates. With Mabel's open and friendly western ways, the pair soon attracted a lot of attention from upperclassmen, as well as some of the staff. Although Dorothy refused to take personal credit for her good looks, she always enjoyed the resulting attention.

In February 1897, she wrote home:

> There are three Yale boys, in our class. And they almost went mad with delight last week, when they abstracted some of the eggs we keep in a pail outside the back window, and put them back boiled. It was funny, but we never intimated we had discovered it. I am glad you liked my sampler and hope it will make up well—love to Bessie and Will. Keep up the courage and believe me—your angel babe—Dorothy.[81]

In her second year, the dry bones were left behind and Dorothy made her first exciting contact with practical medicine—in the laboratory and at the autopsy table. At the end of the nineteenth century, pathology represented the apex of medical science and formed the basis of the scientific approach to medical practice that the faculty at Hopkins espoused. It is the study of the causes and mechanisms of disease and provides an introduction to clinical medicine and surgery. In those days it also included the relatively new and very important subject of bacteriology, which held the key to understanding infectious diseases, which then accounted for the majority of deaths.

The major course in Dorothy's second year was pathological histology. She studied the basic pathological processes of inflammation, thrombosis and infarction, wound healing, and tumor development and spread. With the aid of her microscope, she began to understand the cellular changes in disease and how they brought about the patient's signs and symptoms and ultimate demise. Every Monday morning in January and February, she attended Dr. Welch's eleven o'clock lecture. Arriving late, a little breathless, and without notes, he would pick up exactly where he'd left off the week before, saying, "Last time, I was..." almost as though he had never left the room.

Dorothy never forgot:

The clarity, simplicity, and remarkable synthesis of his material—made the most perplexing and difficult problem seem simple. Always pointing out, however, how much needed still to be cleared up and how incomplete was our knowledge of apparently simple phenomena. His memory was encyclopedic—we thought he knew everything there was to know.[82]

And he came close, as he read both the American and German literature. His lectures enchanted Dorothy; pathology became her field.

Welch, known behind his back as Popsy, was an enigma to his students, a status summarized in this ditty:

Nobody knows where Popsy eats,
Nobody knows where Popsy sleeps,
Nobody knows who Popsy keeps,
But Popsy.[83]

Welch, at this period in his life, was a soft-spoken balding man with a full beard (later replaced with a well-trimmed goatee), and a twinkle in his eye. He lived in the hospital together with Osler and Councilman, sharing with the latter a passion for baseball. Later he rented a couple of rooms, moving only once, when his landlady changed houses. He never owned anything resembling the spacious Victorian mansions that housed his senior colleagues, and as a result he could never entertain the students in his home the way they did. Warm personal contacts were not his forte; he kept his inner feelings to himself. Probably because of this, he never developed the close friendly rapport with the students that Osler and many faculty members achieved. A self-indulgent clubman, every night he ate dinner at the Maryland Club, which was renowned for its food, with a consequent annual expansion in his girth. His only regular female contact was with his sister; he never married. It has been said that he was basically lonely but covered his loneliness with a veneer of activity. Every year he took a solitary two weeks' vacation at the Hotel Dennis in Atlantic City, New Jersey.

Under Welch's leadership, the pathology department, with its active research program and commitment to teaching, became the model for other medical schools. Its principal responsibility was to autopsy deceased patients, a task shared by all staff pathologists. Besides determining the cause of death, an autopsy was an important teaching tool and provided valuable data for research and quality control. For the first time, Dorothy came in contact with patients, albeit dead ones on the autopsy table. The mortuary at Hopkins was two stories high, light, and airy. A spartan, sparsely furnished place, it possessed a distinctive odor. Large stone-topped tables, each surmounted by a smaller wooden one, occupied the center of the room. The latter would fit over the deceased's legs and was where the pathologist dissected the organs after they had been removed from the cadaver. Nearby was a scale; the weight of each organ, diseased or not, was recorded meticulously in pounds and ounces. A cabinet for the saws, knives, forceps, and scissors and a sink and bucket completed the basic equipment. A well-drained tile floor allowed easy cleaning. Dorothy and the other students stood on a tiered viewing stand to watch the daily autopsies. She felt with her bare hands the diseased, blood-dripping organs as the pathologist explained the cause and manner of death. Generally, an autopsy confirmed the clinical diagnoses, but sometimes it did not; frequently it would reveal diseases or abnormalities totally unsuspected by the attending physician. In addition to her attendance in the deadhouse, she spent a lot of time in the laboratory, looking down her monocular microscope at the myriad of cells that, according to recent Germanic theory, formed the building blocks of the body. She learned to correlate what she saw at the autopsy table and with her microscope with the deceased's clinical symptoms and the findings of the physical examination. The pathology museum, with its rows of glass jars containing pickled specimens, both human and animal, that demonstrated every kind of pathological process and congenital abnormality, fascinated her. After she had moved on to clinical work, she returned regularly to the pathology department to follow up on her cases. Welch noticed her enthusiasm and suggested she undertake a research project that involved injecting mice with *Bacillus pseudotuberculosis* and studying the resulting disease microscopically. In 1901, she presented her findings at a symposium honoring Welch on the twenty-fifth anniversary of his graduation from medical school.[84]

The discovery of bacteria in the latter part of the nineteenth century led to a new understanding of infectious disease. In her bacteriology course, Dorothy learned the principles of sterilization and antisepsis as well as how to safely grow and identify the various disease-producing microorganisms. She heard about immunity, vaccination, and serum therapy, some of which she would later forget, with near-fatal results.

In their second year, Dorothy and Mabel moved into a six-room house, where they were joined by two freshmen, Mabel Simis and Pat Long, Dorothy's dear friend from Smith. Although the two women remained friends for life, their relationship was complex. Dorothy ranked Pat as "the most honorable person I know." Even so, she had tried to dissuade her from coming to Hopkins, as she thought her ill-suited to medicine and incapable of the sustained effort required. "She never was a balanced personality," Dorothy wrote. "Of all the women I have known, she had no feminine traits—no liking for clothes, or interest in the other sex. She should have been a man."[85] Pat thought so, too. For most of her life she wore men's clothes. During medical school she spent so much time in Washington playing host for her father, the affable John Long, a former governor of Massachusetts and now secretary of the navy, that she graduated a year late. Eventually Pat established a family practice in Denver, Colorado, and gave Dorothy's children, who called her Auntie Pat, enough money for them each to buy a summer home.

Life in the Pillbox, as the rented house was called, was infinitely more complicated and challenging than in lodgings. Maids came and went with great rapidity; one stole Dorothy's rings, and she had to go to the police court to retrieve the pawn tickets. On Saturday nights the girls ate dinner at an oyster house before going to the theater; on Sunday mornings they shopped at Lexington Street Market for that night's dinner.

One evening, at a reception given by President Gilman, Dorothy, wearing her best dress, was standing rather forlornly in a room crowded with graduate students when she spied the familiar face of Charles Mendenhall. In her direct way, she asked him why he had not contacted her. He said he had tried, but she had moved from the address she had given him. She thought his excuse ridiculous, as he had only to ask the school for her address. Despite this confrontational beginning, the pair found they had a lot to talk about, and after the party broke up, she took him back to the Pillbox. They soon began spending Sundays together, often taking long walks in the lovely, still-unspoiled Maryland countryside before returning for dinner. Charles, with his already thinning head of hair and slim figure, seemed out of place in that unconventional, boisterous household rife with medical jokes, but with his genuine interest in people and his quiet sense of humor, he soon endeared himself to the group. While the girls teased Dorothy about her "beau," Charles continued his visits, and a close friendship developed. In later years, Charles claimed it was love at first sight, but Dorothy insisted that during those Sunday visits, there was "never the slightest hint of love between [us]."[86] After Charles finished his PhD, he took a position at Williams College. They corresponded regularly.

He invited her to his family's home in Worcester, Massachusetts, where his father was president of the Polytechnic Institute. On her arrival, Dorothy realized his parents assumed they were engaged. The next day, she—using a letter from her mother as her reason for returning home—was "laughing to [her]self…safely on the train bound for Talcottville."[87] Her subsequent excuse that she had no idea a visit to the son of a family friend could be so interpreted is, of course, nonsense. Perhaps she thought it best to escape from a difficult situation, or possibly it was glee at the idea of thwarting the plans of his mother, for whom she never cared. Either way, her reaction seems extreme.

An event midway through Dorothy's second year caused her severe emotional trauma. Mabel Austin suggested they attend one of the bimonthly meetings of the Hospital Medical Society, which always attracted a large crowd. At the last minute, Mabel could not go, so Pat Long accompanied her. They sat, as Dorothy always did, in the front row. Dr. Simon Flexner introduced the speaker, Dr. John Mackenzie, clinical professor of laryngology at Hopkins and president-elect of the American Laryngeal Association. As he rose to speak, Dorothy realized with horror that they were the only women present. Mackenzie, as was not uncommon, began his talk with a risqué story; from there matters went downhill. He had recently published a paper on the relationship between erectile tissue in the nose and that in the genitalia; suitably embellished, this formed the topic of his lecture.[88] He took full advantage of the endless opportunities for lewd humor, noting for example a correlation between a large nose and watery nasal discharge with "excessive indulgence in venery" (and masturbation). Individuals in the audience were singled out to provoke laughter.

Dorothy recalled:

We sat just opposite the speaker and the chairman, so that the flushed, bestial face of Dr. Mackenzie, his sly pleasure in making his nasty points, and I imagine the added fillip of doing his dirt before two young women, was evident. I knew that we could not go out—not only should not, but I doubted that I could make the distance to the door without faltering. The decision to sit it through was the right one, so I fastened my gaze on [Dr.] Simon Flexner and prayed that he would not laugh. Roars of laughter filled the room behind us at every dragged-in joke of Dr. Mackenzie and at every allusion to the similarity of the nose to the male reproductive system. Through it all Simon Flexner sat like a graven image, his face absolutely impassive like the profile on an old Roman coin. All my life have I been grateful for this man's decency, which at the time seemed to be an anchor to buoy me through this ordeal. Somehow the talk came to a close. I got up and, followed by Pat, made for the door through a sea of leering, reddened faces. We got outside and started to walk down the parkway in the center of Broadway. I cried all the way home—hysterically—and Pat swore, [and] characteristically put it down to the natural bestiality of men and ignored it entirely.[89]

Mackenzie's performance in the presence of two young Victorian ladies was inexcusable. Unfortunately, lectures of this type at medical-student society meetings remained common for many years afterward.

The next day, Dorothy, unable to face the class, stayed home. She understood that the mere admission of women to medical school was not going to alter the attitudes of the vast majority of male physicians. What upset her most was the realization that men she liked and respected were no different from the rest. She considered abandoning medicine, but never a quitter, she began to think how best to cope with it. By week's end she had regained enough composure to go down to the lab to catch up on her work. While she was looking down her microscope, an instructor, Dr. Carter, the son of the president of Williams College, came up and asked if she needed help, and after a pause he added, "Miss Reed, I want to say every decent man at the meeting Monday night felt the way you looked. I want to apologize for being at such a meeting."[90]

In the early months of 1898, mass hysteria, fanned by the newspapers of Joseph Pulitzer and Randolph Hearst, gripped the nation and precipitated the Spanish-American War. Fervor to alleviate the sufferings of the Cubans and indignation over the sinking of the *Maine* engulfed the medical students. Immediately after hostilities began, Dorothy, Pat, and the two Mabels (Austin and Simis) volunteered for the navy. Nothing happened for a time, and then suddenly the Department of the Navy ordered them to report within seven days to the Brooklyn Navy Hospital, where they would act as nurses. Thrilled to be part of the war effort but more than a little apprehensive about their lack of clinical training (they were still in their second year), the girls raced around, finishing classes and taking exams. They bought nurse's uniforms and packed their bags. With good wishes from their professors and cheers from their fellow students, they boarded the train for New York.

The navy yard consisted of a large, rambling collection of old buildings with a lawn on one side and pine trees that sloped down to the water. Half-empty in peacetime, the yard now was packed with sailors. On their arrival, an armed sentry escorted them to the office of the medical director, who, uncertain of their role but unwilling to argue with the secretary of the navy (Pat's father), assigned them officers' quarters that included a private dining room staffed by a black mess attendant. They found their first meal unnerving, as every time someone spoke to the attendant, he dropped whatever he was holding. The next day, they learned that he had been asleep below decks when the *Maine* blew up and later was found clinging to floating wreckage in the harbor. After his rescue, he remained hospitalized, suffering from what today would be termed posttraumatic stress syndrome. The girls solved the meal problem by never looking at or addressing him directly. They soon met the medical officers, whom Dorothy thought "were an indifferent lot and avoided us"; more likely, their duties left little time for medical students.[91]

The four young women, in their long dresses, starched white aprons, high collars, white bow ties, and Hopkins-style nursing caps, helped bathe and feed the patients and dress their wounds, bringing to that austere male establishment a touch of femininity that must have cheered the sailors. After Dorothy left at the end of July, she received this letter from the surgeon general of the United States Navy:

You were the first women nurses ever employed in a Naval Hospital. You have broken the tradition of years, but you have done it with the gentleness that always accompanies women's work.[92]

The Friday Evening group of well-connected young ladies who spearheaded the drive to open Johns Hopkins Medical School to women. Mary Elizabeth Garrett is in the center wearing spectacles; clockwise from top left are Mamie Gwinn, Bessie King, Julia Rogers and Carey Thomas

The four medical students who served in the United States Navy during the Spanish-American War. Dorothy is at the back, and Margaret Long, wearing spectacles, is in the center, together with Mabel Austin and Mabel Simmis

CHAPTER 6

Progression

Hands-On at Last

DOROTHY SPENT THE REMAINDER OF the summer in Talcottville, where she thought a lot about the year ahead. She knew the first two years of medical school were the hardest and was certain she could handle the intellectual side; what worried her was dealing with the men. The few women in the first three classes had found the clinical years tough going; now that they made up nearly one-third of the class, the men generally had left them alone, at least so far. Sexual antagonism had not vanished; it simmered beneath the surface. Dorothy fretted about working under male interns and residents, who, irrespective of their personal ideas and beliefs, were compelled to work with the female students. There remained many at Hopkins who thought women had no business in medical school. The remark attributed to William Osler, "Human kind might be divided into three groups—men, women, and women physicians," may be apocryphal, but it represented a common attitude.[93] A male student from a later class wrote:

> I hear that one of our "hen medics" is to be married soon. She is following a wise course. I hope that about four others in our class (and that's all of them) will have some such hard luck as that. A woman has no business going into Medicine. She can't do it without unsexing herself.[94]

71

Doubtless, this man was not alone in his thinking; others seemed happy enough with the situation. Bertram Bernheim, class of 1905, in a memoir written many years later and perhaps rendered more benign by hindsight and the passage of time, admitted that there had been rough stuff in the past but thought that nobody could totally escape the women's "softening" influence. Nor did he observe any coarsening or lowering of standards on the part of the women and felt that "an interesting, entirely wholesome camaraderie developed." He considered that the admission of women to Hopkins was "a happy event," and perhaps for the men it was; it was not always so pleasant for the female minority.[95]

After a lot of thought, Dorothy developed an approach to her male colleagues that served her well:

> As long as I was in medicine I would never object to anything a fellow student or doctor did to me or in my presence if he would act or speak the same way to a man. If he were a boor, he would act like one—be loose in his conversation or jokes, slam a door in your face, hog the best of everything, be oblivious of any of the niceties of life or the courtesies—but if he discriminated against me because I was a woman—tried to push me around, was offensive in a way he wouldn't be to a man, I would crack down on him myself—or take it up with the authorities if he proved too much for me alone. On the whole, this was the right way to take the position of women in medicine in the nineteenth century. It made life bearable, allowed me to make friends with some men who were not very pleasant persons—but knew no better, and earned me the respect and friendship of many of my associates. It didn't endear me to one or two I fell afoul of, and undoubtedly I developed independence, even arrogance, which was foreign to my original nature. I was distinctly not such a "nice" person, but a stronger one, after Johns Hopkins.[96]

This paragraph contains the germ of Dorothy's intense feminism, which continued strong throughout her life.

With the onset of clinical work, Dorothy was thrust into a bustling hospital environment crammed with medical personnel all stratified by subtle variations in dress or uniform, rushing hither and thither. The effect was more than intimidating; it was overwhelming. But when her first patient called her "Doctor," she swelled with pride and delight. Her troubles were forgotten. Her goal was in sight.

Clinics and ward rounds replaced lectures and laboratories. Her third year began with History Taking and Physical Diagnosis. The class was divided into small groups so that everybody could get hands-on experience. Dorothy learned the four basic methods of physical examination: inspection, palpation, percussion, and auscultation with the stethoscope. At a time when x-rays were a novelty and few laboratory tests were available, every diagnosis had to be based on the history and physical. Without a diagnosis, the prognosis could not be predicted, and without either of these, there could be no rational treatment or measure of its effectiveness.

Dr. William Osler, chief physician to Johns Hopkins Hospital, bore responsibility for all medical cases. Whenever he met Dorothy in one of the long hospital hallways, he would take her by the hand and say, "I am *so* sorry, *so* sorry to see you."[97] His original enigmatic remark as she got off the tram was undoubtedly influenced by the fate of the three women in the first class: one married the professor of anatomy and the second gave up medicine to become a Christian Scientist, leaving only the third to graduate (with honors). Osler's 1891 article in *Century Magazine* probably more accurately delineates his position: "This is right: if any woman feels that the medical profession is her vocation, no obstacles should be placed in her way of obtaining the best possible education."[98]

William Osler, a Canadian, obtained his medical degree from McGill University, where he was appointed professor of medicine at age twenty-five. After two years at the University of Pennsylvania, he moved to Hopkins to become the leader and, at age thirty-nine, the oldest of the famous four founding professors. Osler, his eyes sparkling with the joy of living, infected everyone with his energy and high spirits. He loved practical jokes. A classmate of Dorothy's described him:

> In his frock coat with his scrupulously neat appearance, he was typically the consulting physician, honored and esteemed by all who came in contact with him, but there was no austerity in him. His twinkling eye, his quick steps, his frequent quips, his friendliness of manner, his habit of putting his hand on the shoulder of assistants, students and friends as he talked and talked, all brought into his clinics and ward visits a delightful tone of informality.[99]

Osler dominated clinical teaching at Hopkins. "The student," he explained, "begins with the patient, continues with the patient, and ends his studies with the patient."[100] Books and lectures were tools— a means to an end. The outpatient clinic, he believed, was the best place to learn, and observation was the first skill for the medical student to master. At the end of the nineteenth century, one man could master the entire field of internal medicine; Osler was such a man, and he single-handedly wrote the standard textbook.[101]

The patients who thronged Johns Hopkins Hospital and its clinics presented a sorry sight: distressingly poor, clad in little more than rags, often undernourished, ravaged by drink and venereal disease, and all too frequently unwashed. Their children suffered from vitamin deficiencies and hookworm. Those fortunate enough to have work delayed visiting the doctor or hospital as long as possible because they could not afford to take time off. For most of the students, this was their first exposure to debilitating poverty and devastating disease, which left their mark in a hospital mortality rate of over 50 percent. The impact on Dorothy and the other young gentlewomen accustomed to the quiet dignity and formal manners of the Victorian parlor must have been tremendous.

Three days a week, Dorothy attended the dispensary, where she would be assigned a case to examine and present to "the Chief," who would perch on the edge of an oak table, one leg dangling, with the patient lying before him on a wicker couch. This way, the sick person could hear his voice, but his expressive hands and face, which often said so much more, were visible only to the audience. He delighted in quizzing the students and assigning them articles to review and reports to make; he expected them to follow up with their patients when they returned to the clinic or were admitted to the hospital. If somebody failed to keep an appointment, the student had to visit that person at home. Osler could be severe and biting if the occasion demanded but never with the students, whom he skillfully drew out so they always felt they had done their best. He possessed many of the qualities that Dorothy found attractive in men, and over the years they developed a close collegial relationship.

At noon on Wednesdays, Dorothy attended his clinical demonstrations to the combined third- and fourth-year classes. His favorite teaching cases included pneumonia, typhoid fever, and syphilis, which, together with tuberculosis and malaria, accounted for the majority of infectious diseases seen in Baltimore. Osler loved to discuss cases of lobar pneumonia, then a very common disease, remarkable for its dramatic onset—the patient would be going about his or her business and suddenly start to shiver violently, and within a few hours, he or she would be lying critically ill and close to death.

Twice a week, Dorothy took Clinical Microscopy, where she learned how to count blood cells, analyze urine, and search specimens of stool for parasites. She had her own place in the laboratory, with a microscope and set of reagents, and could go there anytime to examine a specimen from one of her patients. She attended lectures on a wide variety of clinical subjects, including psychiatry, hygiene, and the history of medicine.

On the domestic side, the group eventually gave up the house-keeping hassles of the Pillbox, and Dorothy and Pat Long rented an apartment on Saint Paul Street. One warm spring Saturday evening, Dorothy was working at Pat's desk, as the light was better, when Harry, the janitor, came upstairs to ask a question. She answered and thought nothing of it. When he kept returning on one pretext or another, she began to wonder why. As darkness fell, the reason flashed across her mind—Harry knew that Pat was away and she was alone. Panic-stricken, she pulled Pat's six-shooter from the drawer and placed it on the desk. Again she heard footsteps on the stairs. Harry appeared, "talking rather foolishly," and started toward her. Terrified but struggling to appear calm, Dorothy placed her hand on the gun. After a moment's hesitation, Harry said he must be going. He turned and left. Dorothy jumped up and locked the door and windows.

The next morning her landlady summoned her to the phone. Patsy was calling, frantic over a newspaper story—a woman had been raped and murdered in their alley, and the police had arrested Harry. The crime apparently had taken place soon after Dorothy, his original target, had scared him away with the gun. Years later she remembered the incident:

> I have never come closer to death, but as happened to me several times in my life, God has given me the sense at the right moment to make the right gesture. In this case, it was the hand on the gun that I did not know how to fire.[102]

Dorothy studied surgery under Dr. William S. Halsted, whom she found a "queer, distorted character and difficult to understand [who] frightened the students to death and made them feel like fools."[103] As a young surgeon, he had investigated the anesthetic properties of cocaine, using himself and his two assistants as guinea pigs. All three became addicts. Welch had brought Halsted to Baltimore and put him to work in his laboratory, hoping that he could break the habit. About the time he taught Dorothy, Halsted had substituted morphine for cocaine and was taking three grains (sixty-five milligrams) daily (ten times the usual dose), which probably accounted for his strange demeanor.[104] In the end, he conquered the habit, but his two assistants died tragic deaths. A meticulous operator, Halsted designed and perfected the radical mastectomy, the standard treatment for breast cancer for over sixty years. He introduced experimental animal surgery into America and revolutionized surgical training.[105]

Dorothy dreaded obstetrics "as being very personal" and was prepared to dislike the professor of obstetrics, whom she suspected of having different standards for men and women. Dr. J. Whitridge Williams was a member of one of the snobbish first families of Virginia (an ancestor had administered the oath of office at George Washington's second inauguration). His tall, handsome figure and his colorful and gruff hard-driving personality captivated Dorothy, as it did so many of his patients.[106] He always began his lectures with a dirty story and never missed a chance for burlesque-type humor. "The jokes were truly humorous," she wrote, "after all, humor is humor—smutty or not. I laughed heartily at most of his jokes."[107] Such was the broadening effect of three years of medical school. After she did well in the examination, Williams offered her a summer fellowship. Since it was the first time he had offered it to a woman, she took it. The experience was to prove invaluable. The male students upset her by saying she got the job because she laughed at his jokes. "Apple polishing," she wrote, "was very distasteful to me, always."[108]

Before beginning obstetrics, Dorothy, at Dr. Welch's suggestion, spent a month working in the laboratory of Dr. Tracy B. Mallory, a distinguished Boston pathologist. She made the long trip north by coastal steamer, accompanied by Mabel Austin and Gertrude Stein, her good friend from the class below. In idyllic weather the three young women lay on deck under the stars while Gertrude in her deep voice recited Kipling's "The Conundrum of the Workshop" and other poems.

Gertrude lived with her brother, Leo, in a house on Saint Paul Street, to which they often would invite the female medical students. In many ways Dorothy and Gertrude were opposites: the one dumpy, homely, and unfashionable; the other trim, good looking, and well dressed. Gertrude was the philosopher, the cerebral one, but lazy and overreliant on other people. Dorothy, in contrast, was practical, pragmatic, energetic, and independent. While Dorothy knew and loved art, it is hard to envision her collecting Picassos and other impressionist art the way the Steins did at the beginning of the twentieth century.

The obstetrics faculty refused to pass the clinically inept Gertrude. Dr. Mall, the anatomy professor, thought she deserved a second chance and gave her a summer problem that, if completed successfully, would enable her to graduate. Gertrude struggled for weeks trying to reconstruct the human embryo brain from hundreds of serial microscopic sections. After she submitted her work, Mall puzzled over the results for several days before he gave up and asked Florence Sabin, who had worked on a similar problem, to try to unravel it. The human embryo lies curled up in the fetal position, and when Gertrude began to make her microscopic sections, she failed to uncurl it, with the result that the tail end of the spinal cord was included in the sections of the brain.[109] Dorothy's account is at variance with that given in Stein's third-person autobiography:

> The last two years of medical school she was bored, frankly openly bored...She always says she dislikes the abnormal, it is so obvious. She says the normal is so much more simply complicated and interesting.[110]

Whatever the reason, Gertrude abandoned medicine to lead a unique literary life in Paris with Alice B. Toklas.

In Boston, Dorothy learned to make microscopic slides and assisted with autopsies, eventually becoming competent enough to perform one unaided, including sawing open the skull and removing the brain. She stayed in Concord with the family of a friend from Smith who knew all the literary families—the Alcotts, the Thoreaus, and the Hawthornes. They took her to call on Miss Emerson, who showed her the great man's study. Dorothy spent the weekends wandering about the countryside, canoeing on the river, and visiting the revolutionary battlefields around Lexington, where her Reed ancestors had fought the British.

From Boston, Dorothy and Mabel Austin joined Mabel Simis, who was working at King's County Hospital in Brooklyn, an enormous building flanked on one side by an insane asylum and on the other by an institution for mentally retarded children. The three women attended ward rounds, watched many operations, saw numerous autopsies, and even visited the leper ward. Today, it is impossible to imagine the squalor, the smell, and the suffering in those old charity hospitals. But this was nothing compared with the horror of the home for retarded children, where the more severely afflicted were tied in beds or chairs while others lay on the floor in their soiled clothes, some howling, some performing purposeless repetitive movements, and others staring catatonically into space. Dorothy remembered it as "quite the most sickening place [she had] ever been in," where nothing could be done then for those poor children.[111] Half a century later, little had changed.

When Dorothy returned to Baltimore to begin her obstetric fellowship, summer was at its most oppressive, humid height, and everybody who was able had long since left the city. The two students on service were assigned to two rooms with an interconnecting bath in the home of the superintendent of grounds. As Dorothy was the first woman to rotate onto the service, the super and his wife viewed the arrangement with great suspicion. She found her classmate, Glanville Rusk, already installed in the room without the night alarm, as he thought it more decorous for her to come to wake him. A gentle, thoughtful man with many sisters, he contrasted sharply with the obstetric extern—a tough, disagreeable man from the unpopular class ahead who made passes at the female students. Dorothy disliked the latter intensely and snubbed him on every occasion, although she was beginning to wonder whether that had been the wisest course. The extern took the day calls, leaving the two medical students to handle the night work on their own.

Initially, when the alarm rang in her room, Dorothy would get up and knock on Rusk's door, but she soon found the only effective way to wake him was rush into his room in her nightgown, shake him and sit him up, and then dash back to her room and put on her uniform. Rusk generally just pulled a pair of pants and a white coat over his pajamas. Usually the patient's husband would come for the "doctor," and the students, who worked in pairs for their own safety, would set off on foot for the poorer parts of town or the tenements bordering the harbor, lugging their birthing kits. On arrival, they generally would be shown into a dingy, candlelit room, where they would find the patient, usually well along in labor, lying in bed or, not uncommonly, on a pile of filthy blankets on the floor, surrounded by a group of female relatives and neighbors. Dorothy would send the onlookers away, retaining a couple of women to fetch hot water and, she hoped, clean towels. The pair would take turns; one delivered the baby while the other acted as nurse. They had no telephone and no way to call an ambulance, so they had to manage as best they could. One of their earliest deliveries took place in a notorious alley where bare-breasted women stood at windows hoping to attract business. "A policeman wouldn't go down this joint alone at night," said Rusk, "and here I am with a white woman to protect."[112]

Dorothy recalled one case:

We followed an old crone to an attic room with no light, no stove, and no running water. A young Negress was on the floor—no bed—in labor...We got rid of all but two of the women [whom we] sent for boiling water. I got out the solutions...and Dr. Rusk cleaned up and examined the patient. Her face looked gray in the light of two tallow candles stuck in bottles and held in a precarious way by the two drunken women. I felt a crisis.

"What is it?" I whispered.

"Post presentation and no time to lose," he replied. It was too late in labor to maneuver the baby into a different position. The lusty mother was bearing down and the baby would come quickly. I passed instruments and Dr. Rusk delivered a fine big boy—and then I gave the anesthetic while he sewed up a tear in the patient's rectum, which seemed to us entirely unavoidable under the circumstances.[113]

Luckily, both mother and baby did well.

On another occasion, Dorothy found herself called to a house only to find the patient gone. Following the drops of blood on the floor, she arrived at the outdoor privy, where she found both mother and baby lying on the floor, apparently none the worse for their experience.

Once when only Dorothy was available, a man appeared and said that his wife was in labor. Had the man not been white, it is doubtful that Dorothy would have been allowed to go alone, even in daylight. But she picked up her bag and followed him into the harbor tenements to a three-story house. He gave a strange knock, a blind moved, and the door opened. As she climbed the stairs in the dim light, she saw men asleep on the bare floor. With a shudder, she realized she was in an opium den. On the third floor, she found a woman in labor, who, fortunately, since Dorothy was by herself, delivered easily. She gave instructions for the woman's care and said she would return next day. The man objected, but after some discussion he agreed, provided she told him the precise time she would arrive. On every return visit, she saw the blind move before the door opened.

The two students delivered two or three patients a night, returning home at dawn exhausted from their exertions, the heat, and the lack of sleep. Every morning Rusk's mother sent her butler around with a wicker basket of food—delicious white rolls, cold meats, fruit, and a bottle of wine. This was often their first meal since breakfast the day before, and the pair would sit on the superintendent's doorstep, eating, drinking, and watching the sun rising over the hospital dome. By summer's end, Dorothy had delivered about seventy babies.[114]

Unlike at the other medical schools of the period, the fourth year at Hopkins was devoted to clinical work. Dorothy spent most of her time as either a clerk (pronounced "clark") on the medical wards or a dresser on the surgical ones. On both services, she was assigned a number of patients. Her task was to take their histories, do physical examinations, and write up progress notes. On the surgery service, she learned to apply dressings, suture wounds, and lance boils, and she assisted at operations. She spent time in the special departments—dermatology, ophthalmology, otology, pediatrics, and psychiatry—but as a woman, she did not attend the genitourinary clinic.

On the medical service during her final year, Dorothy attended the Chief's rounds three times a week. On Saturday nights, Osler invited his clerks to his home; Dorothy initially thought these visits optional but soon realized they were command performances. At eight o'clock, everyone assembled round the dining-room table. After some small talk, Osler would ask, "What did you find of special interest in the wards this week?"[115] The students knew the routine and had searched all week for suitable cases. Once a topic was brought up, Osler would launch into a long discussion, often bringing out rare books from his extensive medical library to illustrate a point. At ten o'clock, the butler would bring in chocolate cake and serve lemonade to the women and beer to the men, who were always trying to get Dorothy to ask for beer. She never did.

Dorothy's biggest problem during her clerkship was her intern, a large, disagreeable man from the class ahead. He was, to her horror, much too attentive and would ask her for dates. The last straw came when put his arm around her shoulder as they were leaning over a desk:

"Dr. Leutscher, please remove your arm."

"Miss Reed, you forget that you are speaking to an intern."

"I thought that I was speaking to a gentleman."[116]

Normally, this exchange would have passed unnoticed. But, there were witnesses, and by noon it was all over the hospital. Jack Yates, Dorothy's friend from the same class, told her that everybody hated Leutscher and would never let him forget her snub.

In her fourth year, Dorothy spent additional time in pediatrics, which she enjoyed greatly, as she loved children. Gynecology followed under Dr. Howard A. Kelly, the youngest of the four founding professors. A brilliant surgeon with a large, highly remunerative practice, he spent his spare time collecting snakes and conducting religious crusades in the worst parts of town. When Dorothy was on his service, Kelly was busy writing a textbook, so she saw little of him but a lot of his first assistant, Dr. Elizabeth Hurdon, an Englishwoman who in 1899 was the only female first assistant at Hopkins.

Finals consisted of a written, practical, and oral exam in every subject, including anatomy, physiology, medicine, surgery, obstetrics, and gynecology. Grades were not given at Hopkins, so students never quite knew where they stood unless they were in danger of failing. On the night before a big examination, Dorothy would join several other women. They would pose difficult questions to one another; this way they discovered their weaknesses and resolved many problems. For the organized Dorothy, written exams (invariably in essay form) presented few problems. She read all the questions carefully and apportioned her time before putting pen to paper and tackled first the questions she knew best. In Dorothy's final clinical examination, Osler, without giving her any history, asked her to examine a young child. She went over the patient meticulously, and when she failed to detect any abnormalities, she repeated the examination since clearly *something* had to be wrong. When Dr. Osler returned, Dorothy told him that although the child was small, he was well developed and apparently healthy. Looking grave, Dr. Osler said, "Take ten minutes more and go over the chest." Dorothy percussed and auscultated for dear life. On his return, he asked, "Now, what do you find?"

"Nothing abnormal, sir."

"Did you listen to the heart?"

"Yes, sir, but it seemed perfect to me."

"Good girl," he replied, patting her on the back. The child was in for surgery and was medically quite normal—it was another of Dr. Osler's practical jokes. Even so, it gave Dorothy one of the worst moments of her life.[117] It was also a shocking example of male chauvinism and paternalism so prevalent in those far-off days.

On June 13, 1900, commencement ceremonies took place in one of the Baltimore theaters. The graduating medical students, thirteen women and thirty men, sat in a semicircle at the back of the stage while proud parents and relatives filled the auditorium. Dorothy's memoirs make no mention of the presence of her mother or sister; presumably they wanted no part of her "descent" into the medical profession. The theater was stiflingly hot and the proceedings long and tiresome. William Osler, resplendent in his scarlet robes, gave the commencement address on the physician's role in inspiring confidence and the importance of the patient's faith and will to recover:

> We physicians use this power of faith every day. While we often overlook our faith cures, are we not a bit too sensitive about those performed out of our ranks? We have no monopoly in this panacea. Faith in the Gods or in the Saints cures one, faith in little pills another, suggestion a third, and faith in a plain doctor a fourth. In all ages the prayer of faith has healed the sick, and the mental attitude of the suppliant seems to be of more consequence than the powers to which the prayer is addressed.[118]

President Gilman announced the name of each graduate, and after what seemed an interminable length of time, he reached the medical-school class. Dorothy held her breath while he read first the list of names of students graduating with honors. To her great delight, it included Florence Sabin's and her own.

The most important decision facing a new medical graduate, then as now, was the choice of internship. Hopkins offered twelve: four each in medicine, surgery, and obstetrics and gynecology, with those in medicine reserved for honors graduates. Dorothy's first inkling of a potential problem had come earlier in the year when Welch had sent for her and pointed out that since she and Florence Sabin were both honors candidates, conceivably there could be two female medical interns, and this would mean that one of them would have to take charge of the black wards—a possibility that filled the male white faculty with horror. Certainly Dr. Hurd, the hospital superintendent, would not have wanted one of his daughters exposed to what he believed were "nameless perils." Welch proposed a series of alternatives: he conveyed "a cordial invitation" from Dr. Halsted, who said Dorothy was "needed on the surgical wards," and, if this did not please her, both Dr. Williams and Dr. Kelly would be delighted to have her on their services. "He was kindness itself," wrote Dorothy, "really solicitous for my future and desirous of helping me make the decision."[119] Dorothy had neither interest in nor aptitude for surgery, although she certainly possessed the "surgical personality," nor was she interested in a career in obstetrics and gynecology. Asking for time to think it over, she searched out Florence Sabin, who told her that Dr. Franklin Mall had said she could begin her fellowship in anatomy without an internship. This way, the problem could be averted. Dorothy thought it unfair and unreasonable to ask Florence to miss her year with Osler. "No," she declared. "If you won't take the internship, I won't either, so why talk about it." Returning to Dr. Welch, she thanked him very much for his interest, and Dr. Halsted and Dr. Williams for their offers, and told him that medicine was what she wanted, and that if she couldn't have it at Hopkins, she would see what New York offered. Unhappy and uncomfortable, Welch told her to do nothing without discussing it with him first.[120]

The morning after graduation, the service chiefs and other professors assembled at nine o'clock in the hospital, surrounded by newly graduated doctors anxious to learn if they would get internships. The first man called wanted surgery; Herbert Allen and Florence Sabin both took medicine. Dorothy and William Sowers tied for the fourth place.

"Miss Reed," asked Dr. Osler, "what is your choice?"

Looking him straight in the eye, she replied, "Medicine, sir." Sowers also took medicine.

Later, Dr. Osler took Allen and Sowers aside and said, "Boys, these girls will have a hard time and I expect you both to give them any help you can to make it easier."[121]

The men in her class were very unhappy because two of the plum Osler internships had gone to women. Henry Christian, who later became dean of Harvard Medical School, wrote Dorothy a very courteous letter asking if she was certain she wanted hers, adding that if he could not work with Dr. Osler, he would leave Baltimore. Another man told Dorothy that it seemed very hard to have to take obstetrics while she got medicine. But her friend Rusk immediately countered, "Miss Reed deserves what she was given—she was a better student than you every year."[122]

The whole episode left Dorothy with a bitter taste. "It was the first time," she wrote, "that I personally was made to feel that I was not wanted in the medical profession and my first realization of the hard time any woman has to get recognition for equal work."[123]

Nor would it be the last. The status of women in the medical profession would not change in her lifetime.

CHAPTER 7

Gratification

On the Firing Line

DOROTHY RETURNED TO BALTIMORE ON the last day of August 1900, eager to begin the practice of medicine after so many long years of study. She describes her attitude as "full of resolves and enthusiasms to begin [her] year's service."[124] The moment she encountered Florence Sabin, her optimism vanished. The first thing Florence said was that she was not going to take up her internship. A timid, nonconfrontational person, she had given in to pressure from Dr. Hurd, the hospital superintendent, and Dr. Tom McCrae, the resident in charge of the medical service during Dr. Osler's summer vacation, and had agreed to go directly into anatomy, as her ultimate goal was an academic career in that field. It will be recalled that the authorities were terrified by the notion of a white woman in charge of the male Negro ward, and by reducing the number of female interns to one, the problem would be averted. Dorothy was furious. No man was going to treat them as second-class citizens and deprive them of internships they had rightfully earned. "If anybody went," she declared to Florence, "I would be the one—but, after all, Dr. Osler had given me the position and Dr. Welch had congratulated me on it." Never afraid to stand up for what she thought was right, the combative Dorothy announced, "I will talk to Dr. Hurd."[125]

By chance, she encountered him that very afternoon. Hurd invited her into his office and said that he understood she wanted the colored wards. He told her that "it was unheard of for a woman to be in charge of the Negro wards. It would end in disaster—it couldn't be done—he wouldn't stand for it."[126] In a rude and offensive way, he recalled his experiences with another female physician who harbored what he considered sexual perversions and, in so doing, made perfectly clear his opinion of female physicians. Hurd went on to point out that the white nurses on the male Negro wards were always in danger and that the male intern was responsible for their safety. Refusing to be intimidated, Dorothy told Hurd that she had come to Baltimore to learn a profession and had fulfilled every requirement for the medical degree. Dr. Osler had appointed her and Florence interns, confident that they were fully capable of running both the white and Negro wards. Dorothy continued,

> Until he returns, Sir, I shall be the intern of the colored wards, and I shall do my best. If in October I find that I cannot successfully perform my duties I shall tender Dr. Osler my resignation.[127]

Overcome with frustration and the enormity of the situation, she burst out:

> Dr. Hurd, it was a difficult decision for me to go into medicine—there were unpleasantnesses that I was told might occur, but I waited four years to be treated unfairly, and the first insult I have received was from the Superintendent of Johns Hopkins Hospital.[128]

With tears of anger streaking down her cheeks, Dorothy stalked out of his office to find Florence waiting in the corridor. "Come with me to Dr. McCrae," she ordered, and marched off, trembling with rage at the idea that a man would categorize all female physicians as sexual perverts.[129] Later Dorothy realized that by becoming emotional she had made a fool of herself and, in so doing, had likely confirmed Hurd's poor opinion of women doctors.

The two women found McCrae fair, businesslike, and helpful. After a long discussion, they both agreed to go ahead with their internships and that Dorothy would start on the black male ward. "Dr. McCrae," she declared, "until Dr. Osler returns I shall do my best to give satisfaction and to perform all the duties of an intern, as I have been taught them on these wards."[130]

As an intern, Dorothy wore the regulation uniform of white skirt, blouse, and jacket, which on her first day she brightened up with a red tie, since she did not care for the customary blue one. ("Ladies" did not wear pants in those days, and Dorothy never did.) When she first entered the doctors' dining room, she was surprised to see all the men at one of the tables rise and remain standing until she was seated. Shortly afterward, she received this note: "Miss Reed has unanimously been chosen an honorary member of the surgical staff."[131] It turned out that by custom, surgical interns always wore red ties while medical interns wore blue. Dorothy, throughout her medical internship, continued to wear red.

She and Florence had adjacent rooms in the doctors' quarters that were simply furnished with a bed, bureau, two chairs, and a table; the bathroom and doctors' lounge were situated one floor up. Given their recent experiences with Dr. Hurd, the two women never visited the house officers' lounge, preferring to use the nurses' sitting room instead. Fifty years later, Dorothy thought their boycott "a bit silly," but at the time the two women felt they were there on sufferance and had best keep a low profile.

Dorothy's first task was to enlist the support of the ward staff. The head nurse, Miss Calvert, was a young gentlewoman who, emboldened by the examples of Florence Nightingale and Clara Barton, had made nursing her career. Anxious to see Dorothy succeed in the chauvinistic male environment at Hopkins, she gave her all the help she could, including chaperoning her whenever she performed a rectal or genital examination. With a five-dollar tip, Dorothy ensured the help of Nathan, the male orderly. Besides maintaining order, she wanted him to tell her about any unusual activities or strange findings in the bedpans or urinals.

For a new intern, the first days are always overwhelming. Dorothy was expected immediately to be up to date on the twenty or so patients she inherited, as well as to handle a steady flow of new admissions, each of whom required a complete workup. That first month was "agony," according to Dorothy. She worked from six a.m. until after midnight. Every morning, she made rounds with the resident in charge and rounded again each night. She took histories, did physicals, ordered medications, and charted her patients' progress. She counted their blood cells and analyzed their urine. All too often, she pronounced them dead. If she had an exceptionally sick case, she would sleep in the patient pavilion in an unused room. Then, as now, elderly patients tended to become confused and restless in the wee hours of the morning, and frequently Dorothy could be found leading a poor old black man clad only in a nightshirt down the long, dim, deserted hospital corridors back to his bed.[132] The oppressive late-summer heat and humidity added to her burdens, but she was determined not to fail in any of her duties—including protecting the nurses—and to gain the respect of the other interns and residents.

Shortly after her return, she encountered her old friend Jack Yates, who had just completed his internship and now, as a fellow in pathology, had rooms down the hall. He greeted her warmly, adding, "Call on your Uncle Dudley if anyone bothers you."[133] Before long, she was glad of his help. Late one night, after the monthly surgical-staff meeting, she heard men laughing, shouting, and running in her hallway. Knowing the pranks hard-drinking residents could get up to, she was terrified. Then she heard Jack's door open, followed by the crash of crockery as the former Yale pitcher dispatched the intruders with a few well-aimed plates; her room remained inviolate. A little later, she responded, with some trepidation, to a knock at her door to find an orderly with a tray of sandwiches and half a dozen bottles of beer, "with compliments of the surgical staff."[134] She went next door and awoke Florence to share a late-night drink and snack.

By the time Dr. Osler returned, Dorothy was on top of her work. Her ward was well under control; she knew everything about her patients. When he complimented her on her work, she glowed with pride. After she told him of her unpleasant interview with Dr. Hurd, he looked serious and admitted, "Hurd was a crabby soul," adding she could always rely on his support.[135]

Dorothy greatly admired Dr. Osler and took immense delight in being his intern; an easy camaraderie quickly developed between them. She always arrived early for his thrice-weekly ward rounds in order to update her notes and add the latest blood count or urinalysis. While Dr. Osler always started promptly at nine o'clock, his progress, depending on the cases, was erratic, so Dorothy never quite knew when to expect him. The murmur of the crowd of fourth-year students, graduate students, medical and scientific assistants, and visiting doctors would herald his arrival. The Chief would appear "dressed in a gray morning coat and top hat, a flower in his buttonhole, sometimes with a walking stick or umbrella in hand," frequently propelling a student or intern by the arm down the seemingly endless corridors that connected the different pavilions.[136] Dorothy, accompanied by her "clerks," would meet him at the entrance to the pavilion and follow him on patient rounds. At each new case, the clerk would read the history, she would describe the physical findings, and then the Chief would ask for her diagnosis. A masterful teacher, Osler held everyone's attention while Dorothy stood by enthralled. A fellow student described the scene:

On ward rounds Osler would often stand at the head of a patient's bed, gracefully using his beautifully shaped, small, brown hands, with their tapering fingers, to accentuate what he had to say. He was fond of enumerating, as first, second and third in order of probability, the situations in which such and such a condition might occur; frequently the last possibility was totally unexpected and entirely irrelevant. In examining a patient, he would sit at the side of the bed, watching the motions of the chest or abdomen and looking for moving shadows in different lights, to which procedure he attached great importance…Much time was also devoted to the palpation of the chest and abdomen. Osler was likely to use both hands and to point out the advantages of doing so.[137]

On occasion, rounds would be interrupted by word that an autopsy was in progress on one of his patients, whereupon Osler would take Dorothy's arm, saying, "Come, let's go and see our mistakes."[138] Then, at his usual rapid pace, he would lead her and his entourage down to the morgue, where he would stand with his cuffs and sleeves pushed back and blood dripping from his bare hands, as he explained the pathologic changes in the patient's heart or other diseased organs to the surrounding students.

Interns were responsible for admitting the patients, and Dorothy had been cautioned never to accept a patient with delirium tremens brought about by chronic drunkenness or to mix patients of different races. One day Dorothy admitted a man with the typical symptoms of pneumonia. As soon as he was in bed, he upset the whole ward by trembling violently, talking agitatedly, and hallucinating. She quickly realized her mistake and transferred her case to a secure psychiatric facility. That same day she saw a former coal miner who was over six feet tall, with red hair, blue eyes, and freckles. Suspecting silicosis, or black lung disease, she admitted him to the free white ward, as she knew the case would interest the Chief. Shortly afterward, the intern there called her and asked, "Did you know you sent me a Negro?" Astonished, she went to his ward to find the patient sitting on a chair in the corridor and, in her most tactful and solicitous manner, asked: "Have you colored blood?" He replied, "Sure, I'm a nigger."[139]

After she had transferred him to the Negro ward, the two interns agreed that neither of them would have thought him black, but the highly sensitive antennae of the southern white male had immediately detected the man's origins. He was a model patient—courteous, cooperative, and full of jokes—who got on famously with Dr. Osler. Unfortunately, nothing could be done to help him. Some months later, Dorothy was called to the operating suite, where she found her former patient lying on the floor, covered in blood. When she asked what happened, he replied, "I went to a strawberry festival and the other colored 'genneman' drew his razor first."[140] Like many black folk at that time, he dreaded surgery, and he would have none of it unless the "little white lady doctor" from ward M would tell him that it was the only hope. Dorothy held his hand while the anesthetic was given. The surgeon sewed up half a dozen intestinal perforations, but he developed peritonitis and died. When she saw him for the last time, he pressed his wallet full of bills into her hand, saying he wanted her to have it. "My old woman ain't no good," he told Dorothy.[141] Of course, she refused it.

The most common admitting diagnosis was pneumonia, which, in those preantibiotic days, carried a very high mortality; next in frequency came chronic heart disease due to rheumatic fever or syphilis. Dorothy recalled a young woman with typhoid, a common disease in Baltimore during the fall, who was bleeding from her vagina. Pelvic examination revealed she was pregnant; removal of the fetus and placenta produced a torrential hemorrhage that necessitated packing the uterus. When she came under Dorothy's care, her skin was cold and clammy, her temperature subnormal, and her pulse imperceptible: she was dying. Dorothy stayed up all night pushing fluids and injecting cardiac stimulants, chiefly strychnine. The next morning her patient's fever was up to 105 degrees. Later, when Dr. Osler made his rounds, he was astonished to find her still alive; after scrutinizing her chart (which was for him most unusual), he remarked, "I hope she doesn't have strychnine poisoning."[142] After her discharge, the patient returned with a thank-you gift for Dorothy—two live chickens.

Not everyone was so appreciative. Dorothy had worked hard to save a young, hard-drinking, drug-using barmaid with pneumonia. After an early crisis (a sharp drop in temperature, usually accompanied by striking clinical improvement), the patient, to everyone's amazement, asked to be discharged. After Dorothy explained the risks involved, the woman replied that the sailor she lived with was due to return from sea the next day and that if she didn't see him first, the "bitch" who worked with her in the bar would get all his money.[143]

Good nursing and diet formed the mainstays of treatment. In his classic textbook, *The Principles and Practice of Medicine*, Osler devoted very little space to therapy, as few effective medications existed.[144] He opposed the then-prevalent "blunderbuss" therapy, believing a drug should be prescribed only if there was a physiological basis for its action or it had proven to be clinically effective. Only a handful of such drugs existed: opium, a sedative used since antiquity; digitalis for the treatment of heart failure; quinine to reduce fever and combat malaria, then prevalent on the shores of Chesapeake Bay; and mercury and potassium iodide given together for syphilis. Young women with anemia took iron pills. In the absence of specific treatment, typhoid patients received fluids and egg albumin shaken up in ice by mouth; if their temperature rose too high, they were immersed in an ice-cold tub. Hospital stays were measured in weeks; the mortality rate among poor, black, and elderly patients exceeded 50 percent.

One Saturday morning when Dorothy arrived late at Dr. Osler's clinic, he greeted her cheerfully: "Here's Dr. Reed. She can report on what she has done on the Negro wards."

"Six deaths from pneumonia on the men's ward, sir," she replied, whereupon everyone broke into laughter.[145] Dorothy flushed with embarrassment—she hated to be laughed at. Dr. Osler, anxious to support his intern, pointed out that many of Dorothy's patients were syphilitic and alcoholic and that it was remarkable that she saved as many as she did.

A very serious problem occurred when overnight one of her black patients developed a deep-seated hard rash with small blisters over his entire body. Dr. Futcher, the medical resident, diagnosed chicken pox and told Dorothy that Dr. Osler would want to show the case to the students. As soon as the Chief and his entourage of students and doctors had assembled round the patient's bed, the resident whipped back the sheet. Instantly Dr. Osler's habitual expression of pleasure and whimsical good humor changed to one of grim horror. "My God, Dr. Futcher!" he cried. "Don't you know smallpox when you see it?"[146] Confusion ensued. The onlookers melted away. The stricken man was isolated and the ward quarantined. Every contact—patient, doctor, nurse, and student—was vaccinated. Osler had good reason to be alarmed; he had seen three thousand people die of the disease in Montreal. Although several new cases developed on the ward, his prompt actions averted an epidemic. Nobody who was there, including the mortified medical resident, would ever miss smallpox again.

One fall day, Dorothy heard the bell in her room give one long ring and seven short rings—an emergency. Racing to her ward, she found men fighting in the spaces between the beds, cheered on by patients too sick to join the melee. Swinging a crutch wildly to keep the men away, she plunged into the fray, shouting, "Back to your own wards." At once the fighting stopped, and a dozen bleeding men, their clothes slashed to pieces, limped past her, back to the surgical ward. Half a dozen more lay on the floor, too badly hurt to get up. In those days, it was difficult to stop Baltimore blacks from bringing their favorite weapon—a straight razor—into the hospital. Keeping a close lookout, Dorothy backed down to the telephone and asked for the surgical resident, only to be told that he was operating. Finally she got through and asked him to come at once—there had been a riot on her ward. Then she noticed there were no nurses. Several patients explained that, terrified for their lives, they had locked themselves in the linen room. The surgeons summarily discharged all the patients who had taken part in the fight; Dorothy spent the rest of the afternoon sewing up lacerations and bandaging wounds, as her patients were mostly too sick to go home—besides, she thought the cuts and bruises, black eyes, and sprains were punishment enough. Her fellow interns ribbed her unmercifully about the battle in her ward, but, as she put it, "While it lasted, it was far from funny for me."[147]

On one occasion passing by the children's ward, Dorothy heard a commotion and ran in to find a little girl blue in the face from a paroxysm of coughing. Grabbing the child, she jumped on a chair and, holding her upside down, whacked her across her back. A plum stone, which the child had aspirated earlier, flew out of her mouth and pinged against the window. Dorothy's prompt action saved the little girl's life, as the surgical instruments necessary to extract it did not exist then, and death from aspiration pneumonia would have been inevitable. As the girl's ecstatic parents carried their daughter home, she was still clutching the stone.

Dorothy found the male Negro patients generally easy to handle and enjoyed their sense of humor. Undoubtedly they were surprised to find a female physician in charge of their care, but they treated her very respectfully. A retired Pullman car attendant helped her immeasurably. After spending several months on her ward with a cardiac condition, he would explain authoritatively to new patients the ward routine and ensure they followed the rules. Unaware of Florence Sabin, he cheerfully extolled the abilities of "the onliest lady doctor in the hospital."[148]

After she had grown more used to the work and her responsibilities, Dorothy began to develop a social life. Beautiful, intelligent, and high-spirited, she presented an interesting challenge to some of the men. Medical students and house staff in those days worked hard, played hard, and drank hard. They had a reputation for boisterous behavior and were determined to live up to it. With the memory of her brother's drinking fresh in her mind, Dorothy would take just one drink and smoke an occasional cigarette "because comradeship required it."[149] The house staff, when they were not on call, often visited the Baltimore Country Club or some beach resort. Dorothy always avoided twosomes and took care that somebody stayed sober enough to drive her home.

During her medical-student years, Dorothy's social life had stagnated, and her wardrobe had deteriorated. Every year, Johns Hopkins Hospital gave a splendid party, hosted by Dr. and Mrs. Hurd. Dorothy had never forgiven Hurd for his remarks at the beginning of the year; she thought Mrs. Hurd a nonentity and considered their two daughters plain. The Hurds frequently entertained the male interns but ignored her and Florence. It was time, she decided, to make an impression. She had her black lace gown refurbished and her hair done specially for the occasion. Looking quite stunning and sophisticated, she saw herself as the "belle of the ball," dancing every dance. In retrospect, she admitted that she probably looked like a tart and had not enjoyed the party all that much.[150]

After six months, Florence asked to take over the male colored ward. This surprised Dorothy, as during their interview with Hurd, she had declared that "she would never attempt running the Negro service."[151] They traded places, and Dorothy moved to the white women's ward. She found the patients there harder to manage than the menfolk, in part because the unit included obstetric and orthopedic patients who were not physically sick. She did not especially enjoy this part of her internship. "There were," she wrote, "personal reasons why these months dragged for me, which chiefly involved my mother and my sister."[152] There was, too, a more cogent, unmentioned reason: she was in love.

On New Year's Day 1901, the house staff gathered in the rotunda of the hospital for drinks and hors d'oeuvres. There Dorothy encountered a young physician recently returned from the "obligatory" year's study in Germany. As she knew the country well, they had a lot to talk about. After the party broke up, they moved to the reading room and continued talking. Dorothy felt aroused as never before. When she returned to her room, she threw herself on her bed and cried her heart out. "I knew," she later wrote "I had met my man and that fate was against us." Thus began an affair that was, in Dorothy's words, "to change my entire life and to so twist my character through sheer misery that I wonder how I had the strength of will to go on living."[153]

Dorothy, at twenty-five, asserted that she had had no sexual experiences of any sort—except for a few daydreams—and that no man had kissed her (at least not seriously) or laid his hand on her twice.[154] During her youth she'd had had little contact with boys her own age and had never experienced the heart wrench of calf-love. Prematurely thrust into adult society, she claimed to have received three proposals of marriage, but in Victorian times intimacy was not a prerequisite. In retrospect, she thought that despite her exceptional looks, she was too independent to attract men. Incurably romantic, she expected a knight in shining armor to carry her off, little realizing that the age of chivalry was long dead.

She kept the affair a secret all her life. She always referred in her memoirs to her lover as "AJ" and never revealed his identity to a soul. She described him as tall, well-bred, handsome, personable, and, on occasion, very amusing. As a young man, he had already published outstanding research. Working and living in the same place, their passion for each other developed quickly. Since grass and trees surrounded the hospital and the country lay within walking distance, they found it easy to be alone. With a surprising display of common sense, Dorothy continued to go out regularly with her classmates and fellow house officers, but it is unlikely she fooled anybody, as gossip spreads quickly in medical communities.

Consumed by passion, she chose to overlook AJ's imperfections—his egotism and vanity. Perhaps she thought that, with her love, he would change. Dorothy described herself at this time as "virginal in body and mind."[155] It is very doubtful that this was true of her friend, who had long been interested in girls; now in his middle twenties, he would have had many opportunities to prove himself. Success with Dorothy did not come easily; he had to overcome her moral scruples, and she soon realized that once she succumbed to his advances, she would lose her hold. Victorian morality required young women to remain virtuous before marriage, although their intendeds were allowed more latitude. The exact nature of Dorothy's relationship with AJ can only be conjectured. Since her memoirs were originally written for her young granddaughters, it is hardly surprising that explicit details are lacking.

Dorothy's former beau, Charles Mendenhall, after a stint at Williams College, had accepted an assistant professorship of physics at the University of Wisconsin in Madison. That summer he returned to Baltimore. Sitting in the hospital yard, he asked her to marry him. Behind every tree Dorothy saw the shadow of her lover, AJ, and she refused Mendenhall. Brokenhearted, he departed, leaving her more upset than he realized. She could not help but compare the loyal, quiet, selfless, and reliable Charles to the dazzling, conceited, and self-focused AJ. If only Charles had asked her a year ago, life would have been so much simpler. But he was too late. Her passion for AJ enslaved her.

The advent of summer in Baltimore, when the heat and humidity became unbearable, was a signal for the faculty and many interns to leave that low-lying southern city. The male interns who stayed hosed one another down with a fire hose in an effort to stay cool. When Dorothy would go to bed, always after midnight, she would tie her long braids to the bedposts in the hope that they would dry out by morning. When she arose at six, the temperature in the shaded hospital breezeways was still one hundred degrees. Remembering Dr. Hurd's remarks about the irresponsibility of women, she soldiered on to the last day of her appointment.

Portrait of Doctor William Osler, professor of medicine, Johns Hopkins School of Medicine, painted in 1908. This picture, and those of Hurd and Welch show the subjects as Dorothy knew them.

Doctor Henry Mills Hurd, superintendent of
Johns Hopkins Hospital, taken in 1906.

Doctor William H. Welch, professor of pathology and dean of Johns Hopkins School of Medicine, taken in 1893.

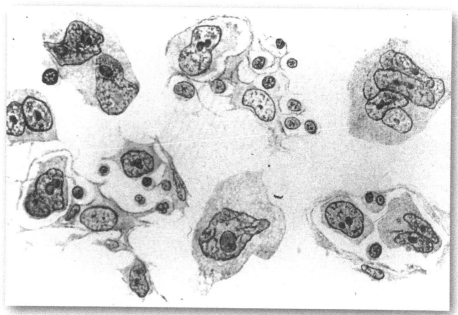

One of Dorothy Reed's original drawings of the characteristic giant cells in Hodgkin's disease, taken from her seminal paper in 1902. These are now universally known as Reed or Reed-Sternberg cells.

CHAPTER 8

Disillusionment

Men Dominate Medicine

DOROTHY, TOTALLY EXHAUSTED BY HER internship, returned to Talcottville for a short rest. What a joy it must have been to breathe clean air tingling with country smells, to sleep in cool, dry sheets, and to know that the hospital alarm bell would never ring. She had every reason to feel triumphant. She had fulfilled all her obligations as an intern as well as any man, including quelling the riot on her ward single-handedly. With one of the most eligible bachelors in the hospital as her lover, she was the envy of many on the nursing staff. Dorothy kept a diary during her internship but later buried it at Talcottville, so the feelings she recorded during that tumultuous emotional period can never be known.

At the Old Stone House, Dorothy found a series of problems awaiting her: Grace Reed needed money (when did she not?), her sister Bessie lay critically ill, and her brother-in-law's paper mill had gone bust.[156] As if this was not enough, the residue of the family fortune no longer produced enough income to meet everybody's needs, and Dorothy felt compelled to give half of her own share to her mother. Despite all these worries, Talcottville worked its usual magic, and Dorothy returned to Baltimore rested, relaxed, and eager to begin the next phase of her career.

In the spring of her intern year, Dr. Welch had offered Dorothy the university fellowship in pathology. He knew of her keen interest in the subject, as she had completed a student project on pseudotuberculosis in mice in his lab, and he recognized her intelligence, industry, and academic potential. Since Dorothy's motivation to enter medicine was based more on her interest in biology than an urge to heal the sick, the prospect thrilled her. When she learned that she would be the first woman to hold an appointment at Johns Hopkins University, which, unlike the medical school, did not yet admit women, she was ecstatic. At the next faculty meeting, Welch gave an enthusiastic account of her abilities and accomplishments, and her appointment, supported by Osler, passed without difficulty. Dr. Gildersleeve, the professor of classics, had a question: "Is the candidate good-looking?" Welch flushed with embarrassment. Amid much laughter, the meeting broke up.[157]

Welsh's staff consisted of two associates, Eugene L. Opie, MD, and William G. MacCallum, MD, and two assistant pathologists, Harry T. Marshall, MD, and John L. Yates, MD. Welch's approach to pathology was the most advanced of anyone's in the United States. He was one of the first American pathologists to introduce Germanic scientific methods, including the use of experimental animals. In his department, microscopic examination of diseased tissues was standard in all autopsies. He was also the first to employ frozen sections for rapid diagnosis—not intraoperatively, as is customary today, because of the then high risks of prolonged anesthesia, but to quickly resolve questions arising during the course of a postmortem. At Hopkins the faculty taught medical students, performed autopsies, and did research. As academic pathologists, they considered surgical pathology, the routine examination of tissues and organs removed from living patients, beneath their dignity and delegated this task to a member of the surgery department.

Welch assigned Dorothy space in Jack Yates's lab, which, since Yates was renowned for his love of practical jokes, made her apprehensive. The previous summer he had embarrassed her with a series of flamboyant postcards from Italy addressed to "Dorothy Reed, Ps.D." On his return, she asked him what it meant. "PhD means plain *he* doctor," he explained, "and PsD means plain *she* doctor."[158] Jack took a lot of guff from the staff and students over his friendship with Dorothy. He lived in Baltimore with his mother, who daily sent over sandwiches for lunch, which they washed down with tea that Dorothy laced with rum from a bottle kept in the lab labeled "aniline oil." Understandably, lunch became a popular feature of laboratory life. By year's end, Jack had become a close colleague and, as Dorothy put it, "as good a friend as I ever had [and] one of the most original and delightfully unpredictable humans I have ever known."[159]

Dorothy's duties included teaching and performing autopsies, much as they would today. In second-year pathology, the department's main course, she helped students in the lab use their microscopes to study disease-induced changes and answered their questions. Gross pathology (the alterations produced by disease that are visible to the naked eye) was, and still is, an important subject, particularly for surgeons; Dorothy quizzed students on the abnormalities and diagnoses of fresh tissue specimens from the morgue as well as on "potted" ones from the departmental museum.

In those days every pathologist did autopsies, often several hundred a year. Because of Dorothy's prior experience in Boston, Welch soon allowed her to perform them unsupervised. Nobel laureate Payton Rous, on a visit to Hopkins before he entered medical school, described how he was taken to the morgue: "And there was Dorothy examining a cadaver! She was strikingly beautiful and not less so because her [bare] arms plunged almost to the elbows in the viscera of a corpse"—not your everyday picture of a Victorian gentlewoman.[160]

In addition to performing postmortems at Hopkins, Dorothy traveled by streetcar across town to perform them at Bay View Asylum.

After completing her examination, she would haul all relevant specimens back to Hopkins in glass jars. Initially, Jack Yates or another pathologist accompanied her to that remote basement morgue with its cabinets full of saws and razor-sharp knives. Dorothy assumed that once she had acquired more experience, she, like her predecessors, would go alone. When she realized that because she was a woman this was not going to happen, she complained about the unfairness of it to Jack Yates. After he pointed out that the janitor who assisted them was a hospital inmate and a sexual pervert, she reluctantly agreed to allow a medical student to accompany her. Her escort, for his part, was happy to spend a half day in the company of an attractive and relatively important personage and perhaps enjoy a little flirtation; besides, he would open the skull—a job she hated doing—and lug the heavy specimens back to Hopkins.

Every pathologist, even today, runs a certain risk in performing an autopsy. One hundred years ago, the danger was immeasurably greater. Many more patients died from uncontrolled infections, and as a result pathologists were exposed to every type of microbial disease, including smallpox and tuberculosis. In the preantibiotic era, the nearly inevitable accidental small cuts were not infrequently followed by fulminating septicemia and death. In those days before the widespread use of rubber gloves, tuberculous infection of the skin of the pathologist's hand was common. Dorothy performed thirteen autopsies at Hopkins and an unknown number at Bay View, successfully escaping all these hazards. Her handwritten reports, which are still on file at Hopkins, demonstrate her progressively increasing levels of pathological skill and sophistication.

Shortly after Dorothy joined the department, Welch sent for her and initiated a long discussion about research, during which he brought up Carl Sternberg's recent paper on Hodgkin's disease. He recalled a number of cases and suggested that she retrieve them from departmental files to see what they showed, probably expecting her to confirm Sternberg's findings.[161] Dorothy had no idea of the significance of his request or how it would enshrine her name in the annals of medicine.

The story of Hodgkin's disease began in 1832 with a presentation to the London Medico-Chirurgical Society entitled "On Some Morbid Appearances of the Absorbent Glands and Spleen." In it Thomas Hodgkin, then curator of the museum and lecturer in morbid anatomy at Guy's Hospital in London, described the autopsy appearances of seven most unusual cases.[162] Every one showed striking enlargement of the lymph glands[#] and spleen; the latter, when cut into, contained numerous irregular white, "lardaceous" deposits. Although Hodgkin owned a microscope, the resolution of his instrument was poor and techniques for examining human tissue were rudimentary, so he based his report solely on his naked-eye observations.[2]

For more than twenty years, Hodgkin's work was forgotten, until Samuel Wilks drew attention to it in two papers in 1856 and 1865. In the first, entitled "Enlargement of Lymphatic Glands Combined with a Peculiar Disease of the Spleen," Wilks included three of Hodgkin's original cases. By way of postscript to his paper, Wilks laments that Dr. Hodgkin did not affix a distinct name to the disease. Nine years later he published a second paper as part of a series designed in part to establish and enhance the reputation and prestige of Guy's Hospital and its medical school. He titled his second manuscript "Cases of Enlargement of the Lymphatic Glands and Spleen (or Hodgkin's disease)"; the name stuck and is still in use today.[163]

Very little progress occurred in our understanding of the condition until Sternberg's 1898 paper, which contained the first detailed and reasonably illustrated description of the microscopic changes in the affected lymph glands and spleen.[164] Sternberg discussed the nature and cause of the condition. Since eight of his cases also manifested

---

The terms *lymph glands* and *lymph nodes* are synonymous; although *nodes* is more correct and is used today, the term *lymph gland* is retained here as Dorothy employed it.

active tuberculosis, he thought the two conditions causally related and concluded that Hodgkin's disease was an inflammatory process. Working in Vienna, he naturally wrote his paper in German, with the result that it received little attention in America or England.

Dorothy, delighted to have a research project, set to work enthusiastically and began by reading Sternberg's paper in the *Zeitschrift für Heilkunde*; as she spoke fluent German, this did not present a problem. Welch furnished her with a microscope fitted with the new compound lenses that corrected for both spherical and chromatic aberration. Her prior experience in "modern" bacteriological and histological techniques in Boston gave her a head start.

She found the medical records of eight cases of Hodgkin's disease in the archives at Hopkins. She reviewed the clinical notes and studied with her microscope the pathological changes in lymph glands removed from six patients during life, as well as autopsy tissues from one of these who had died and two other cases in which only postmortem material was available. Dorothy experienced considerable difficulty in getting good sections prepared from some of the old specimens, but with the aid of the two "pathological janitors" and, one suspects, a generous tip, she got the job done. Because Sternberg had postulated that Hodgkin's disease was a form of tuberculosis, Dorothy attempted to culture the tubercle bacillus from her cases and also injected tuberculin (a recently described extract of tubercle bacilli) into the skin of five patients still living.

Dr. Welch met repeatedly with Dorothy to review her work and sent away for articles to the Surgeon General's Library in Washington, DC, so she could complete her literature search. To her surprise, the project went "swimmingly," and by the early part of 1902, she was compiling her results and beginning to write them up. Her paper went through the usual rewrites and revisions; Welch, of course, had many suggestions and corrections. She showed her manuscript to Dr. Osler, who found the latest version so much better. Later he included one of her drawings in his famous textbook of medicine.

The results of Dorothy's research, "On the Pathological Changes in Hodgkin's Disease, with Especial Reference to Its Relation to Tuberculosis," appeared in *Johns Hopkins Hospital Reports* in 1902.[165] Dorothy's paper consisted of twenty-four pages of text and a fifty-nine-page appendix containing clinical details and photographs of her patients as well as the pathological findings, autopsy reports, and technical methods.

Clinically, all her patients suffered from progressive enlargement of their lymph glands and spleen, often accompanied by intermittent fever. Six of her eight cases ultimately died, and one was lost to follow-up. She reviewed the gross autopsy findings and found they were just as Hodgkin had described them. The centerpiece of her paper was her description of the microscopic appearances of diseased lymph glands illustrated by five sets of elegant drawings she made herself. Dorothy found the normal glandular structure completely destroyed and replaced by an abnormal cellular tissue that included many types of cells—lymphocytes, endothelial cells, plasma cells, and eosinophils. The latter, she stressed, were present in great numbers and reinforced the diagnosis. The most striking finding was the presence of varying numbers of extraordinary "giant lymphoma cells," which she described in detail:

The nucleus is always large in proportion to the size of the cell. It may be single or multiple. If single, it is usually round. Bean-shaped and irregularly indented nuclei are common. If multiple, the nuclei may be arranged peripherally in the cell, or heaped in the centre. Eight or ten nuclei have been seen in a single cell. The chromatin network is prominent in these nuclei, and one or more large nucleoli are always present...[These] always take a contrasting stain to the nucleus in the double stains, they have an affinity for acid dyes. No definite mitotic figures were ever seen in these cells [here she was wrong]. *These giant cells, so far as our observation reaches, are peculiar to this growth, and are of great assistance in diagnosis.*[166] (author's italics)

The microscopic changes seen in what Dorothy called "metastatic" nodules and Hodgkin termed "lardaceous deposits" in the spleen and liver were identical to those seen in affected lymph glands.

Dorothy's microscopic findings were similar to those of Sternberg, but her illustrations were infinitely better and her conclusions quite different. She could find no evidence linking Hodgkin's disease to tuberculosis. Only one case demonstrated both diseases, which she attributed to chance, as tuberculosis was widespread in Baltimore at that time. She concluded that Hodgkin's disease was a specific pathological entity, unrelated to tuberculosis, which could be diagnosed only when microscopic examination of affected lymph glands revealed the presence of the characteristic "giant lymphoma cells." The nature and cause of the process were unknown—as they are to this day.

In an addendum to her paper, Dorothy described the case of an eight-year-old boy in whom, for the first time, the diagnosis was made by microscopic examination of a surgical biopsy. She made two important discoveries that were overlooked by the medical community for many years. The five patients who received tuberculin injections were all nonreactive, a remarkable finding at a time when nearly everybody showed a strong positive response; she was thus the first person to report the now well-known failure of the immune system in Hodgkin's disease. This phenomenon was rediscovered in the early thirties.[167] She also clearly described the progressive spread of Hodgkin's disease from one anatomic group of lymph glands to the neighboring one, a phenomenon that was rereported from Stanford more than sixty years later.[168]

Dorothy's research on Hodgkin's disease was her most important contribution to medicine. Her paper, the first in English to give an accurate account of the microscopic findings, is fundamental to our understanding of the condition. Today the diagnosis of Hodgkin's disease still depends on the presence of the "giant cell" she described, which is now known worldwide as the Reed cell, the Reed-Sternberg cell, or the Sternberg-Reed cell.

In addition to her paper on Hodgkin's disease, she published a report of a case of acute leukemia in which, far ahead of her time, she postulated the existence of a totipotential stem cell in the bone marrow.[169]

As the year progressed, Dorothy found herself worrying more and more about the future. One of her motivations for entering medical school had been to become financially independent. Her visit to Talcottville the past summer had made it abundantly clear that she would have to support not only herself but also her mother and sister. This need for money contributed to Dorothy's dilemma over the direction her career should take. Pathology attracted her the most, and her future there appeared bright. In those days the vast majority of physicians were in general practice, and very few positions existed for pathologists, the majority of which were in academia and relatively low-paying. Since the American Specialty Boards with their standard training and certification programs had yet to come into existence, her year of training at Hopkins would have qualified her for most of them. Dorothy had enjoyed her clinical internship despite the long hours, and, like most physicians who switch from clinical to laboratory medicine, she felt ambivalent about giving up patient contact. She resolved to explore some of the clinical opportunities.

Like many young gentlewomen of the period, Dorothy felt genuinely concerned about the grinding poverty that afflicted the majority of the population, who lacked the means to adequately feed and clothe their children and had no access to health care except under the direst circumstances. Influenced by another female student who planned to become a medical missionary and by Smith College's liberal tradition and strong emphasis on social work, she asked Welch for a month's leave to work at the Henry Street Settlement House on New York's Lower East Side. Opened in 1895 by Lillian Wald, who raised the necessary funds from rich New York bankers, it had become a landmark among outreach programs. Initially Wald was a medical student, but after an encounter with a sick woman in a tenement, she switched to public health nursing, where she felt she could help more poor folk.[170] The logic behind Dorothy's action is not clear, as social work would never have allowed her to support her mother and sister. Besides, she had seen plenty of the downtrodden, depressed, and diseased among the patients at Hopkins and had not evinced any particular empathy with them. Her stay in Henry Street quickly clarified her views:

> I knew definitely that I could never stand the unmitigated gloom of living and working with the down and out. The under[dog] has always had a great appeal for me, but without the impetus of religion and the joy of converting lost souls, I do not see how anyone can live as well as work in the slums. Missionarying even at home—I found bothered me.[171]

Shortly afterward, a unique clinical opportunity presented itself: Bryn Mawr College was searching for a college physician. Years earlier, Carey Thomas, the president, had spearheaded the drive to open Johns Hopkins Medical School to women and had almost certainly met Dorothy at one of Mary Garrett's grand receptions, to which female medical students were regularly invited. Dorothy found the prospect of working with young women attractive and wrote Carey Thomas, who invited her to visit the college.[172] Carey's brother, whom she knew at Hopkins, encouraged her to look the place over. When she arrived at the "Deanery," where Carey lived, it quickly became clear that it was Miss Thomas who was doing the looking. Seated in her study facing the window, she subjected Dorothy to an hour of merciless scrutiny and questioning. Over lunch, an impressive monologue followed on how a young professional woman should behave and establish herself in the community. Carey stressed the need to belong to a church; it increased one's standing and brought in patients. Did Dorothy drive? She did not. "You must learn at once," Miss Thomas told her. "A car is needed in general practice and it looks so affluent."[173] An appointment at the college, she continued, would quickly lead to a good livelihood in a pleasant community.

On her return to Baltimore, Dorothy, sensing that conflict between the two strong-willed women was inevitable, wrote a polite note declining the position. Miss Thomas, used to getting her way, was annoyed.

In late spring, Welch invited Dorothy into his office and after giving her "measured praise" for her work, asked her to remain for a second year as university fellow. He understood something of her financial problems and suggested that if the university stipend of $500 a year was insufficient, he would get her a Rockefeller fellowship that paid nearly twice that sum. Even so, given the state of her sister's health with its potential for additional financial burdens, Dorothy was not sure she could manage. Leaning strongly toward a career in pathology, Dorothy went back to see Welch again and asked just what her prospects in the department and her chances of advancement in the medical school were. Welch looked puzzled and then embarrassed. Dorothy wrote, "I explained that the man who had had the fellowship just before me had done no research but had been made an assistant in pathology the next year and both he and Jack Yates could look forward to promotion in the Medical School— if they wished it. Why not I?"

After a moment's pause, Welch explained, "No woman had ever held a teaching position in the School and he knew there would be great opposition to it."[174]

For Dorothy, this was the moment of truth:

Suddenly, as I saw what I had to face in acceptance of injustice and in being overlooked—I knew that I couldn't take it. And I told Dr. Welch that if I couldn't look forward to a definite teaching position even after several years of apprenticeship, that I couldn't stay. I just couldn't take it.[175]

Dorothy realized then what she had suspected since the beginning of medical school, but until this moment had never quite believed—medicine was a man's world.

In the years that followed, only two women held medical-school appointments higher than intern or resident, neither of whom ever married. Florence Sabin continued on as fellow in anatomy (supported by Mary Garrett's money) until she was promoted to associate professor of anatomy in 1905, but even then she was without a vote in faculty meetings.[176] On the death of the professor of anatomy, Hopkins selected an outsider to fill the chair. While Florence's gender undoubtedly influenced the decision, her nonconfrontational personality and her association with Mall, whose department was notoriously lax in teaching practical surgical anatomy to medical students, also would have damaged her candidacy.[177] Subsequently, Sabin moved to the Rockefeller Institute for Medical Research in New York at a salary of $10,000 a year, where she remained for the rest of her distinguished scientific career.

The other was an Englishwoman, Elizabeth Hurdon, a graduate of Toronto University Medical School, whom Dr. Kelly, the gynecologist, had brought to Hopkins in 1897. She became an assistant in gynecology a year later and subsequently received a medical-school appointment. Much of her success at Hopkins and in her later career in England came because "she understood and was able to successfully contend with the difficulties attached to the rather unwilling acceptance of women's work in some quarters of the [medical] profession"—something Dorothy never learned and perhaps never wished to learn.[178]

Dorothy was at a critical turning point in her life. Three interrelated issues affected her decision—her career, her family problems, and her love affair. Still, her passion for AJ consumed her—never before had she felt such a desire for a man (nor would she ever again).

She wanted him desperately and could not bear to see him every day if she could not have him for her very own. Her roommate, Patsy Long, was often away with her father in Washington, so the pair frequently had the apartment to themselves. Almost from the onset, the more rational side of her brain kept warning her. She saw all too clearly his conceit, his intellectual superiority, and his self-absorption; she still hoped he would change. Gradually Dorothy realized that AJ regarded women as playthings and had no desire for a home and children. "Marriage," she wrote, "was offered because that was the only way he could have me."[179] The final blow to their affair came when she found he was a cheap philanderer, even making passes at her girlfriends. Although they remained secretly engaged, she decided she could never marry him. The intense physical attraction persisted; she found his very presence heart-wrenching.

After a lot of anguish, Dorothy decided to leave both AJ and Baltimore. When she told Dr. Welch, he seemed relieved. It seems likely that he, and probably everybody else in the department, knew about her affair and was happy to have avoided a potential conflict between ex-lovers. Never comfortable around women, the idea of the organized, domineering, and outspoken Dorothy as a permanent member of his department probably filled him with horror. He set to work at once to find her another position. She would have liked to stay in academic pathology, but few opportunities existed for women then, and those lucky enough to hold a medical-school appointment usually found their careers capped at assistant professor.

Welch had a number of ideas. He told Dorothy that the Mayo brothers were looking for a pathologist, but she thought Rochester, Minnesota, too far from her family. He also knew of opportunities at the Woman's Medical College of Pennsylvania and the New England Hospital for Women and Children in Boston; neither appealed to her, possibly because she wanted to avoid working exclusively among her own sex. Welch, on his return from a trip, told her that Dr. L. Emmett Holt, the leading pediatrician of the day, was in need of a resident physician at the new Babies Hospital then under construction in New York. Initially Holt offered one hundred dollars a year. Later, probably under pressure from Welch, he raised it to fifty dollars a month plus the usual room, board, and laundry. After a lot of thought, she decided to accept his offer and move to New York City.[180]

Dorothy had made her mark at Hopkins; she had many friends among the house staff and loyal supporters on the faculty, including Welch, Osler, and Williams. She recalled her last night in Baltimore.

> Dr. Futcher, who had been my resident when I was intern, invited me to be the guest of honor at dinner at the Hotel Stratford. All my friends were there and the kindness and affection shown to me at this farewell party, and the lighthearted fooling of Jack Yates did much to break my grief at going. A deputation of these same friends saw me off, and I looked my last at the dome of the hospital as I sped out of Baltimore—at least for the last time as part of a great institution to which I owe a great debt—"The Johns Hopkins Medical School."[181]

Dorothy regarded Memorial Day 1902, when she departed Baltimore, as the lowest point in her life of nearly twenty-eight years:

> I turned my back on all I wanted most and started to make a new life for myself. My house had come down on my head.[182]

CHAPTER 9

Reorientation

New York and an Offer of Marriage

ONCE DOROTHY DECIDED TO LEAVE Hopkins, her immediate challenge was to find something to do before she started at Babies Hospital on January 1, 1903. Without a stipend and with her mother to support, money was a serious issue. Fortunately, Whitridge Williams, the head of obstetrics, knew that the New York Infirmary for Women and Children needed a replacement for its resident medical officer, who had contracted tuberculosis—an occupational hazard for physicians. With his strong recommendation, she secured the post.

When Dorothy arrived in Livingstone Place off Stuyvesant Square, she thought the place looked familiar. Indeed it was. She and her mother had stayed with a great-aunt in one of the mansions that now housed the hospital. This small specialized institution was worlds apart from the university-associated medical school she had just left. Gone were the bustle and excitement and all the familiar, helpful faces of the serried ranks of professors, assistants, interns, and students. At the infirmary Dorothy, aided by four interns, bore responsibility for all the inpatients. The attending staff volunteered their time. Since they did it primarily for the prestige, they would breeze in, give their orders, and breeze out; they did not teach. In the all-female hospital, founded by the first American woman physician, Elizabeth Blackwell, protocol loomed large: an attending would leave the elevator first, followed by Dorothy as the senior house officer, then the interns in order of seniority, and finally the nurses. Dorothy rounded with the attendings whenever they appeared and with the interns every morning and again last thing at night. The hospital served the same class of poor, indigent patients as Hopkins; whenever Dorothy worked in the outpatient clinic, she found herself deeply conflicted between "[her] sympathy with [the patients'] pitiful condition—deserved or not—and irritation with their feeble will or lack of mentality which got them into the situation and seemed bound to keep them there."[183]

Dorothy soon made friends with the four interns. She particularly enjoyed Caroline Finley, the obstetrics-gynecology intern, a rather plain, heavyset woman with a sharp mind and a ready wit, whose approach to life was unhampered by social standards or any sense of appropriateness. She took Dorothy to meet her tailor father—her first visit to a working-class home. Dorothy took a close interest in the obstetric service, the busiest in the city, and covered for Caroline when she was off duty. She recalled admitting an older married woman, who between Hail Marys and the characteristic cries of second-stage labor, fervently denied pregnancy. When Dorothy examined her, the uterus felt far too big even for a term pregnancy. She persuaded herself she could feel multiple arms and legs, and despite hearing only one heart, she diagnosed triplets. After the patient had delivered a two-pound baby, the uterus remained unchanged. The subsequent removal of a six-pound fibroid uterus explained Dorothy's dilemma.

Time passed quickly and happily. On hot summer nights, the house staff would all sign out to the roof and sit up there, happily smoking and talking. Caroline organized expeditions to Coney Island, the Palisades, and the theater. Dorothy became friendly with an ob-gyn attending whose companion invited her to visit her parents' palatial establishment on Oyster Bay, not far from President Theodore Roosevelt's home. She enjoyed both her work and life in New York City and now was anxious to start her training in pediatrics. Still, she pined for Baltimore and AJ.

On New Year's Day 1903, a taxi deposited Dorothy and her bags at the door of the newly opened Babies Hospital on the corner of Fifty-Fifth Street and Lexington in New York City. Miss Smillie, the assistant superintendent, met her: Yes, she was expected. No, there was no other doctor on duty. Dr. Holt was in Florida and would not be back for a week.[184]

After this inauspicious exchange, Miss Smillie showed Dorothy to her quarters: a large room on a high floor with two closets and its own bath. The social freeze continued throughout lunch. Afterward the laconic Miss Smillie took Dorothy on a tour of the hospital, the first in New York devoted exclusively to infants. The rows of white-painted wrought iron cribs with brass knobs could accommodate fifty small patients; above each cot hung a temperature chart, and in front of each place stood a tiny rocking chair.

As Dorothy made her way back to her room, she wondered why she had been treated more like an outside visiting physician than a colleague. Miss Smillie had spoken only in generalities and provided none of the practical specifics that the new resident physician needed to know. She had told her nothing about the patients, perhaps because as head of the already famous nursemaid training program, she had little to do with them. Undaunted by her reception, Dorothy unpacked her uniform; then, properly attired, she set out for the wards. Her first task was to learn the diagnosis of every case—a formidable obstacle with nobody to help her. The temperature charts were all up to date, but when she asked for patient histories and other records, she was met with blank stares. There weren't any! Alone in a strange hospital full of little patients without a single diagnosis or treatment plan and only her brief medical-school course in pediatrics and limited experience at Hopkins to guide her, Dorothy felt overwhelmed.

Quickly regaining her self-control, she began in her conscientious, practical, and methodical way to examine the infants one by one. In those days, patients, who often remained in the hospital for weeks, were customarily grouped by disease. She easily identified those with pneumonia, diphtheria, and rheumatic fever. She left the big group with feeding disorders to the care of the experienced ward staff. Even so, a disturbingly large number of sick infants remained undiagnosed. Fortunately, a small redheaded nurse of Scottish descent offered to make rounds with her. After Dorothy explained what sort of clinical information she was looking for, the nurse told her that Dr. Holt frequently wrote on the back of the first page of the temperature chart. There she found brief notes on the family and some orders, but nothing about the physical examination or laboratory findings. Helped by the nurse's native intelligence and retentive memory, Dorothy succeeded in piecing together the majority of the cases. New admissions she handled just as she would have done at Hopkins, writing the history, physical, diagnosis, treatment plan, and progress notes on blank sheets of paper.

Several days later, the hospital superintendent, Miss Marianna Wheeler, a poised, clever, autocratic woman, returned from vacation. Gradually Dorothy established good collegial relationships with both her and Miss Smillie, and mealtimes became positively cordial. Later she discovered that her cool reception had had nothing to do with her and everything to do with the dismissal of her predecessor, Miss Wheeler's relative and protégé, whom Holt felt lacked the necessary personality and ability.

At the end of what seemed like a very long week, L. Emmett Holt returned. Dorothy remembered him thus:

A small man, immaculately dressed, gray hair worn pompadour, small, tight features and very keen, sharp eyes—light as I remember them and missing little that there was to see. He did not radiate kindliness, but a brusque businesslike interest in what was going on.[185]

Holt, the leading pediatrician of the day, had interned at Bellevue Hospital in New York City when Welch and Halsted were there.

Through his membership in Fifth Avenue Baptist Church, he knew John D. Rockefeller and was instrumental in persuading him to endow the Rockefeller Institute for Medical Research and together with William Welch was one of the original members of the Board of Scientific Directors. This probably explains Welch's success in getting Holt to accept Dorothy as his fellow and pay her a relatively large stipend. [186]

Holt led a well-ordered, busy life. Every morning after his horse-back ride, he would enter his office and, without a word of greeting to his secretary, begin work. He never gave praise. He had taken the medical directorship when Babies Hospital was in danger of closing and transformed it into a flourishing enterprise. Four attending physicians volunteered their services, including Dorothy's cousin Dr. Reuel Kimball, whose wife had written Dorothy when she first arrived in New York to explain that her position at the hospital made it impossible for them to receive her socially.[187]

Holt's forte was practical advice succinctly given. An excellent teacher, like Osler he skillfully drew out the students and provided them with every opportunity to learn more. The spontaneity of children intrigued him, as well as their remarkable ability to learn from the world around them—two qualities notably absent in adults. Deeply concerned about the health and well-being of children, he lacked imagination and had no time for sentimentality. He once remarked, "The best way to make friends with a child is not to try."[188]

The nutritional problems and infectious diseases that dominated early twentieth-century pediatrics were Holt's principal interest. After working together for many years, Holt and Miss Wheeler realized that if mothers and nursery maids knew more about the dietary requirements of infants and the spread of infectious disease, the number of sick children would drop dramatically. At the suggestion of a member of the hospital board, they established the Practical Training School for Nursery Maids. Young women of reputable background paid to attend the four-month course (later increased to six), where they learned the basics of nutrition and feeding, hygiene, and infectious disease as well as the practicalities of childcare. The program soon achieved national recognition, and its graduates were much in demand as nursemaids for the children of the rich. As students, these young women helped take care of the patients in the hospital, and the best among them stayed on the staff, supervised by Miss Wheeler and Miss Smillie, the only trained nurses at Babies.

In 1894, Holt published *The Care and Feeding of Children: A Catechism for the Use of Mothers and Children's Nurses*.[189] Originally based on Miss Wheeler's lecture notes, this extraordinarily popular work went through seventy-five printings, including Spanish, Russian, and Chinese editions, and in 1946 was included among the hundred most influential books in America.[190] Written in question and answer format, it addressed in a straightforward and succinct way all aspects of the first two years of a child's life, from bathing to bad habits:

> *What is the best infant's food?*
> Mother's milk.
> *What must every infant food contain?*
> The same things which are in mother's milk.
> *What are the symptoms which indicate that a child who is nursing is not nourished?*
> It does not gain weight, cries frequently, sleeps irregularly and always in short naps, suffers from colic and the movements contain undigested food. [191]

To Victorian mothers, this little book was a revelation. It dealt with feeding: when and how much, which foods were allowed, and which were forbidden. It answered questions on crying, explaining in a few words how much was normal and how it might be helpful. Holt espoused a regimented, regulated way of childrearing that would not be well received today. He was among the first to recognize that the pediatrician's responsibility extended beyond the care of the sick child and included monitoring normal physical and mental development as well as confronting associated problems such as domestic violence and child abuse. Dorothy thought that he had taken advantage of Miss Wheeler, as she had first used the then-revolutionary "catechism" style to instruct her uneducated nursemaids. But the ideas and terse style were clearly Holt's.

There could, of course, be no comparison between the university-associated Johns Hopkins—with its many departments and large staff—and Babies Hospital, which depended on the skill and energies of one man. Nonetheless, Holt's aim was similar to that of the larger institution, namely to make Babies Hospital preeminent in its field. Dorothy soon found that he would accept any suggestion of hers couched in terms that intimated that it was what Osler would do at Hopkins.

Both Dorothy and Dr. Holt possessed strong personalities and opinions, and since neither of them had a sense of humor, they never developed a close collegial relationship. When Dorothy complained about being left alone on her first day to assume responsibility for the whole hospital, Holt seemed surprised. "Most unfortunate," he mumbled, and he continued on his rounds.[192] His cold, constrained personality contrasted sharply with that of the friendly, fun-loving, youthful exuberance of Osler. Holt, unlike her former chief, never once invited her into his home and treated her more like a servant than a colleague. Dorothy missed the camaraderie of the large house staff at Hopkins. Her heart still ached for AJ.

Because of Holt's reputation, many physicians visited Babies Hospital. Once when he was showing a group over the hospital, Dorothy heard a German accent, and, turning, she saw Dr. Gustave Manning, the son of her former Berlin landlady. They talked in German, and she felt pleased to have one-upped Holt, who spoke only English.[193]

Babies Hospital, with nearly six thousand outpatient visits and close to one thousand admissions a year, bustled with activity.[194] Bronchitis, pneumonia, and gastroenteritis accounted for the largest number of hospitalizations, followed by diphtheria, scarlet fever, gonorrhea, syphilis, and tuberculosis. Unfortunately, no specific treatment existed for any of these except diphtheria. Holt treated gastroenteritis with rice water and pneumonia with inhalations, mustard poultices to the chest, and time in the steam room—one of Holt's innovations. Marasmus, failure to thrive, and malnutrition were also common diagnoses and causes of death, reflecting the terrible social conditions existing in the nation's big cities at the beginning of the twentieth century. For most patients bed rest and good nursing remained the only treatment available, with the result that only 72 percent of the little folk returned to their parents.

The surgical load was fortunately light. Dorothy's duties included giving the anesthetics, which she did by dropping ether onto a piece of gauze stretched on a wire frame held over the baby's face—a method that remained in use for the next fifty years. Hernias and tonsillectomies—the latter, in Dorothy's opinion, done chiefly for financial reasons—accounted for the majority of the procedures. They also operated on a few cleft lips and cleft palates and orthopedic cases.

Not only was medicine different at the beginning of the twentieth century, but the culture was also. Miss Wheeler had warned Dorothy about women who dumped unwanted babies on the hospital. Initially she found this hard to believe, but she quickly learned to recognize the desperate faces of the usually youthful and frequently unwed mothers, often newly arrived in the city with neither family nor money. They would explain that the baby, who did not appear ill, was suffering from some sort of gastrointestinal problem, or perhaps convulsions. The complaints were always vague, and under questioning the stories would change. Dorothy would explain that the risk of contracting an infection in the hospital was very high and direct them to the nearby Foundling Hospital, to which a surprisingly large number of mothers would take their babies.

Catholic nuns took nursemaid training at Babies. They believed the next best thing to saving the child's life was assuring its place in heaven and asked Dorothy if they could baptize any dying infant if they knew it had not been done. She agreed, as she knew they would anyway. Undoubtedly a large number of children of other faiths were received into the fold.[195] In one sad case, obviously poor, ignorant parents asked if they might bring in a faith healer to pray daily with the child. After the patient's death, Dorothy was horrified to learn that he'd billed the parents twenty-five dollars a day—far more than the cost of hospital care.[196]

One woman who had read about Holt's extraordinary abilities arrived with her baby at the hospital after a four-day train journey from Oregon. The child was clearly retarded, and the physicians out west had pronounced him an incurable idiot. Dorothy recalled a similar case in Baltimore and called in Holt, who confirmed her diagnosis—cretinism. Once started on dried thyroid gland, the child's flaky, dry, coarse skin gradually became soft, and hair grew on his head. After a year in the hospital, he looked and behaved like any other child his age.

All too often an infant would be brought to the clinic screaming from excruciating pain in the bones and joints. Dorothy never failed to marvel at how a few teaspoons of diluted lemon juice would quiet the baby long enough for her to find the characteristic gum hemorrhages of scurvy. Both it and rickets remained common diseases until mothers routinely gave orange juice and cod liver oil to their babies, a practice that Dorothy later would help pioneer.

The regular outbreaks of infantile gastroenteritis that every summer swept New York City convinced Holt that breast milk was the best and safest food for babies. He arranged for the hospital to retain a wet nurse. When she could no longer keep up with the demand for her milk, Dorothy prepared a short paper justifying the need for an additional person. Holt took her proposal to the ladies' board that governed the hospital. As he read Dorothy's last line—"See what a single woman can do"—the board broke into laughter and promptly voted to hire two "single women."[197]

Shortly after her arrival, Dorothy became aware of several cases of gonorrheal vaginitis among baby girls and arthritis among the boys, which she thought were probably all due to the same cause. Only too well aware of the long-term dangers of gonorrheal vaginitis, Dorothy discussed the problem with Miss Wheeler, who told her the hospital was never free from it. A crisis arose when one of Holt's private patients contracted the disease. Dorothy finally tracked down the culprit—the night superintendent, who, during the regular nurse's supper break, would change diapers in the isolation unit and then, without washing her hands, move to other parts of the hospital. Dorothy instituted routine vaginal smears on all admissions, which together with the isolation of positive cases, mandatory use of rubber gloves (then relatively new), and sterilization of all equipment and diapers, effectively controlled the disease. Dorothy had hoped to write up her experiences—and had actually sent the manuscript to Dr. Welch for his opinion—but her cousin, Dr. Reuel Kimball, who had done nothing except complain about the problem, seized her material and, with bare acknowledgment of her help, published it.[198]

Probably in order to justify Dorothy's salary, which was six times Holt's original offer, she was also appointed assistant pathologist. Before long, Holt began handing her pathologic specimens, generally with the words, "From a very interesting case I saw this morning. Please let me know what you find."[199] Dorothy soon found herself devoting a considerable amount of time to his private patients, to the detriment of her own work. One day she mentioned this to Dr. Martha Wollstein, the hospital pathologist, who laughed and said, "Little Emmett always likes to get something for nothing; he used to have to pay me for the work you are doing."[200] Dorothy, who always resented any attempt by a man to take advantage of her, straightaway decided Holt would not get his pathology for free. She kept a record of everything she did and, using Wollstein's fee schedule, sent Holt an itemized bill. He paid her promptly but never gave her another specimen. The next year, she was dropped as assistant pathologist. In fairness to Holt, he had secured a large stipend for her and probably felt she owed him something in return.

From the outset, Martha Wollstein was friendly toward Dorothy, who enjoyed working in the laboratory and covered for her when she was out of town. A rather timid, unassertive woman, she typified, in Dorothy's mind, the early female professional woman—single, very bright, and extremely hardworking but embittered by years of discrimination from the male members of the profession, accentuated in her case by an Orthodox Jewish heritage. Wollstein also worked part time at the Rockefeller Institute, where she published numerous papers. After she failed to achieve the rank of member, she returned to full-time work at Babies Hospital. She was the first woman elected to the American Pediatric Society and arguably the first pediatric pathologist in America.[201]

The arrival one night of a poor white woman carrying an infant wrapped in a shawl heralded Dorothy's biggest problem in New York. She diagnosed pneumonia and explained to the mother the seriousness of the child's condition. During the night the baby died. Two postcards asking the mother to pick up the body produced no response. Dorothy asked administration to have the city remove the body, but then she remembered that Holt liked postmortems on such cases. Since the pathologist was away, Dorothy, without a permit, performed the autopsy herself. Just as she finished, the mother arrived. Dorothy explained to her that the baby's lungs were so badly diseased that recovery was impossible; the mother said she would bury the child. A week later, Dorothy was called to the hospital office, where a big, brutish-looking man handed her a summons charging her with the murder of the child. Visions of professional ruin with her picture in the newspaper flashed across her mind. The hospital's attorney heightened Dorothy's anxiety by pointing out that she had performed an autopsy without a permit and that the hospital could incur substantial damages. Accompanied by the hospital's aristocratic-looking lawyer, she was forced to appear in many sleazy courtrooms, including the infamous "Toombs," where she faced the child's mother, the black man with whom she lived, and their seedy attorney. On several occasions, she noticed the presence of a burly man, who one day flashed his police badge and said, "There is only one way to settle this. Go and see the woman."[202] Dorothy, despite the protestations of the hospital lawyer, hired the detective for ten dollars plus expenses.

A cab deposited them at the edge of the notorious "Hell's Half Acre," where the detective did nothing to allay Dorothy's fears by asking a policeman to come after them if they did not return within the hour. They walked through dirty tenements and up an evil-smelling staircase before they found the place. When the woman answered the door, the detective told her that she had no case and could never succeed in blackmailing a rich corporation, adding that Dr. Reed would be the only one to suffer. This last argument struck a sympathetic chord; the woman invited them in. Sitting at the kitchen table, Dorothy told her story, omitting her role in performing the autopsy, and pointed out that in a lawsuit, the word of a physician would always be believed. The woman explained that the man she lived with, the baby's father, drank excessively and was very rough with her and the infant. He was the one who had persuaded her to bring the suit after their lawyer had promised them big money. They talked and talked. Finally the woman said, "Let's kiss and forget it—I've nothing against you. You was good to me."[203] A thankful and greatly relieved Dorothy paid the detective and returned to Babies Hospital.

As far as her duties at the hospital would allow, Dorothy led an active social life. Her friends included two Smithies: Patsy Long, now an intern at the New York Infirmary for Women and Children, and Sophia Bigelow, who was managing Patsy's grandmother's fine house on Eighty-Sixth Street. Almost every week, she met with Caroline Bacon (another Smith graduate) and her husband for a dinner or theater outing.

Early in Dorothy's first summer, Babies Hospital sent her to its country branch at Oceanic, New Jersey, to take charge of both the medical care of the children and the administration. She welcomed the break from the oppressive city heat and the summer epidemic of diarrhea; besides, she had relatives in nearby Red Bank, including Edmund Wilson's mother and Paul Kimball, MD (brother of Reuel Kimball at Babies), who practiced nearby (and who had been in love with her sister, Bessie). A lonely Dorothy welcomed his frequent visits; he, in turn, let her use his horse and buggy when he took vacation. His kindness extended beyond cousinly affection, and when he proposed marriage, Dorothy reputedly laughed and said she would just as soon think of marrying her brother.[204] She also enjoyed the company of a young female cousin until an amused Paul told her that when the girl wanted to "party" all night, she told her parents she would be staying with Dorothy. Outraged at the idea that she might be considered "loose moraled like all women doctors," she went to see the girl's father.[205]

Family responsibilities continued to weigh heavily on Dorothy. Before leaving for Oceanic, she had examined her sister's sputum and found it teeming with tubercle bacilli. Bessie had failed to respond to sanitarium treatment in the Adirondacks and was now at Talcottville in their mother's care. The challenge of a seriously ill patient and three rambunctious children in an old manor house with neither indoor plumbing nor sanitation was quite beyond Grace, with her childlike approach to life and utter inability to deal with anything unpleasant. Dorothy feared that soon she would have to support not just her mother, but the whole family. At the beginning of August, Dorothy took leave and headed upstate. When she arrived, she could barely contain her anger at her mother, whose snobbish notions and extravagance had brought the family to its knees. Brother Will, meanwhile, continued his merry downhill course, moving from one promising but ultimately unsuccessful business venture to the next. All he ever did was ask for money. Bessie, concerned about her children's welfare, made a will appointing Dorothy her executor and trustee and the children's guardian. As his wife neared the end, Willard, who had recently lost his paper mill through lack of interest and sloppy business practices, came to stay in the Old Stone House.[206] Kneeling by his wife's bed, he promised her that Dorothy would bring up the children.[207] Immediately after the funeral, he announced that the children were going to live with him in Winchester, Massachusetts. When his sister-in-law reminded him of his promise, he replied that he'd made it so that his wife might die in peace; he did not have to honor it. On hearing this, Grace took to her bed and refused to see Willard again. His behavior did not surprise Dorothy, who had long recognized his flawed character. After many long and irksome discussions, she finally told him it was her duty to do all she could to help. "Let us start," she said, "from tonight—forget the past and work together to bring up the children."[208] A Boston attorney told her Bessie's will was worthless, as it made no mention of her husband; the best solution would be for her brother-in-law to sign a release. Dorothy knew he would not agree but thought if he were asked to sign a paper by the lawyer, he would do so without bothering to read it, which he did. Later Willard told her he knew the document was illegal but felt things would work out best if she became his children's guardian. Dorothy took her responsibilities seriously and worked hard to help bring up and educate her sister's children; she even paid for her niece, also named Dorothy, to go to Smith College. Willard Furbish never made anything of his life. Dorothy claimed he embezzled from his employer and his daughter and that her husband had to repay the money to prevent him from going to jail, but there is no evidence for this.

Back again on the mosquito-ridden Jersey shore with a crowd of convalescent kids, Dorothy soon grew bored and introspective. In the long, quiet summer evenings, after the ocean breezes had stilled the scourge of mosquitoes, she would sit out under the stars and try to revive her spirits from the despair that engulfed her.[209] The problem of her medical career remained. She still had to figure out what course it should take and how she could best earn a living. She had gone through the pros and cons of general practice when she visited Carey Thomas at Bryn Mawr, and nothing had happened since to change her mind. Clinical work was never her real love. She had seen how male physicians treated their female colleagues and was determined that nobody was going to treat her as a second-class citizen. She preferred pathology, particularly investigative work, but the chances of finding a position appeared slim. After long discussions with Paul Kimball, she decided to stick with pediatrics.

Dorothy—now twenty-nine years old, unmarried, and meeting few eligible men—felt trapped in a career she wasn't sure she wanted to pursue. In those days, young professional women had to choose marriage *or* a career; those who elected the latter generally lived in institutions, leading frustrated, lonely lives—the last thing Dorothy wanted. Her father's early death and her mother's peripatetic round of relatives and rented houses had reinforced her nesting urge; she wanted a home and children of her own. In the still of the night, she yearned for the passionate embraces of AJ.

Probably she thought too of Charles Mendenhall. After she rejected him, he had written:

Dear Dorothy…I have decided to try and write you what I said this morning I would tell you. But I cannot wait…It is this. Let me have what is left of you—far more than I deserve— and let me give you all there is of me—which is next to nothing. My life will have its inspiration, then, in doing all the small things I could for you, very very [*sic*] small compared with what I had hoped to do for you but still, perhaps I could make your way easier—might even make you happier a little...For pity's sake D, don't reject this at once—let me plead it with you...It *can't* be worse than the utter blank which you assume is the only possibility, can it?[210]

A year later, he wrote again:

Dear Dorothy, I have found my bearings, as you told me to do—and they are just the same—they can't be any different. A little bit of light finally came out of the blank you left me in—and I am living on that...I must tell you about it. So won't you, Dorothy, let me see you as soon as I can...I am so miserable.[211]

Another year passed; she did not hear from him again.

Early in September, Dorothy and her little patients returned to New York, where she happily immersed herself in the hectic routine of hospital life. Shortly afterward, she received a cable from Charles Mendenhall announcing he was on his way home from Germany. She arranged for time off. Wearing her smartest coat and hat and feeling both excited and a little apprehensive, she waited for him on the dock.

As Charles's slight figure and serious face appeared at the top of the gangway, a wave of renewed hope swept over her. They exchanged enthusiastic greetings and talked nonstop about shared experiences in Germany, as well as his promotion to associate professor in the physics department at the University of Wisconsin in Madison. She told him of the tragic death of her sister, how Willard had schemed to take control of the children, and about her troubles at Hopkins and Babies. He took her to dinner, and afterward they went by taxi to Morningside Heights, where they sat on a park bench talking about their lives and hopes. "It was good," she remembered, "to talk freely with one who knew my family and with one whom I knew cared deeply for me and mine."[212]

When the time came for him to leave, she accompanied him to the station; he bought her a pass, and she helped him board the coach. As they said their good-byes, a thought suddenly crossed her mind: Why not make this the solution? Isn't it obvious? As the porter moved the steps, the locomotive gave its first great puffs, and the car began to move, she cried out, panic-stricken, "Take me with you."

Charles, scarcely able to believe his ears and likely wondering if he had heard correctly, answered, "Now?"

Running beside the train as it gathered speed, she shouted, "Next time."[213]

As the train sped past the backs of tenements and out of the city, Charles, startled and confused, reflected on what she had just said. Had he heard correctly? Was she really going to marry him? Did she really mean it? It was too late to ask. He lay down but could not sleep, his mood swinging repeatedly from ecstasy to scientific skepticism. When the train stopped at Albany, he jumped out and sent her a telegram, asking if he had heard correctly and whether she meant it.

In Edwardian times, well-brought-up young ladies did not ask men to marry them. Dorothy spent the next week anguishing over her actions—the most important decision of her life. Finally, after multiple drafts, she mailed Charles this letter:

Dear Charles, I've tried half a dozen times to write you a decent letter and I can't. The last week has been an ordeal; everything mounted up at once, as it always does. One trouble followed on the next, and I quite lost my grip on myself. Today I feel more sane, but my brain feels sore and I feel tired and forlorn...I've worried about you between everything else. You don't know me at all, there are two sides to me—like everyone else—and there is a passionate pagan imaginative childish side to me that you don't know or want, and yet it's the source of all the strength that makes the thinking soul possible. I can't explain it to you. No one but Mary [Strong] knows them both, but I am too foolish and inconstant and changeable to suit you. I couldn't make myself over and be always what you expect me to be and even my dramatic instinct wouldn't meet the requirement of playing a part all the time.

My dear, I would make you very happy one day and very miserable the next, and I could not help it any more than I could being and besides I don't want to be bred just for the woman that everybody knows but for the child that never had a chance for happiness his way.

Perhaps what you mean about my disliking you comes from this feeling. This young savage inside of me always weighs the balance. This sounds like perfect rot, but it's true. I think you are making a great mistake, and if you knew me all, you wouldn't love me all in all, and I know that if you didn't love all in all, why I should never make you happy. You know, I've made you pretty miserable up to now, and can't you see why it is. Dorothy.[214]

After an exchange of letters—Charles always wrote Dorothy beautiful, passionate letters, expressing emotions in ways he never could do in person—they agreed to postpone a decision until they met again. At Christmas, he came to New York, where they had a marvelous time, including a wonderfully romantic night at the opera *Parsifal*. After long and serious discussions, they decided not to announce their engagement until she had officially broken up with AJ.

Later that winter, Dr. Osler invited Dorothy to Baltimore to give a talk to the Medical Society on Hodgkin's disease. She was delighted but feared the visit would open old wounds. Her talk went well, and she enjoyed the ovation afterward. Dr. Welch asked if she was keeping up with the literature, as he did at every subsequent meeting, possibly with the hope that one day she would return to pathology.

The Oslers had invited her to stay with them. When her former chief inquired about medicine in New York, she said that nothing at Hopkins had prepared her for "the smallness of New York," adding that she found the physicians there petty and focused on money.[215] She also thought that the medical students, who mostly possessed only a high-school diploma, compared unfavorably with the college graduates at Hopkins.

Holt, too, was interested in the differences between the two places and, on her return, asked her the same question. Catching her on a day when she was particularly irritated by his meanspirited approach to life, she replied,

> Well, Sir, it is hard to point out the essential differences, but you may understand when I say that in six years in Baltimore I never heard money mentioned in regard to the practice of medicine. Here, when any attending or a visiting physician is taken around the hospital, the conversation always reverts to the almighty dollar, how much a man received for an operation or how much less or more was being made this year or last.[216]

Dorothy never hesitated to speak out against anything she thought wrong, although in later years she acknowledged things might have been better if she had held her tongue.

In Baltimore she saw AJ, who once again aroused her passion. As they visited their old haunts together and remembered the good times they had shared, her resolve, so easy in his absence, melted away. She still hoped he would change. April found Dorothy still undecided, her soul in turmoil, her dilemma unresolved. On Good Friday 1904, "in utter despair of being able to make anything out of the broken pieces [of my life]," she walked up Lexington Avenue to the Episcopal Church.[217] Uplifted by the service, she returned to the hospital to learn that a gentleman was waiting for her—it was AJ. He, too, had been moved by her visit to Baltimore and had come to New York to try to rekindle their love. Their meeting was a disaster. Discussions became bitter and rancorous. In the heat of the moment, they both said things better left unsaid. Finally, emotionally exhausted by the death of her sister and the long months of indecision, Dorothy told AJ she "would prefer death to living with him."[218] He stormed out.

Many years later, Dorothy wrote, "He did love me I knew then and I know now—but he made evil his choice and it couldn't be mine."[219] She kept AJ's identity a secret all her life. Who was this man? A search of the students and faculty at Hopkins during that period reveals nobody with the initials AJ. The first hint of his identity came from this undated letter in Dorothy's archives, which must have been written after she announced her engagement to Charles:

Dear Dorothy,

I had not heard of your engagement—apparently nobody liked to tell me—and it was hard to grasp for a while. Since you are going to be married though I cannot think two ways about your state of mind and I most sincerely pray whatever powers there are that you may find entire happiness in loving and being loved by this man…I shall not forget it or feel any the less remorseful, any more than I can forget you for as I look back over my whole life what little love was given me of love for a women I in turn gave to you and now for the rest I am left I think absolutely indifferent and careful only of things in the laboratory. I regret it but believe me you should not. I—about to continue in this loveless life—congratulate you and am glad with you that you are to have someone else's love than mine, I am grateful to you for your kindly feeling for me altho [*sic*] I don't see why you should have it. I haven't much to look forward to. I shall achieve a mediocre success I suppose in my work—not more probably and I shall always be alone and live in or about a hospital. Already I have lost interest in nearly everybody and feel old. W.[220]

This is a classic letter from a rejected lover. There were of course many people with the initial W at Hopkins, including Welch and Osler; among men her own age were William MacCallum and William Thayer (who later married). Dorothy never mentioned her affair to anybody, nor does she identify her lover in her memoirs. Margaret Long, who almost certainly knew the truth, said not a word. The riddle would not be solved until long after Dorothy's death.

That summer, Dorothy spent a month at Talcottville with Charles, where in the beautiful rolling upstate countryside, she gradually regained her mental composure, and Charles's innate goodness, tenderness, and unswerving devotion conquered her misgivings. They became officially engaged. It might be imagined that theirs was a marriage of convenience, at least on Dorothy's part, due to her urge to have a home and a family. Her letters to Charles show otherwise:

Dearest, I tried to write last evening but couldn't. I felt too much the touch of you in my arms and more than the touch of your lips on mine. And I was dazed by the way you whisked me up and down from the heights to the depths, with everything tumbling around. Just a word and a touch—a living tingling touch—how much does that mean to you, dear, which means everything on earth to me. I need you so much sweetheart—can't you see by taking yourself away from me for even just a little while what an objectless, aimless craft I'll be?

And if anything can make my love more true and kind, dear—make me want to be everything to you.[221]

Neither family was happy with the match. The Mendenhalls never approved of Dorothy, whose college education, professional training, and independent, outspoken ways symbolized the "modern woman." They thought their son deserved better. Grace Reed, too, was unhappy. She had tried unsuccessfully to marry Dorothy off to several rich men and had opposed every step of her medical education. Now she upbraided her daughter for giving up a promising career to marry Charles, who, despite his many fine qualities, had fallen short of her ideal—a good-looking, affluent, and socially prominent husband.

Dorothy returned to Babies Hospital and continued working there until the end of 1905. Hospital regulations required the admission of every severely ill baby or infant. Frequent overcrowding resulted, and Dorothy had more work than she could handle. Using her usual technique of explaining how Osler ran his service at Hopkins, she was able to persuade Holt to appoint two female interns, who relieved much of the pressure and allowed her more time for the interesting and unusual cases.

One day while at dinner with the hospital superintendent and her staff, Dorothy collapsed under the table, conscious but in cardiac and respiratory arrest. Repeated injections of cardiac stimulants revived her. Holt was called but was unable to explain the episode. For several days afterward, her eyes remained swollen, her fingers were painful and stiff, and a rash covered her body.[222] A physician friend from Hopkins diagnosed a hypersensitivity reaction. Cases of diphtheria were very common at Babies and were treated with injections of a diphtheria antitoxin that was raised in retired racehorses. Because of her continued exposure to the disease, Dorothy was in the habit of giving herself a little shot when injecting antitoxin into her patient. In so doing, she had become sensitized to horse serum and had suffered an anaphylactic reaction. "This near fatality," she wrote, "proves what I have long known—my life is charmed." As Jack Yates told her years earlier, "You are born to be hung."[223]

In midsummer 1905, Dorothy eagerly looked forward to her future with Charles:

> Dearest, It is hard to start a birthday letter in all the rush of the day's work...Where will we be next year for our birthdays—it will be our first anniversary together dear and we must celebrate in an especial fashion—I wish you could be here now for this one. To tell the truth I am a bit cross for I believe you could be just as well as not...I am terribly homesick for you...Isn't it odd to think two years are about up since we started to care together—love isn't love until two love.
>
> Dearest, I'm shutting my eyes now and trying to put my arms around your neck and feel again your face close to mine, and kiss you on both shut eyes for your eyes will have to be shut if you are pretending too and then your mouth, dear—And then you will hold me close and kiss me too—and more and more—and I don't see how you can stay as far away, when your girl wants you so...Dearest man, I'm so glad of you— and thankful to be your girl—I don't want anything or anybody but you and I never have or can ever love anybody else so much. Kiss me dear, Dorothy.[224]

Toward the end of Dorothy's time at Babies, Holt decided to place the hospital under the control of the College of Physicians and Surgeons of Columbia University, where he was professor of diseases of children. This upset Dorothy; she feared the two internships would go to men. This would be a major loss for female medical graduates, as they were excluded from all but a handful of such positions, mostly at women's hospitals—a situation that would persist until the outbreak of World War II. In order to ensure that after her departure the position would not fall into male hands, Dorothy persuaded a female friend who had graduated with honors from Hopkins to come to Babies as an intern. Once the new arrival had proven herself,

Dorothy gave one month's notice and resigned. Holt, unable to find a replacement on such short notice, was forced to appoint her the new resident medical officer.

It is not clear if Holt knew of her scheme. Surely he was angry over the abrupt manner of Dorothy's departure and was disappointed to learn that the woman he had worked so hard to train was abandoning pediatric practice. Everyone was kind when she left New York, but her mood was somber and sad: "It was the end of 10 years in medicine, and leaving them behind was not easy."[225]

CHAPTER 10

Devastation

Tragedy and Resurgence

ON VALENTINE'S DAY 1906, DOROTHY awoke, scraped the ice off her window, and peered out. She had chosen this as her wedding day not for the usual romantic reasons, but because it was her father's birthday. Although the temperature was well below zero and snow covered the fence posts, the plow had cleared the road in front of the Old Stone House, so everybody should arrive in time for the ceremony. On this special day, her conscience was not entirely clear: she had told the Reverend E. F. H. J. Masse that her intended, Charles Mendenhall, was a baptized Christian; he was not—he was a Quaker.

Dorothy's ancestral home, decorated with masses of greenery, looked its best. In front of a blazing fire in the north parlor stood the same prayer bench her grandmother and sister had used at their weddings. Merwin K. Hart gave away the bride,[226] who looked radiant in a fashionable cream organdie dress with a pigeon-breasted bodice and three-quarter-length sleeves covered with tiny appliqué leaves; handmade lace formed the stand-up collar and cuffs, and an heirloom lace shawl and veil completed her ensemble.[227] Three classmates from Smith—Mary Strong, Ethelyn McKinney, and Sophia Wells—and several relatives from Boonville and Utica attended the ceremony. Neither her brother, Will; her brother-in-law, Willard;

142

nor her Mendenhall in-laws, who had retired to Italy, could attend. After feasting on panned chicken, peas in butter, potato balls in cream, and currant jelly, the guests left to catch the afternoon train from Boonville, leaving the bride and groom behind in Talcottville.

The Quaker Mendenhalls had settled in Delaware County, Pennsylvania, in 1686. Later, Charles's grandfather moved to eastern Ohio, where his father, Thomas Corwin Mendenhall, was born. As a youth, TC, as Dorothy's father-in-law was always called, showed a remarkable aptitude for mathematics; following just one year of higher education, he graduated *instructor normalis* (IN). After a decade of teaching high school, Mendenhall senior became the founding professor of physics and mechanics at Ohio Agricultural and Mechanical College—later Ohio State University.[228] His marriage to the meek and submissive Susan Allen Marple was a happy one, fostered by her skill at predicting his opinion on any particular subject and then, when it was brought up, agreeing with him. The Marples traced their ancestry back to before the Revolutionary War; it was through their friendship with the Kimballs that Dorothy first met Charles.[229]

Dorothy and TC never got along. She resented his attitude of male superiority and disliked his domineering approach and the way he treated women. He thought their place was in the home, waiting on their husbands—a role his wife, a first vice president of the National Association Opposed to Women's Suffrage was only too happy to fulfill.[230] TC, for his part, refused to acknowledge that Dorothy was a professional woman with a doctorate, of which he was probably envious, and never alluded to her important contribution to the pathology of Hodgkin's disease.

The Mendenhalls' only child, Charles Elwood, was born on August 1, 1872, two years before Dorothy. When Charles was six, the emperor of Japan appointed his father professor of physics at the Imperial University, and the family moved to Tokyo. TC found the three subsequent years very agreeable; he particularly approved of the way Japanese men treated their womenfolk. These years were also scientifically interesting and profitable; among his other achievements, he measured the weight of the earth from the top of Mount Fuji. When his contract ended, the family returned to Columbus, where TC continued his distinguished academic career. He received numerous honors, including membership in the National Academy of Sciences and the attachment of his name to an Alaskan glacier. Organized, efficient, hardworking, and frugal, he insisted Charles work his way through college at a time when he was making $10,000 a year as a college president. TC possessed a fine tenor voice and a deep love of music and, surprisingly, was much in demand as a witty after-dinner speaker.

Charles, after spending three years without siblings or playmates in a culture unchanged since the Middle Ages, grew up withdrawn and lacking in social skills. Dorothy remembered seeing him at a children's party in Columbus looking forlorn and lonely. He had not wanted to attend, so his mother told him he must write his regrets. Charles demurred—how could he when he had none? He preferred to stay home. His mother insisted, "If you don't send your regrets, then you have to go."[231] The Quaker ethics of truthfulness and integrity formed the backbone of his character even though the family no longer belonged to the Society of Friends. His rigid upbringing, introverted personality, and lack of experience with women made him difficult to live with; Dorothy frequently felt isolated and misunderstood. A workaholic, Charles always felt guilty about enjoying things. He would, for example, habitually leave the part of a meal he liked most, saying "it was delicious, but perhaps not good for him because he enjoyed it so much."[232] Before his marriage, he never danced or played cards.

In many respects they appeared an ill-matched couple. Charles, soft-spoken, shy, and unassuming, was a good conversationalist who could be quite funny. Dorothy, opinionated and dogmatic, had a loud and penetrating voice with a commanding manner. Her cousin, the author Edmund Wilson, remarked on her curious accent: she said "lahst" and "bahth" and used the German pronunciation for some words such as "nerve" for *nephew* and "funger" for *finger*.[233] She always spoke in complete sentences and never used slang. She eschewed nicknames or diminutives, except for her elder son, whom she called Tom; after he married she always called his wife by her proper name, Cornelia, when everybody else, including her parents, called her Nellie. Although Dorothy laughed at jokes, it was never clear that she got the point. Nellie claimed, "She did not have a funny bone in her body."[234]

The couple shared a deep love of nature. In their later years, Dorothy would wander off looking for wildflowers while her husband fly-fished. Incurably romantic, she adored poetry. Charles loved music—something Dorothy never really cared for—and enjoyed playing his violin in amateur ensembles. All his life, his work and his students came first. The need to match his distinguished father's achievements drove him relentlessly.

On February 19, 1906, the newlyweds set sail from Boston for Naples, where they joined Charles's parents, who, since TC's retirement, had led a peripatetic existence, migrating like birds with the changing seasons between hotels and pensions throughout Western Europe. During their long honeymoon, Dorothy became acutely aware of her husband's forgetfulness and proclivity for procrastination. After Charles caused the group to miss the train for a planned excursion for the third time, his father became so enraged he had to retire to his bed with a "heart attack." Leaving Charles's parents behind, they crossed the Bay of Naples in a terrible storm to Sorrento. They explored the still-unspoiled island of Capri and spent two weeks in the enchanting village of Ravello, suspended between sea and sky high above the Amalfi Coast. In Salerno, they searched in vain for traces of the old university and its once famous medical school, the first in Europe.

The day after they visited Pompeii, Mount Vesuvius erupted. When Charles heard the rumbling of the mountain and saw its seething plume of smoke and streams of red-hot lava, he set out immediately to get a closer view, leaving Dorothy alone with her recollections of the volcanic destruction of Pompeii, rendered all the more vivid by the hordes of refugees praying and singing hymns. After Charles returned safely, they fled by train to Rome, where they spent a month exploring Dorothy's favorite capital, which, although swollen to almost half a million people, still retained much of its earlier charm and something of its pastoral atmosphere.[235] They took numerous excursions and several short walking tours into the Campagna before heading north to Padua, Florence, and Venice. Dorothy found the art galleries an absolute revelation. Possessed of a vivid visual memory, she often recalled the art and architecture she had seen on her honeymoon. They joined up again with Charles's parents in Lugano, Switzerland, and together took a train to the foot of the Simplon Pass and ascended by stagecoach through vivid flower-filled alpine meadows to the summit. It was midsummer now; they had planned to stay longer, but Dorothy was pregnant and feeling increasingly unwell. After a short stop in Holland to pick up new equipment for Charles's laboratory, they crossed to England, where they boarded a ship for home.

Landing in Boston, they took the train westward across upstate New York, disconcertingly close to Talcottville. Stopping in Chicago, they visited Marshall Field's, purchasing a dining-room set, beds, and a few chairs. Dorothy had never been to Madison, so Charles tried to keep up her spirits by talking of the beautiful rolling countryside. Madison occupies an attractive position between two lakes, with the university perched on the top of bluffs overlooking Lake Mendota. A faculty wife who arrived a few years before Dorothy described it:

The town itself, when we first saw it, was little more than the site of the capitol and the university. It breathed an air of dignity and moderate prosperity...Many of the buildings were of local sandstone, so that as one looked down from "the Hill," as the university was called, the town resembled an Old World settlement, as if it had been there for generations.[236]

Dorothy, fresh from the scenic beauty and architectural glories of Italy, failed to see the resemblance. As they drove from the depot, her heart sank. How could Charles have brought her to such a place? Why on earth had she married him? He had never thought of Madison as a place to live; it just happened to be the location of his laboratory.

The university, set in an intrinsically liberal and socially progressive state, provided a powerful intellectual stimulus that pervaded the city. The forward-thinking faculty, recruited from leading eastern universities, was determined to build a great university in the heart of the Midwest. As Dorothy would discover, their wives included a remarkable collection of highly intelligent women who lived in imposing Victorian homes, surrounded by children. Ample domestic staff afforded them the leisure to pursue their varied interests. The state government and supreme court increased the number of intellectually curious people who read books, listened to music, marveled at the new wonders of science, and debated the issues of the day. The city was far from a backwater; Isadora Duncan danced in the Fuller Opera House in 1909, and former president Theodore Roosevelt visited there in 1911. Its citizens, resplendent in evening dress, indulged in ten-course dinners served on fine china and crystal and disported themselves at grand charity balls. In the winter of 1901–02, no fewer than eighteen Madisonians wintered in Rome. Although not immediately apparent to Dorothy, "There was always something in the air, call it the hum of culture."[237] In time, she would be at the center of things.

For the moment, the stirrings of her baby and the need to find somewhere to live occupied her. She found setting up house a new and challenging experience:

No one ever knew less of housekeeping than I did. I have always avoided manual labor—using my head to save my heels. My mother never taught either of her girls how to do anything domestic.[238]

She learned quickly, growing, in her own estimation, into "an efficient if rather irregular housekeeper."[239] A good German maid soon made her life easier.

Dorothy married in order to have children, and, despite not feeling well, she was happy to be pregnant and was looking forward to the birth of her baby. A faculty wife suggested a well-trained but, Dorothy thought, rather careless physician, supposedly the best in town. In those days, Madison possessed one small hospital and lacked specialists in both obstetrics and pediatrics. At Hopkins, she had learned that most babies came naturally and without complications. Even so, she decided on a hospital delivery and engaged a nurse to help afterward at home.

The weeks dragged. Although other young faculty wives were kind and attentive, they could not provide the companionship and intellectual stimulation Dorothy needed. Her husband's experiments took up most of his waking hours—he was rarely home. When President Theodore Roosevelt asked Charles to join the Mint Committee in Philadelphia and help weigh the gold and silver coinage, he readily agreed. Having little experience with women, it never occurred to him that his wife, about to deliver her first child, needed him at home. While he was away, he wrote regularly, but somehow his letters never arrived. By the week's end, Dorothy was a nervous wreck; Charles's absence provided incontrovertible evidence of his warped, callous, and selfish personality—proof positive he did not love her. Her mother, who was spending the winter with them and had never cared for Charles, did nothing to disabuse her of this notion.

A week later, Dorothy, still upset, went into labor and entered the hospital. She was horrified to see her physician ignore the nurse's proffered bowl of disinfectant and perform a pelvic examination without washing his hands or changing his dirty, spotted clothes. As her confidence ebbed, Charles, back home at last, called her old friend from Hopkins, Jack Yates, now a surgeon in Milwaukee, to ask his advice. He was out of town. Dorothy endured intermittent contractions for three days before her physician took her to the operating room. She recalled "turning [her] head into the pillow and thinking this [would] be the end." She thought, "I shall die; he doesn't know what to do."[240] Her doctor performed an internal version, rotating the fetus in the womb, and delivered the infant with forceps. The next thing Dorothy knew, she was back in her room, and Charles was saying they "had a lovely little daughter, perfect in every way."[241]

She dozed off. Suddenly she realized something was wrong. Her baby was breathing irregularly. She gave the child artificial respiration until the doctor came and took her away. The next morning, Charles told her their little girl had died from a cerebral hemorrhage.

Dorothy always mourned Margareta Lilac; the infant remained ever present in her mother's mind. She never forgave the doctor but knew enough about the outcome of severe neonatal brain hemorrhages to be thankful that her only daughter was spared the fate of a helpless spastic. "The little time I had her on my knees," she wrote, "she was a comfort to me. She was a beautiful, tiny child, dark hair growing in a widow's peak like many of the Kimballs." Dorothy eulogized her baby in a poem, reproduced in part below:

She newborn dear, as timid and alone
In thy deep-pitying breast my little one enfold.
Make the [sic] her lips to smile, the heart within to sing.
Keep her secure from dreary dark and cold
Warmed by thy love and sheltered neath thy wing.[242]

Dorothy, not surprisingly, developed a severe case of childbed fever and spent several weeks in the hospital. Her physician assured her she'd suffered no permanent damage; later, after she complained of difficulty in holding her urine and feces, he admitted that she had sustained a large perineal tear. When she told Dr. Bolivar De Lee, the famous Chicago obstetrician, how her Madison physician had concealed the information, De Lee replied, "It was lucky for you he did nothing. Your only hope of living was free drainage, and it was a miracle you survived such obstetrics."[243]

For a long time after Margareta's death, Dorothy remained severely depressed and, by her own admission, "hell to live with." She blamed herself for her choice of obstetrician and the death of the little girl she had looked forward to for so long. A photograph (probably taken at this time and available only in proof) shows all too clearly the furrowed brow, the deep-set sad eyes, and the drooping mouth.[244] Charles felt their loss deeply too but found it difficult to articulate his feelings or comfort his wife. He became withdrawn, spending more and more time in his laboratory. Dorothy seriously considered abandoning her marriage and moving back east to return to medical practice.

That summer, the couple took a canoe and fishing trip to the North Wisconsin woods, where the serene, quiet beauty and lack of outside distractions helped mend their marriage. The following spring (1908), Dorothy, who never took steps "to interfere with the natural results of intercourse," found herself pregnant again and suffering from terrible nausea.[245] Taking no chances in Madison, she put herself in De Lee's hands, who, for fear of premature labor, insisted she spend the last month of her pregnancy in Chicago. Again, labor was prolonged, but Dorothy had confidence in a physician who personally sterilized and dated his own rubber gloves. On the fifth day, he delivered with forceps a fine eight-pound baby boy, Richard Corwin. Dorothy thought him "a beautiful baby...an angel child— sweet-tempered, good, and needing little correction."[246] Years later, Dorothy asked De Lee why he had not performed a cesarean section. He replied, "At that time [1909], I couldn't be sure of our techniques and I wanted to take no chances with you."[247]

Since neither she nor Charles wanted Richard to grow up as an only child, she soon got pregnant again, and on June 14, 1910, again under Dr. De Lee's care, she gave birth (without any difficulty) to her second son, whom they named after his grandfather, Thomas Corwin Mendenhall.

The family now lived in the Astronomer's House on Observatory Hill, one of the oldest buildings on campus. By fall, Tom, nearly five months old, was gaining weight steadily, and Richard was growing into a beautiful, sweet-tempered little boy. Suddenly, Dorothy's world fell apart:

> One morning, the ninth of November 1910, Charles and I were at breakfast and Richard was in his high chair at my right. He was eating a soft boiled egg, and I remember that he had messed it over his face and bib. Suddenly, looking at him I had a hideous sense of impending doom. I burst into tears. Charles came around from his end of the table to find out what was the matter. All I could say between sobs was that I knew Richard would never live to grow up. I had seen him dead. Both of us felt I was very foolish. At eleven o'clock a colored man was putting on screens and washing windows. We were both in the nursery—the front bedroom at Observatory Hill house. The door opened and Lucy, his nurse, came in followed by Richard running. She tried to grab him but he dashed past her out of the window and threw himself on the [low] railing running around the portico over the front door. He balanced a second and fell over, head first onto the concrete [twenty feet] below.[248]

Charles rushed the child to the hospital, where he died from a fractured skull. "Too stunned even to cry," Dorothy spent the day being driven around country lanes in a horse and buggy.[249] After the funeral attended by all their friends, Dorothy received a letter from Mrs. Mendenhall, advising her to put Richard out of her mind and concentrate on Charles and Tom. Infuriated, Dorothy replied that she "was trying…to remember each little loving thing and not to forget any day she had him."[250] Charles took her to Minneapolis for Christmas to try to avoid the mental anguish that thoughts of an absent Richard opening his presents would cause.

Apparently, Dorothy and her brother had patched up their differences. In August 1909, he wrote her on the stationary of the Reed Construction Company, of which he was president. He began by announcing he was sending a pedigreed puppy, which he hoped the baby would enjoy. After commenting on their mother's better spirits, he came to the point. Reed Construction, he boasted, was doing very well and was planning to raise more capital. To preserve his one-third share in this now profitable enterprise, he needed $3,500, of which he must have $1,500 in the next couple of days. In a postscript he told Dorothy not to mention this to their mother. She did not take his advice, and when she told Grace, she nagged her until she sent the money. He gave her his IOU.[251]

Later, Grace Reed received a letter from Will's wife, Clara, who addressed her as "Mother." She was sorry to hear about Richard's death. Will had disappeared the preceding April, taking some of the company's money with him, leaving his wife with twenty-five dollars in cash, two horses, and some cows—and three hundred dollars in debt. She thought she could make a living running a dairy business but needed a loan to get started. Her letter concluded thus:

> I am very sorry to tel you a bout Will is why I did not wright and tel you a bout it sooner I hope this will find you well with love from Mrs. Clara Reed.[252]

Dorothy at once asked her old friend in Columbus, Walter Martin, to investigate. Apparently Will had put about $700 into the firm and probably used the balance of the money Dorothy had sent him to settle pressing debts. Martin thought Will's partners had not reported his absence—at least he had not seen it in the papers—and their failure to pursue him suggests he had not taken a large sum from the firm. His wife did not appear in any particular need and was well able to look after herself; he thought it would be a mistake to start giving her money.[253] Will's IOU for $1,500 remains in Dorothy's papers, unredeemed. She never heard from him again.

That spring, she visited Jack Yates in Milwaukee, who noticed Tom playing with an inflamed mole on her face. "Dorothy," he said, "you ought to have that off."

"Take it off if you want it," she replied, "and please take the large mole off my shoulder if you want the little one, too."[254] As he injected the local anesthetic into her shoulder, feeling an intense burning pain, she cried out. "Keep your shirt on, girl," admonished Jack, thinking she was overreacting. Dorothy felt the same excruciating pain as he injected her face, but she kept quiet. By the time she arrived back in Madison, her eye was swollen shut, and the skin on her back had turned black. She called Jack, who ordered her to return immediately. After one look at her face, he admitted her to the Milwaukee General Hospital for what proved to be a long stay. Apparently, a junior nurse had filled the syringe with carbolic acid instead of local anesthetic. Dorothy's face was paralyzed, the skin sloughed, and saliva dripped out over her cheek. To everybody's great relief, movement eventually returned to her face, the fistula closed, and the wound healed.

When she finally returned home, mentally drained and physically weak from her long hospital stay, she was dismayed to learn that her mother, suffering from a bad heart, was coming to stay. Too weak to be of any help, she added to Dorothy's troubles by continually rehashing the tragedy and suggesting various remedies to restore her daughter's good looks. Dorothy and Charles hired a nurse to look after Grace Reed. On her second night, the woman came running to Dorothy. She had just given Grace her new medication, terpin hydrate. Immediately afterward, her patient had developed difficulty breathing. Dorothy raced to her mother's bedside to find her dead.[255]

With her mother gone, the additional responsibility for her sister's children as well as her own changed Dorothy's attitude from one of utter despair to one of determination to survive and face up to her responsibilities. Slowly she regained her health and strength, and the sadness and strain left her face. She got pregnant again, spending the last month of her fourth pregnancy in Chicago. On May 8, 1913, at the age of thirty-nine, she delivered an eight-pound boy, whom they named John Talcott. Two weeks later, mother and child, accompanied by a nurse, took the train back to Wisconsin. The heat was stifling; the nurse fanned the baby to keep him cool. Suddenly Dorothy looked down. John's arms were twitching—he was having a convulsion. They debated whether to get off the train; Dorothy decided they should continue on to Madison. Despite the continuous application of cold towels, John was still having fits when they arrived home. When Dorothy, emotionally and physically exhausted by the trip, tried to feed him, she discovered her milk had dried up. She made up a formula and tried to get him to take it. In the days before either evaporated or dried milk were widely available, artificial feeding presented a challenge. She literally took cow's milk apart, trying to find components John would tolerate; she tried all the tricks she'd learned at Babies Hospital—to no avail. Then she remembered that Holt had used peptonized whole milk. She gave it to her baby. It worked, but it took six months for John to regain his birth weight. A milk allergy was confirmed a year later when his mother again fed him cow's milk and his symptoms returned.[256]

Looking back over this period of her life, Dorothy wrote the following:

> I wonder that I had the courage to go on and I realize that I was enabled to go through this period without breaking into maudlin grief or taking up an irrational way of life, by

hardening myself, which produced intensity and bitterness which must have been difficult for others to live with. I don't blame Charles as much now as I did then. He was always inarticulate—his way of suffering was to shut it up inside of him, never to speak of it, perhaps even never to think of it. He loved me, but didn't know how to help me in my sorrow. As a result, I was bitter and hard on him—probably cruel when my suffering went unnoticed or when I turned to him vainly for comfort or even understanding. I realized then, and even more so now, that we were drifting apart.[257]

Time lessened Dorothy's grief. Gradually she regained her mental equilibrium, and her energy returned; she felt again the joy of parenthood and the urge to do something outside the home. In those days, professors' wives did not work, although an exceptional few with artistic or literary talent pursued their avocations in a ladylike manner. Dorothy could easily have opened a badly needed pediatric practice in Madison, but that was never her ambition. Years later, she wrote, "The practice of medicine had never attracted me. Laboratory work or some form of research...was the field in medicine which appealed to me."[258] All her life, she boasted that she had never billed a patient.

Two unexpected events led to a resurgence of Dorothy's medical career. In 1913, Julia Lathrop, chief of the newly formed US Children's Bureau, asked her to review a health-care guide for farm mothers written by J. Morris Slemons, MD, a Hopkins man and an excellent obstetrician.[259] Dorothy thought his book displayed a complete lack of social conscience and was out of touch with the realities of country life. His notion that pregnant women "should not work nor lift nor run a sewing machine" was unrealistic, except for those who could afford domestic help; from the poor, overworked farm wife's point of view, it verged on the absurd. Most mothers opted to do the laundry within a few days of delivery; otherwise they would face a double load a week later. Farm women, Dorothy thought, needed guidelines that told them what they could safely do and how their menfolk could help with the heavy-duty lifting and carrying. Miss Lathrop thanked Dorothy for her comments and asked her to be sure to call on her when next she came to Washington.

About the same time, Abby Marlatt, head of the department of home economics at the University of Wisconsin, asked Dorothy to lecture on health to women in neighboring farming communities. Her first talk took place in Stoughton, a small town eighteen miles southwest of Madison. Reading from a prepared text in her best Hopkins manner, she delivered a comprehensive review of infant nutrition. Her lecture sailed right over the heads of her audience of farmers and their wives. "They were very patient," she wrote, "looking at me with the expression of the mother of eleven who had buried seven."[260] They generally breast-fed their babies and had no use for her newfangled ideas. In the question and answer period that followed, they made it clear that their overriding interest was their own health during and after pregnancy.

On her return, Abby asked how her talk went. Dorothy replied, "Those women aren't interested in infant feeding—most of them nurse their babies. What they need to know is the elements of prenatal care."[261] Dorothy repeated some of the tales she had heard of bad obstetrics and its toll on rural mothers in Wisconsin and pointed out that nearly one-half of all newborn babies died before their fifth birthday. The magnitude of the problem caught Abby's attention; she asked Dorothy to undertake regular week-long lecture tours for the Extension Service, with a stipend of one hundred dollars per trip plus expenses.[262] Dorothy and Charles talked it over. Money had been a major concern during her years at Hopkins, when she'd had to support both herself and her mother out of her tiny stipend as an intern and fellow, supplemented by the residue of her father's estate. Her sister's untimely death and her brother's irresponsibility had exacerbated the situation. "For years," she wrote, "I would wake in the night—afraid of poverty."²⁶³ Over the last ten years, she had developed into a good money manager, and, since her marriage, she had been able to add to her capital. Now she needed an extra $1,000 a year to send her niece, Dorothy Furbish, to Smith College, and soon her two nephews, Hart and Ordway, would be college-bound. Miss Marlatt's proposal appeared very attractive; besides, the timing was propitious, as she had two maids and a nurse whom she could trust to look after the boys.

For three winters, the farmer's slack season, Dorothy formed part of a team that generally included a member of the home-economics department and a professor of agriculture. The group would travel by train across the frozen countryside to remote parts of Wisconsin. After leaving the comparative comfort of the railroad car, they would continue on in subzero weather in a variety of buggies, cutters, sleighs, and lumber wagons and, on at least one occasion, by railroad handcar to their final destination. Generally they stayed in local hotels, enduring cold rooms, hard beds, and at best indifferent meals. Occasionally they lodged in private homes that lacked indoor plumbing and sometimes running water. Dorothy dreaded sitting in the kitchen—often the only heated room in the house—surrounded by squabbling kids and the smell of unappetizing food. She remembered spending three very long days marooned by heavy snow in an "unspeakable" farmhouse near Waupaca and another occasion in Janesville, where she slept on a billiard table and the food ran out.²⁶⁴ At the end of a long, tiring week, the journey home was often the hardest part.

Dr. Harper, secretary of the Wisconsin Board of Health, appointed her a deputy health officer so that she could call on local health officials, discuss the prevalence of disease in their communities, and learn of any special problems. The practical, authoritative Dorothy lectured on prenatal care, obstetrics, baby care, and nutrition as well as aspects of child development, all areas in which she had received special training. She learned to speak from note cards in order to add spontaneity and retain the audience's interest. She borrowed Holt's height and weight chart for infants and, with the idea of helping parents face up to their responsibilities, would ask, "Is your child the correct weight for his height and age?"

She examined children with problems, suggesting either a simple remedy or the need to see the family physician. Some cases were deceptively simple. A pasty-faced, painfully thin boy of nine appeared, who would neither play nor take an interest in other children. The only abnormality Dorothy could find was a coated tongue. The family, like everybody else in the community, used an outdoor privy, to which the child was sent every morning, but his mother never checked for any movement. Truth was that for half the year, it was too darned cold for the boy to tarry, and he could not remember when he'd last defecated. Dorothy prescribed a laxative diet with prunes and molasses and had a commode installed in the house; the child quickly became happy, healthy, and regular again. In this remote community forty miles from the railroad, "the only doctor available was a man who slept on a lock of hair from the patient and the next morning told what he dreamed was the trouble."[265]

The plight of women in rural areas nationwide is well summarized by this poignant letter to the US Children's Bureau:

> I should very much like all the Publications on the Care of myself, who am now pregnant, also the care of the baby...I live sixty-five miles from a Dr. and my other babies (two) were very large at birth, one 12 lbs., the other 10 ½ lbs. I have been *very* badly torn each time, through the rectum the last time. My youngest child is 7½ and when I am delivered this time it will be 8 ½ yrs. I am 37 years old and I am so worried and filled with perfect horror at the prospects ahead, so many of my neighbors die at giving birth to their children. I have a baby 11 months old in my keeping now whose mother died— when I reached their cabin last Nov, it was 22 below zero and

I had to ride 7 miles horseback. She was nearly dead when I got there and died after giving birth to a 14 lb. boy. It seems awful to me to think of giving up all my work and leaving my little ones, 2 of which are adopted—a girl 10 and this baby. Will you please send me all the information for the care of my self before and after and at the time of delivery? I am far from a Dr. and we have no means, only what we get on this rented ranch. I also want all the information on baby care the especially right young new born ones. If there is *any thing* what [*sic*] I can do to escape being torn again won't you let me know. I am just 4 months along now but I haven't quickened yet.

I am very Resp. ACP., Wyoming.[266]

It is difficult today to imagine the life of unremitting hard physical labor, interminable pregnancies, and extreme privation—often exacerbated by spousal drunkenness and abuse—that these country women endured. Their lives afforded them no outlet for ambition, no channel for self-improvement, and no avenue of escape. Their plight touched Dorothy's heart; she determined to do something to improve their lot and that of their children.

At that time, the alleviation of social problems was left to local private philanthropy. The Attic Angels, one of Madison's oldest charities, began when the daughters of a retired general began collecting clothing for a poor family with twins. When their father saw them descending the stairs with their arms full of clothes, he cried out, "Here come the Attic Angels!" The name stuck. Membership in the organization was restricted to 150 young, unmarried women, who originally just prepared layettes for babies and Christmas boxes for poor children.[267] Later the Angels sponsored a charity ball, which grew into one of the biggest social events in Madison.

After Miss Sexton, a district nurse working for the Angels, told Dorothy of the desperate need of the city's poor children for better health care, Dorothy persuaded the charity to open a clinic for mothers and their babies and volunteered her services as medical director. As a married woman, she could not join the organization or attend annual general meetings, so they made her an honorary Angel.

The first Attic Angels Health Center opened in May 1915, in an apartment at 805 Mound Street, in the Italian district.[268] Volunteers filled out record cards and undressed the babies while the nurse, Miss Sexton, weighed and measured each one, checking his or her progress against Holt's tables of normal growth. Dorothy's relationships with the mothers were always cheery and friendly but not overly familiar. The mothers treated her with respect and were probably awed by her presence. She recognized at a glance the cool, confident mother and the plump, pink-faced, self-satisfied healthy infant. She quickly identified the agitated, nervous parent, constantly fussing over a sallow-complexioned, whimpering child with seemingly oversized eyes—warning signs that all was not well. She knew the loud, strong cry of anger and the short, sharp yell with the contorted face and contracted legs of the infant in pain.

At a baby's first visit, Dorothy performed a careful examination, looking for congenital abnormalities and signs of disease or dietary deficiencies. She noted the attainment of key milestones: was the infant looking around, sitting up, crawling, walking, and talking at the appropriate age? If the child failed to measure up to the standards for height and weight, her question was always the same: "Why is your child undersized?"

Dorothy, with her special interest in nutritional problems, always dealt with these cases herself. She attributed many of the feeding difficulties among the Sicilian families who lived in the neighborhood to their preference for imported pasta and olive oil over good, fresh Wisconsin-grown farm produce. One of her favorite recommendations was chopped vegetables. She helped mothers with questions about teething, weaning, toilet training, constipation, bed-wetting, and masturbation. She counseled them on sibling rivalry, jealous husbands, and housekeeping. Her approach was straightforward and down-to-earth.

The superstitions and ignorance of some of the mothers was beyond belief. One mother, told "to prepare the cereal in a double boiler, thought she was supposed to cook it twice."[269] She even instituted classes to teach women about healthy foods and how to prepare them.

Dorothy always referred children with serious medical problems to their physicians if they could afford one; otherwise she sent them to the free hospital clinic. Whenever Dorothy encountered a difficult feeding or pediatric problem, she and Miss Sexton would visit the family at home, a practice that, understandably, annoyed the community physicians, who resented her very presence. What had they done to deserve a female graduate from the most progressive eastern school, who, horror of horrors, was advocating community or government involvement in the delivery of health care? The American Medical Association saw her approach as flat-out socialized medicine. The president of the Dane County Medical Society told her that the Attic Angels Health Center would have to close because it was reducing the practice (and more importantly the income) of his colleagues. Dorothy pointed out that the clinic served only children. "That is just the trouble," he replied. "We don't see any more sick babies."[270] On another occasion, the secretary of the Wisconsin State Board of Health told Dorothy that she was wrong to consider medicine a profession; it was a business.

She also ran into trouble over birth control. A Catholic priest accused her of advocating it. She went to see him and explained the purpose of the clinic was to assist in raising healthy babies, not in preventing their conception. Adding that she worried about the long-term effects of birth control and never used any form of contraceptive device herself. At the meeting's end, Dorothy invited him to come to the clinic and see what went on there for himself. Her openness, charm, and practical logic won over the holy father. The following Sunday, he retracted his accusations from the pulpit and urged his parishioners to take their babies to see Dr. Mendenhall.

Dorothy's experiences in Baltimore and New York had taught her that these problems were not unique to Wisconsin. Ever since the death of her precious Margareta, she had thought a lot about maternal and child health. In 1914 she joined the American Association for Study and Prevention of Infant Mortality and attended its meeting in Boston, where, by a happy coincidence, her former chief of obstetrics at Hopkins, J. Whitridge Williams, gave the presidential address on "the limitations and possibilities of prenatal care." He asserted that proper prenatal care provided the best possible guarantee of safe delivery of a normal child.[271] At the same meeting, Dorothy spoke about her own experiences with rural obstetrics in Wisconsin.[272] After emphasizing that nearly one-half of women of childbearing age lived in the country, she summarized the problems facing pregnant women in small Wisconsin towns: inefficient, careless, and poorly trained physicians; few trained nurses or midwives; and the dearth of hospitals—in some cases the closest might be fifty to one hundred miles distant.

Dorothy did more than just speculate. Her training at Hopkins led her to undertake a statewide scientific investigation of infant mortality. She reviewed over twenty-six thousand death certificates from 1915 to determine the causes of infant deaths in the first week of life, the number of babies delivered by midwives, and the prevalence of puerperal fever. She presented her findings to the Wisconsin State Medical Society in 1916 and later published them.[273] Her study showed that although infant mortality in Wisconsin had fallen to 82 per 1,000 live births from 120 per 1,000 live births six years earlier, it still exceeded the national average. She attributed this to parental ignorance and the hardships of rural life—poverty, isolation, and lack of skilled assistance at delivery. One-half of deaths under one year of age occurred during the first month of life because babies were born too weak, too injured, or too diseased to live. Turning to maternal mortality, she reminded her audience that Dr. Bolivar De Lee, the distinguished midwestern obstetrician, thought it "much safer for men to go into battle than for women to have babies."[274] Puerperal fever and eclampsia caused half of all maternal deaths in the state. Midwives delivered one-sixth of all babies in Wisconsin, with no increase in the incidence of fever, possibly because complicated cases requiring instrumentation were referred to a physician. She complained that many death certificates were misleading and obscured the diagnosis of puerperal fever and suggested adding it to the list of reportable infectious diseases.

She also recommended establishing an educational program to ensure that prospective mothers understood the risks of overexertion and lack of prenatal care and went so far as to suggest that general practitioners should not deliver babies—it would be better if obstetrics became a specialty. In her opinion, the citizens of Wisconsin were "too busy perfecting the dairy cow to be interested in conservation of human young," a problem they could ill afford to neglect.[275] Prior to World War I, this was heady stuff for a state medical society, and it provoked long discussions. One physician agreed that the "ordinary cow in Dane County" had better care than many of the mothers, adding,

> I have gone into homes where I have seen the woman lying upon a bed with an old dirty mattress, without sheets, with pillows upon which there were no pillow cases, and saw her lie there in a dirty black gown that was filthy with the discharges of amniotic fluid.[276]

Many physicians in the audience reported similar experiences.

Although Dorothy probably did not realize it at the time, she had embarked on a second career, one that would fulfill her urge to do something with her medical education and improve the lives of mothers and babies. In terms of saving human lives, this would be her major contribution.

CHAPTER 11

Interruption

World War I and a New Career

IN THE SPRING OF 1917, World War I engulfed the United States. The Mendenhalls had often considered the possibility that America might enter the conflict that already had raged in France for almost three years. Charles, a middle-aged Quaker, felt safe from personal involvement, but, to his surprise, in May he was ordered to Washington, DC, where he spent the war as a major doing research for the United States Army Signal Corps and later the United States Army Air Corps. Dorothy missed her unlikely soldier in his rumpled uniform, loose belt, and crooked tie much more than she expected. Desperate to join him, she decided to rent out their Madison home and pay her niece Dorothy Furbish, who had recently graduated from Smith College, to keep the boys in her brother-in-law's house in Winchester, Massachusetts, never dreaming that several years would pass before the family would be reunited in Madison.

After a long search in a city jammed with soldiers, sailors, and bureaucrats, Dorothy found a cramped two-bedroom apartment. When the boys came for Christmas, she found that the oven was so small that she had to cook the turkey in two halves. At the end of their visit, four-and-a-half-year-old John refused to return to Winchester. Nothing would change his mind. Dorothy thought this inflexible determination came from Grandpa Mendenhall, but her friends knew better. Later the family moved to a very ordinary six-room house (1447 U Street NW) within walking distance of Charles's office. They enrolled Tom in the Friends School and hired a nanny for John.

Dorothy, remembering Miss Lathrop's invitation, soon made her way to the Children's Bureau. "The Chief," a middle-aged woman from a wealthy, educated Illinois family, greeted her warmly and soon asked how long she would remain in Washington. Would she be able to help out? Dorothy, delighted at the prospect of real, meaningful work, immediately agreed to become a wartime federal employee without any discussion of hours, salary, or conditions of service. Subsequently the two women became close friends. Dorothy thought her boss "the finest woman I have ever known and one of the ablest."[277]

At the end of the nineteenth century, nearly half of all children died before their fifth birthday. The principal causes were lack of prenatal care, birth injuries, malnutrition, and, as infants grew older, infectious disease and child abuse. In cities, the annual epidemics of infantile summer diarrhea resulted in a frighteningly high mortality rate. Poor hygiene in the milking shed and progressively longer transportation times in unrefrigerated wagons lay at the root of the problem. Initially the only effective prophylaxis was breast-feeding, but for mothers working in shops and factories, this was impossible. Toward the end of the century, the emerging science of bacteriology revealed the infectious nature of the problem, and the newly developed technique of pasteurization provided the means to control it. Regrettably, summer diarrhea remained a problem in the United States, as widespread adoption of the process would take many years.

At this time, the French led the world in social services. The first *crèche*—day nursery—was established in Paris in 1844, followed fifty years later by the first "well-baby clinic" (*consultations des nourrissons*), where infants were regularly weighed and examined and mothers were taught basic infant feeding and hygiene.[278] The French government strongly encouraged mothers to breast-feed their babies and set up depots to distribute safe, clean milk to those who needed it. These measures were not put in place for entirely altruistic reasons: there existed an urge to build up the nation's manpower to combat the ever-increasing military might of her eastern neighbor, Germany. Unfortunately, many of those who owed their lives to these farsighted programs were among the 1.8 million Frenchmen killed in World War I.

In the United States, the development of federal health programs occurred much later, due in part to the country's continuously expanding western boundaries and its decentralized government. At the beginning of the twentieth century, few states or territories registered births and deaths, and the fight to provide better care for children depended on private philanthropy. Children's activists, like Lillian Wald, failed to understand how the US government could spend huge sums of money fighting cholera in hogs and the boll weevil in cotton and do nothing to prevent the deaths of an estimated three hundred thousand infants and twenty thousand pregnant women annually.[279] Politicians, it seemed, could understand farm problems, but the importance of the health of the nation's children escaped them. Perhaps it was because the time frame was longer than either the growing season or the interval between elections and the immediate economic benefits were delayed, and thus less apparent. Significantly, mothers had no vote.

In response to growing concerns over the health of the nation's young, President Theodore Roosevelt convened in 1909 a White House conference, The Care of Dependent Children. Three years later, Congress established the US Children's Bureau with the mandate to "investigate and report upon all matters pertaining to the welfare of children and child life among all classes of our people."[280] These "matters" included the birth rate, infant mortality, orphanages, juvenile courts, desertion, dangerous occupations, accidents, and diseases of childhood. Congress optimistically expected Julia C. Lathrop, the bureau's first director, to improve the lives of nearly thirty million children under fourteen with a staff of fifteen and a budget of $25,000. Lathrop clearly understood that the "mere business of being a baby must be classified as an ultra-hazardous occupation."[281] She therefore decided to focus the bureau's limited resources on reducing infant mortality (deaths in the first year of life), which she estimated at 13 percent.[282] Other issues—such as illegitimacy, delinquency, offenses against children, and the major problem of child labor—would have to wait.

Since no reliable data existed on infant mortality, the Children's Bureau initiated a study in Johnstown, Pennsylvania, and a subsequent one in Manchester, New Hampshire which revealed a rate of 134 per 1,000 live births.[283] The mortality rate was higher among poor and illiterate families and almost double among infants of color.[284] Today, infant mortality is approximately 7 per 1,000 live births.[285] Prohibited by law from providing direct medical care, doubtless at the instigation of the American Medical Association, the bureau's principal activity became the preparation of educational pamphlets; the demand for the first two of these, *Prenatal Care* and *Infant Care*, exceeded 1.5 million copies.[286]

Miss Lathrop was delighted to add Dorothy to her staff. Her training in obstetrics, pediatrics, and nutrition and her experience in working with the poor in both urban and rural settings made her a unique and invaluable addition to the bureau. The tragic deaths of Dorothy's first two children, Margareta and Richard, had left her with a special empathy for mothers and a motivation to improve their lives and those of their children not found elsewhere in an agency staffed largely by single women. Lathrop appointed her liaison officer with the Food Administration, the Department of Agriculture, and the Red Cross. She visited all three agencies daily to coordinate their work with that of the bureau and, when necessary, to enlist their help.[287] She proved herself an industrious and highly intelligent staffer with a retentive memory, who, in her legible hand, wrote easily and well. Her principal interest remained infant welfare and nutrition, but like everyone else on staff, including Miss Lathrop, she responded to some of the thousands of letters received annually from anxious mothers across the nation. The following samples illustrate Dorothy's philosophy and style:

> Dear Sir, I seen in the home and farm paper that you were sending out pamphlets free, for helpful to expectant mothers. I would certainly like for you to send them. For I am expecting to be a mother in July, and I always have such a hard time giving birth to them I stay in labor so long. And I would like to know what causes that.
> Please send them right away.
> Yours truly, B. A., Clay, KY.[288]

On receipt of the booklets, Mrs. A. wrote back, thanking the bureau and enquiring "how much hot salt or hot water that I must put in the babies bed at night to keep it warm."

Dorothy replied for the bureau on June 11, 1918:

> My dear Mrs. A., I am very much interested in your letter and I am sorry that there is very little that I can tell you that will be of assistance to you. It is quite evident that you have rather difficult and prolonged labors. Would it be possible for you to go to a hospital for your next confinement and is there a good hospital in your neighborhood?
> In regard to your question of how to heat the baby's bed at night: it has been my custom in ordinary weather not to use any means of heating the bed. In very cold weather or if the bedding is not perfectly dry I have used hot water to warm the bed before the baby was put in it. If a hot water receptacle is kept in bed with the baby it should be rolled in a blanket and great care exercised to prevent any possibility of the baby touching it directly. I have seen very serious burns on a small

infant from a hot water bag that seemed only pleasantly warm
to the touch.
Hoping you will call upon us if we can be of any further assis-
tance, I am,
Yours respectfully,
Dorothy Reed Mendenhall, M.D.
Director, Division of Hygiene.[289]

She replied to a query from a wounded veteran:

There is no possibility of an acquired injury being inherited
or affecting a child. There is no reason at all why, when your
general health is again restored, you should not have a family
of perfectly healthy children.[290]

Dorothy wrote to a woman asking for dietary advice for a nursing
mother:

In order to produce milk one should take an abundant varied
diet with three or at most four regular meals in the twenty-
four hours. Milk in the mother's diet has been found to be
the best milk producer. You can take this milk as a drink or
as weak cocoa or soup or in the form of butter milk. Usually
it is better to drink all that you possibly can at a meal and
take a large glass of milk after the meal is over or at the end
of the meal.
More important even than food is the taking of sufficient
water during the period. A very good rule is for the mother
to drink one or two glasses of water either hot or cold, at the
time she is nursing her baby.
In this way the intake of water can be increased outside of
regular meal times.[291]

This letter clearly shows Dorothy's interest in nutritional problems, which had begun when she worked with Emmett Holt at Babies Hospital and was later stimulated by her son John's milk allergy and expanded by her experiences with the urban and rural poor in Wisconsin. At the Children's Bureau, Dorothy studied the health of New York's schoolchildren. In an article, "Child Welfare and the Milk Problem," she reported that nearly 10 percent of New York City's schoolchildren were undernourished due, she thought, to decreased consumption of fresh milk.[292] This led her to an exhaustive study of the properties and chemical constituents of milk as well as a comparison of milks from different animals. She crystallized her thoughts in a Children's Bureau publication, *Milk: The Indispensable Food for Children.*[293] "Milk," she asserted, "has no substitute in the diet of a child," and she stipulated that an average youngster ought to receive a pint and a half daily. She considered it a complete food, containing protein for growth and carbohydrates and fat for energy, as well as all the important minerals (except iron), together with "an abundance of unknown dietary factors—the vitamines [*sic*] which control growth and health." In her opinion, breast milk was the best food for babies; she asserted that babies breast-fed for the first six months of life did better than others (now known to be due in large part to the passive transfer of maternal antibodies in the milk). She regarded fresh cow's milk as the best substitute for mother's milk and discussed the importance of pasteurization, which still was not widespread. She dismissed proprietary baby foods and described in detail the properties and use of condensed, evaporated, and dry powdered milks, stressing that they should all be derived from the best-quality milk. The war had caused a severe milk shortage throughout Europe, and powdered dried milk had become the prime replacement to ship there, as it was light, easy to transport, and, importantly, not damaged by freezing temperatures. Dorothy recognized the universal truth behind the belief of Wisconsin dairy farmers that the nutritional status of the cow was reflected in the size and health of her calf. She reminded the mothers of America, "Milk is an indispensable part of the diet of pregnant and nursing mothers and of all young children."[294]

In 1918, with the first Children's Year Campaign approaching, the bureau was searching for new ideas. Dorothy suggested the weighing and measuring test that she had used so successfully in Wisconsin. The bureau printed cards with Holt's height and weight table on one side and, to enhance the sense of responsibility among parents, these questions on the other:

IS YOUR CHILD THE CORRECT WEIGHT FOR HIS HEIGHT AND AGE?
IF NOT WHY NOT?

Seven million cards were dispatched to the nation's mothers, who, for the first time, had a definitive standard by which to judge their own children's development. At the same time, the card conveyed a warning that if their offspring did not meet the appropriate measurements, they had best find out why.

Among the myriad of problems facing the bureau was organized medicine. Physicians were unwilling to transfer such simple tasks as weighing and measuring babies to paraprofessionals, as they feared it would reduce their income. After years of dealing with the jealousy, pettiness, and insularity of doctors, Dorothy came to agree with Miss Lathrop's assessment: "The medical profession was the least socially minded of any of the professions." [295]

With the cessation of hostilities, Dorothy's chief asked for her résumé, as she wanted to appoint her head of the child hygiene division of the bureau, adding that before this could be done, she would have to pass the civil-service examination. Dorothy's response—she had taken enough exams and would take no more—created a potentially insurmountable problem for Washington bureaucrats. Shortly afterward, she learned to her surprise that she had passed the examination and was now an accredited medical officer of the Children's

Bureau.[296] Her colleagues who had studied for and actually taken the test were understandably annoyed.

Dorothy soon realized that the average farm wife had neither the inclination nor the time to read the long and comprehensive publications of the Children's Bureau and began distilling their contents into what she called dodgers, small pamphlets limited to one or two sheets of paper. Among the first were *Minimum Standards of Prenatal Care* and *What Builds Babies?*[297] She continued her active membership in the American Association for Study and Prevention of Infant Mortality. At its meeting in Milwaukee in 1916, she spoke on the work of the extension department in educating mothers about prenatal care and infant hygiene.[298] In Chicago in 1918, she presented a paper, "Nutritional Problems in War Time."[299] Dorothy also reviewed two books.[300] Under the title "Bananas for Babies," she panned *The Health Care of the Growing Child* by Louis Fischer but praised *Painless Childbirth*, in which the author, Carl Henry Davis, analyzed the use of anesthetics in obstetrics and discussed painless childbirth.[301] Dorothy found this book a revelation and concluded,

Dr. Davis has made a real contribution to meet what is one of our most vital problems—the conservation of the life and health of our childbearing women: for here we find not only one of the leading factors in our infant mortality question but the means of measuring the strength and stamina of the coming generation. Civilization may be measured by the safeguards the race provides for motherhood.[302]

Meanwhile, she attended to the needs of her family. Whenever possible, she returned home to lunch with John, sometimes spending the afternoon with her younger son, which, as a part-time employee, she could do if it did not conflict with her work.

In 1919, the government appointed Charles scientific attaché to the London embassy. Deciding the children would be better off in

Madison, Dorothy reopened their Carroll Street house and hired a housekeeper. On her own in Washington, she felt lonely and abandoned. One evening, while dining with some of Charles's scientific friends at the Cosmos Club, she learned that they were about to depart for an important scientific conference in Brussels, Belgium, where Charles would head the American delegation. "Too bad," they said, "you can't be there." Never one to be left out, Dorothy announced she would join them. "Impossible," they replied. "As the wife of a serving officer and government employee, you would be denied a passport."[303] The determined Dorothy was not so easily put off. To her way of thinking, she had spent two difficult years in Washington and now most assuredly deserved some compensatory fun. That night, endlessly turning over the problems in her mind, she scarcely slept. The children, the house, the cost, and her other responsibilities—none seemed insurmountable.

The next morning, she visited Miss Lathrop and explained that her only chance of seeing her husband in London was in her capacity as a medical officer from the Children's Bureau. Miss Lathrop immediately wrote a letter stating she required a firsthand report on the care of war orphans in Belgium and France, together with data on the effect of wartime conditions on the health of British children. Handing it to Dorothy, she asked, "Will that do?"[304]

During her lunch hour, Dorothy went to the State Department, where a clerk took down her particulars and asked her nationality and birthplace. He then demanded if somebody could attest to this; her companion responded that she had known her and her parents for ten years, which satisfied him. Afterward, they went to the British embassy to get a visa. By two o'clock, she had all her documents and was back at work. Her friends got her a passage on the *Aquitania*.

Week's end found her crossing the Atlantic for the seventh time. She shared a cabin with a young, "rangy, plain" actress. As she rose early and her cabinmate stayed up late, their paths hardly crossed. Years later, she encountered the woman in Madison, who recognized her immediately. With the words, "Here is the little doctor," Lynne Fontanne introduced Dorothy to her husband, Alfred Lunt.[305] Now, as the ship hurried north on her great circle route, Dorothy, with only clothes suitable for the hot Washington summer, shivered in the cold. On arriving in England, she went straight out and bought a fur cape.

In July 1919, the Mendenhalls left London for Brussels to attend the first big postwar scientific meeting. The American and British delegations stayed at the same hotel, where Dorothy, as one of only three women, enjoyed a lot of attention. But she had work to do. She called on the chief of the Belgian Bureau of Health, who received her cordially and talked about the devastating effects of the war. She explained her mission. The next morning, she found a young one-armed, English-educated Belgian officer waiting for her with a chauffeur-driven automobile. Taken by surprise, she asked him to return after lunch. By then she had found a companion, as she was not going off alone with a strange man in a foreign country, even if he was an officer.

Over the next several days, they visited all the Belgian orphanages, which were generally built on the cottage system, with a housemother taking care of a dozen or so children. Since the officer kept reappearing, they went on to explore the battlefields, retracing the heroic resistance of the tiny Belgian army that had enabled the French and British to stabilize the line in front of Paris and ultimately, with American assistance, defeat the Germans. Her guide showed her the methodical devastation inflicted by the Hun and told her of the deliberate slaughter of civilians and destruction of priceless buildings and treasures. They visited Ypres and other battlefields, where Dorothy stood in silent awe before the storied rows of crosses marking the graves of a generation of young men.

Dorothy, who loved pomp and circumstance, watched with Charles the great procession celebrating the return of King Albert to Brussels. The sight of General John J. Pershing leading the American contingent of one thousand men, all over six feet tall, brought tears to her eyes. That night, they attended a reception in the fifteenth-century gothic town hall. Diplomats glittering with decorations, officers strutting in splendid dress uniforms, and ladies shimmering in evening gowns filled the great tapestry-lined chamber. Dorothy heard stories of bravery among the civilian population and of the duplicity that led to the betrayal and subsequent execution of the British nurse Edith Cavell, who had helped Allied prisoners of war escape.

Back in London, she called on the minister of health, who insisted she see the movie *Clean Milk*. The British audience seemed excited, but to Dorothy it was all old stuff. What impressed her was a government-run health center where tea was served in the waiting room. A staff member took each patient's history and gave her a physical before sitting down with her to plan her confinement and register her unborn child for the nearest well-baby clinic. She had seen nothing like it in the United States.

Dorothy found the constrained approach to life of upper-class English households trying and the plumbing unbelievable. She wondered how, in the presence of so many servants, the food could be so bad and why it was always served cold. At a dinner party given in their honor, the hostess insisted, to Dorothy's embarrassment, that she lead the women out of the dining room at the end of the meal so the men could enjoy their port and cigars. Their visit to Britain concluded with a trip to Cornwall, where Charles discovered fly-fishing—soon to become his principal avocation.

On the passage home, Charles spent a great deal of time preparing his customs declaration. He included everything he had bought during his six-month stay in England, putting down its full value, even if he had worn it for months. Dorothy's approach was to declare only expensive items bought as gifts for others; she did not mention her purchase of fine old Mechlin lace. Charles possessed a diplomatic passport and could have bypassed customs, but he refused special treatment. The officials thought his long list silly and reduced the value of many items so that they owed very little. This took so long that they barely caught the last train to Washington.

At dinner, Charles remarked, "It is odd to me that a woman has no sense of honesty."

Seizing the opening, Dorothy replied, "That would come better from you if you had declared the one expensive thing you bought in London—your new silk-lined overcoat—and had not worn it off the boat."[306] Surprised, confused, and then angry, Charles barely spoke the rest of the way home.

After the war, Charles was offered the chairmanship of the Division of Physical Sciences of the National Research Council. When John heard he might have to spend another year in the nation's capital, he wrote,

Dere mother Tom and me want to stay home—we're thru playin in parks.[307]

Faced with little choice, Dorothy left them with a housekeeper in Madison while she and Charles spent the winter in another tiny Washington apartment. Every few weeks, she made the long trip to Madison to check on the boys (the fastest train to Chicago then took seventeen hours). Everybody counted the days until the end of Charles's appointment, when the family could all be home together again.

Meanwhile, Dorothy continued with the Children's Bureau. After the war more and more colleges began offering courses on children's health but found their efforts frustrated by the lack of good source material. Miss Lathrop asked Dorothy to oversee the preparation of *Child Care and Child Welfare: Outlines for Study*, published in note form in 1921.[308] It began with "The Fundamental Rights of Childhood" and included all aspects of health and hygiene, as well as discussions on recreation and child labor. In addition to editing the entire work of seven sections (over 300 pages), Dorothy wrote all of the first section, "Health Problems of Mother and Infant," and large parts of several others, about 165 pages in all. In addition to having professional knowledge, she was the only person in the bureau with personal experience of country life.

Dorothy also wrote the Children's Bureau pamphlet *Minimum Standards of Prenatal Care*, in which she outlined in plain English "the least a mother should do before her baby is born."[309] Dorothy advised women as soon as they knew they were pregnant to visit their physicians and schedule regular appointments, which, as the time for delivery approached, should be weekly. At each visit, her doctor should check her temperature, pulse, weight, and blood pressure and test her urine for protein. She advised pregnant women to wear loose clothing and flat shoes and to eat three balanced meals a day that included fresh vegetables and fruit as well as plenty of milk and protein. She cautioned, "It is *not* necessary to eat for two." In the days before washing machines and vacuum cleaners, she thought doing the in housework was exercise enough; heavy lifting and hard labor should be avoided. Later she recommended that at the patient's first visit, a Wassermann test be run to exclude syphilis, which, at that time, was a relatively common disease that affected mothers could transmit to their newborn babies with devastating consequences.[310] All of this is well known today, but at the end of the war, this was hot stuff. The infant mortality rate in the United States was still approximately 132 deaths per 1,000 live births, which put the country in eighth place behind New Zealand—the world leader with a rate of 83.[311] These figures make it abundantly clear that most women either remained ignorant of Dorothy's recommendations, were unable to follow them, or did not wish to follow her advice.

Dorothy testified for the Children's Bureau at the Congressional Committee on Labor Hearings on the Hygiene of Maternity and Infancy. When asked if financial aid should be left to the states, Dorothy replied,

> I think we feel that the rural districts need it most. The rural districts are less able to speak for themselves. I should be a little afraid of some big cities with their powerful organizations if there were any funds to be obtained, they might obtain them and leave little for the country.[312]

The resulting Sheppard-Towner (Promotion of the Welfare and Hygiene of Maternity and Infancy) Act greatly expanded the role of the Children's Bureau and provided matching funds to states that set up child and maternity welfare clinics. It emphasized that the bureau's role was to promote health and well-being among pregnant mothers and children by education rather than by offering direct medical care. Opposition to both the bill and the bureau developed gradually from several areas, including organized medicine and conservative women's groups, notably the Women Patriots (formerly the National Association Opposed to Women's Suffrage), who saw in the bill the forerunner of socialized medicine. In 1929, Congress terminated the maternity and infancy program, and later the bureau became part of the US Public Health Service, thereby ending the dream of a government agency devoted exclusively to the needs of children.

Dorothy also worked hard for a provision to train and license midwives. She knew that in remote rural areas and urban immigrant tenements, where there were few physicians, untrained women were assisting at many births. Since she had experienced firsthand a bad obstetrician, she thought it obvious that properly trained midwives would do a much better job with uncomplicated deliveries and help reduce infant mortality. Physicians, fearing a loss of income, strongly opposed her efforts.

After Dorothy returned to Madison, she continued working for the Children's Bureau as a contract employee and wrote the folder *What Builds Babies.*[313] This was her last major piece of work for the organization—in part because she was offended when the Medical Advisory Committee decided that mothers were too dumb to understand the scientific rationale for their recommendations and determined that these should be omitted from future publications and in part because she found it too onerous to tone down her opinions to suit the cautious bureaucrats who, then as now, appeared more interested in avoiding controversy than actually accomplishing something. It was time to move on.

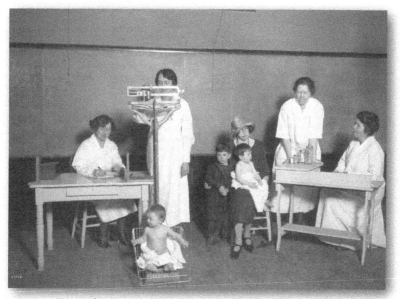

Dorothy (seated on the far right), in one of her
baby clinics in Madison Wisconsin.

Dorothy holding baby John Mendenhall in 1913.

Charles, Dorothy, Tom, and John circa 1919.

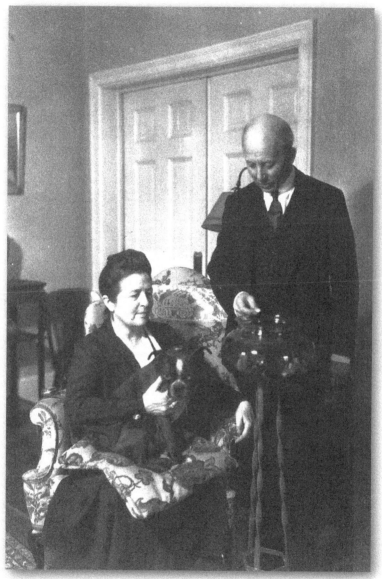

Professor and Mrs. Charles Mendenhall with their dog, Noah, on the twenty-fifth anniversary of their marriage.

CHAPTER 12

Fulfillment

Family Life

THE SUMMER OF 1920 FOUND the family reunited in Madison after an absence of more than three years. Dorothy entered the happiest and most stable period of her life; her husband's career blossomed, and her sons matured into fine young men. At once, she set about renewing old friendships, enrolling the boys in school, and resuming her work with mothers and their babies, juggling her numerous commitments with the needs of Charles, Tom, and John.

Dorothy, with her erect posture, her dark-brown hair piled on top of her head, and her strong jaw and unflinching gaze, commanded respect. Her appearance remained important to her. She loved large hats, chunky jewelry, and the color purple. Although vain, she wore very little makeup and ignored the dictates of fashion, buying only top-quality clothes in the styles she thought best suited her. Her deep-set eyes conveyed a certain sadness that reflected the premature deaths of her father and sister, the problems with her brother, the trying years at Hopkins, and the tragic loss of her first two children. Her life had not been easy. She had been tested and had learned to be tough; she knew what to do and would, if necessary, do it again. As she put it:

> The years of my mother's dependence on me, the responsibility of the Furbish children and the sorrow of my sister's

unhappy life and tragic illness, forged my character into iron. Any sweetness I may have once had—turned into strength.[314]

Once the family had settled back in their old home at 510 North Carroll Street, Dorothy began picking up the threads of her professional life. She resumed her lectureship in the university department of home economics and taught a course, Child Care: Hygiene of Maternity and Infancy.[315] She believed childbearing was the principal biological function of women and thought every woman should understand the physiology of reproduction. In the first of twenty lectures, she listed the fundamental rights of a child: the best possible heredity, basic requirements for mental and physical health, normal home life, education, opportunity for play and companionship, protection from child labor, and moral and religious training. In her direct, unsentimental way, she described the development of the fetus before progressing to prenatal care, delivery, infant feeding, and normal physical and mental developmental milestones. She also gave a course called Modern Parenthood, based on the premise that the family provided the foundation for the development of the human race and twentieth-century civilization. She explained how a child had gone from an asset who could be put to work to a liability requiring medical care and education and discussed the inherent difficulties facing wage-earning mothers.[316] She emphasized the necessity of prenatal care for mother and baby and ended with the basics of childcare and feeding. The university subsequently made her course The Prospective Mother available by correspondence.[317] When the Wisconsin legislature mandated a freshman course on "sex hygiene," Dorothy lectured the female students on reproduction. Since the course was held at eleven o'clock on Saturdays, it was unpopular with the students and never repeated.[318] She declined, with no regrets, an invitation to participate in the agriculture department's winter forays into Wisconsin's backwoods.

The state of her beloved Madison Health Center shocked her. Harry Ray, MD, who had directed the clinic in Dorothy's absence, lacked her enthusiasm, and his own practice kept him fully occupied, with the result that clinic attendance had dwindled to such an extent that the Attic Angels were considering closing it. The one bright spot was the new facility on Park Street, where the janitor took advantage of modern plumbing by storing coal in the bathtub to avoid trips outdoors during the bitter midwestern winter.

Miss Sexton, the health-center nurse, was delighted to have Dr. Mendenhall back. The two women shared the belief that the clinic should go beyond Dorothy's outline in *Minimum Standards for the Child Health Center* and ought to function as "a sort of school for mothers," open free of charge to everyone.[319] To increase enrollment, Dorothy arranged with the Board of Health for Miss Sexton to deliver birth certificates; this way new mothers could learn about the clinic and enroll their babies at the same time. A contemporary photograph shows Dorothy seated in the clinic, listening intently to a mother who is balancing a partially clothed infant on her lap while a volunteer is weighing another infant in a basket. The clinic became a popular assignment among student nurses at Madison General Hospital, as Dr. Mendenhall was "fun to work with."[320]

With Dorothy's return, enrollment soared, and she was forced to hire a second nurse. To raise funds for the nurse's salary, the Madison Kennel Club staged a May Day dog show, which, despite a heavy overnight snowfall, was a huge success. To Dorothy's amazement, Miss Sexton, who had long complained of being overworked, became so jealous of her new colleague that she was forced to assign the newcomer to the recently opened second location. Subsequently, the increasing number of patients necessitated opening a third facility, fulfilling Dorothy's ambition of having "a baby clinic within wheeling distance of any Madison mother."[321]

Eventually the enterprise became too costly for the Attic Angels, and the community took over the funding. Every year, Dorothy appeared before the county board, which readily granted her $1,000 to cover clinic work for patients living on the outskirts of town. Relationships with the city council were never as good, in part because of Dorothy's earlier battle with a former city health officer, who, although he never visited a clinic, took every opportunity to undercut her work. A crisis arose when one of his staff refused to admit a case of scarlet fever to the Contagious Disease Hospital, saying, "[he] wouldn't admit a dirty Dago to the nice new hospital."[322] As the epidemic of what was in preantibiotic days a very serious disease spread, an angry Dorothy saw contaminated milk bottles standing outside patients' homes awaiting collection and caught one patient's father shuttling between his quarantined upstairs apartment and his grocery store below. A story hit the newspaper of a mother who had spent the night with her child in the Contagious Disease Hospital and then was sent home still wearing the same clothes. The board of health summoned Dorothy and Miss Sexton to a meeting at the city's health department, where, in the presence of the city attorney, the proceedings took on the atmosphere of a trial. Dorothy, interrogated for two hours, stood her ground. Shortly afterward both the city medical officer and the director of nursing at the Contagious Disease Hospital resigned.[323]

Dorothy, despite her education and scientific contributions, never became part of the medical establishment. Charles Bardeen, the dean of the medical school—the man who had told her all about Hopkins on that far-off summer day at Smith—never offered her a courtesy appointment. Her only academic title was lecturer and instructor in the department of home economics from 1916 to 1945, when she became emeritus. She refused to join the American Medical Association or the state or county medical societies, as the problems of private practice did not interest her. In later years she admitted that doing so might have helped her reach her ultimate goal—to improve medical care for women and children and stop discrimination by male physicians.

In 1921, the parent-teacher association began "preschool day," when parents were encouraged to bring young children to the schools to be weighed, measured, and medically examined. In Madison, a city of forty thousand, approximately one thousand births occurred annually. During the first three years of the program, Dorothy examined over five hundred preschoolers and reported that while half appeared in excellent health, 10 percent were severely under-nourished; 10 to 20 percent had serious health defects, chiefly enlarged tonsils and adenoids or bad teeth; and almost 10 percent had thyroid enlargement.[324]

In 1923, Dorothy, at the request of the university's department of agriculture, mounted an exhibit at the Milk Show in Milwaukee. In it, she displayed a list of all the ingredients of milk together with the protein, vitamin, and mineral requirements of pregnant mothers and children. At that time many women refused to drink raw milk, so she illustrated other ways for them to include it in their diet. Subsequently, she gave a paper, "Feeding for Mothers and Infants," at the annual meeting of the Home Economics Association in Buffalo, New York, in which she discussed the importance of proper nutrition for the mother and child during pregnancy and lactation.[325] Throughout the twenties, she remained a popular speaker on infant welfare and women's health, as well as a much sought-after judge for baby shows.

Charles, delighted to be back in his old department, set about refocusing his research toward peacetime objectives. Quantum physics dominated the interwar years, but he chose to focus on photoelectric problems, a subject in which his department became preeminent. His graduate students, who eventually numbered more than thirty-five, remained his chief interest throughout his career. He gave them the best research problems and happily discussed their findings long after the other faculty had gone home. A courteous, quiet, kindly, unassuming man with a broad knowledge of physics and unassailable scientific integrity, he always strove to boost the self-esteem of his weakest students.[326]

Gradually he assumed more and more administrative responsibilities, and in 1926 he became chairman of the physics department. Under his leadership the group functioned with a high degree of smoothness and harmony, undoubtedly taking its tone from its leader. Devoid of prejudice, he dealt with difficult issues of promotion and tenure objectively and fairly. In those days, chairmen lectured undergraduates; Charles enjoyed doing this, although he preferred teaching his graduate students. Later, to lighten the teaching load of his colleagues and increase their chances for promotion and tenure, he added the difficult lectures on experimental physics to his own schedule. The prestigious National Academy of Sciences elected him a member in 1918. He chaired the physics section from 1924 to 1927 and served with distinction on the board of the National Research Council that awarded research fellowships in physics, mathematics, and chemistry. He was active in many professional organizations; he greatly enjoyed his friendships with other scientists and regularly attended the annual meeting of the National Academy of Sciences—a function Dorothy placed on a par with an Elks convention.

Dorothy's in-laws, TC and Susan, had spent their early retirement years in Europe. With only basic foreign-language skills, they remained largely disconnected from the world around them, their lives uninspiring and unfulfilling. Eventually they returned to Columbus, where TC's beloved Ohio State University appointed him a trustee and, shortly afterward, chairman of the board. Busy and productive, he was happy again.

Tom, from time to time, would be sent to stay with his grandfather, who, after his wife's death in 1916, lived alone. They made a strange pair. The old man, with his great head fringed with white hair and an enormous mustache, towered over the eager, bright, slender youth. Tom, in the absence of companions his own age, must have found the visits a strain. But there were compensations. Swords, armor, and fierce warrior masks from TC's stay in Meiji, Japan, filled the house. Tom loved his grandfather's huge library but cared little for his well-equipped workshop. The old man did his best to make his grandson's visits enjoyable; he let him help record the twice-daily weather observations and care for the canaries, the only other living creatures in the house. Every day, the pair walked either uptown or in the opposite direction to watch the trains go by. TC always hoped Tom would complete a most unusual three-generational membership of the National Academy of Sciences. Every morning he would set his grandson a series of mathematical problems, but Tom's interests were artistic and literary, and he could never get them all correct. Although TC's grand ambition was not fulfilled, he would have been gratified, had he lived, to see Tom follow in his footsteps and become a college president. On his death in 1924, the old man left an unexpectedly large fortune of over $100,000 (about $1 million today) to his two grandsons with a life interest to Charles. This more than doubled Charles's university salary and brought their annual income to about $15,000, enabling them to live in some style, educate the boys and still allow Dorothy to do what she loved best—travel.

Her own life centered on her two sons—after the tragic loss of her first two babies, how could it not? The boys possessed very different personalities: Tom, carefree, sociable, and physically active, was a great reader. If he had any money, he spent it right away; in later life, he often found himself without cash and would be forced to borrow from an acquaintance for the plate in church, a taxi, or other incidental expenses.[327] John, more conservative and self-reliant than his brother, always had money in his pocket. His mother claimed he was the easiest person to amuse—you just left him alone. He preferred to work out problems by himself and possessed the high degree of self-confidence necessary for a good surgeon. By the time the boys had reached their teens, Dorothy had achieved a reasonable balance between her maternal urge to keep them safe and their need for independence to mature into self-reliant young men. Nonetheless, she always kept an unobtrusive eye on their activities, striving to

bring them into her orbit rather than have them find their amuse-
ments in an environment she could not control. In summer, they
bicycled, swam, and fished, but their great love was sailing. They
owned a C Scow, christened *Pretzel*, and became accomplished sailors. The family joined the Lake Mendota Yacht Club, and Dorothy
went to considerable trouble to arrange for their boat to be towed to
regattas in neighboring lakeside towns.

Both boys were happy in day school in Madison. Tom was dis-
playing unusual academic ability and, perhaps because of his early
education by the Society of Friends, was performing far ahead of his
contemporaries at Madison University High School, where instruc-
tion was poor and discipline nonexistent. When he began to attract
the attention of much older girls, his mother had nightmares of
"adolescent dissipation."[328] Tom did not share his mother's concerns
and failed to understand why he could not accept the invitations of
these forward and attractive young women.

The boys' education always provoked "great arguments," as John
referred to the periodic disagreements that punctuated life in the
Mendenhall household (as in most others).[329] Dorothy's loud and
dogmatic pronouncements contrasted sharply with Charles's softer,
subtler approach, although on occasion he, too, would get upset and
swear like a trooper. His wife always felt that her sons, with their
genetic background and obvious intelligence, were destined for distinguished careers. At Hopkins, she had encountered the products
of renowned eastern prep schools and Ivy League colleges and seen
the cachet, the confidence, and the priceless contacts these institutions afforded. Charles remained oblivious to all this and could
see nothing wrong with University High. Dorothy, who knew the
boys' education was the best investment they could make, decided to
send Tom (at TC's expense) to Asheville School in North Carolina.
Unfortunately, there he became a target of merciless bullying, which
compelled her to bring him home.[330] Mindful of her own experiences as a girl in Berlin, she wanted her sons to have the benefit

of time abroad. She saw great advantages to foreign schools besides learning another language, automobiles were unavailable and "premature social entanglements" (by which she meant adolescent sex) were less likely.[331] After extensive discussions, Dorothy decided (she made all major decisions) to move to France for a year and put the boys in schools there.

In the summer of 1925, Dorothy closed out her commitment to her sister's children by holding at her home the wedding of her niece, Dorothy Furbish, to Malcolm Sharp, who shortly afterward joined the faculty of the University of Chicago Law School. Dorothy remained in close contact with the couple all her life. Immediately afterward, the Mendenhalls left for Europe. On the voyage, Tom, now in his midteens, had the time of his life, dancing every night until the band stopped playing. In France, however, he missed his new friends and developed a severe attack of what his mother called "adolescentitis." No! He did not want to see the Bayeux Tapestries. Dorothy's heart sank. How was she going to travel through Europe with this sulky, uncommunicative, and uncooperative creature who refused to go anywhere with his family? Miraculously, after an exceptionally good dinner, the "peace of Bayeux," as John called it, descended on the family, and life proceeded smoothly again. They saw the sights of Normandy, including Mont-Saint-Michel, which Tom liked so much that they stayed several days, eating omelets and lobsters at Chez Mère Paillard. After another scene with Tom, they left the boys in Brittany and drove to Paris to look for a place for Dorothy to spend the winter and schools for the boys. With Cousin Louisa's aid, they found an apartment overlooking a tiny garden in the Latin Quarter, where, at the owner's insistence, everyone spoke French at meals.

Suitable schools for the boys proved hard to find. Dorothy visited one boarding school that seemed satisfactory until she saw the rows of iron beds in unheated dormitories and the primitive bathrooms and toilets—whereupon she announced she was not sending her sons "into penal servitude."[332] Eventually she discovered for Tom something approaching an American school, where he stayed mid-week with one of the teachers, and a day school for John near their apartment. When Dorothy heard of a vacancy at Le Rosey, one of the preeminent European schools situated at Rolle, a small town on the shores of Lake Geneva, Switzerland, with a winter campus in the mountains at Gstaad, she enrolled Tom immediately. As they had no place for John, she put him in a boarding school in Lausanne.

Dorothy was never one to be involved in the minutiae of domestic life. All her life she had ample domestic staff, and during short absences felt comfortable leaving Charles in their hands. For major events or crises, Dorothy relied on Cousin Louisa, who would function as her lieutenant, taking control of Dorothy's dinner parties and running the house during her long absences abroad.

Louisa K. Fast, an orphan whose guardian had been President William McKinley, was raised by one of Dorothy's Kimball relatives. She graduated from Smith two years behind Dorothy and went to work as a librarian. At the outbreak of World War I, she joined the Smith College Relief Unit and went to France to help women and children made homeless by the Germans. Afterward, she worked for the League of Women Voters before returning to France to manage the club sponsored by the American Association of University Women in Paris, where she knew all the literary expatriates—Gertrude Stein, Sylvia Beech, Hemingway, Galsworthy, and Joyce. Characteristically, when she was needed at home to take care of ailing relatives, she returned without complaint and built a new life for herself in Tiffin, Ohio. After a full and active life devoted to helping others, she passed away at the age of 101.[333]

Dorothy liked living in Paris but found the French egocentric and difficult to deal with. She enjoyed visiting galleries and museums and attended a number of talks at the Louvre. She endeavored to keep up her professional skills by attending some medical lectures and clinics but found Parisian pediatrics woefully behind that of the

United States. When after one lecture she asked why the professor had omitted important British work on vitamin D, she was told he never mentioned any research until it had been repeated in France.

Opera was always Dorothy's passion—she had seen the whole of Wagner's *Ring* at the Bayreuth Festival. When she first took Tom to the Paris opera, he was initially refused admission: he was too tall to be considered a child, and as an adult he had to wear *un smoking* (a dinner jacket). At once his mother called her friend, the Paris secretary of the Rockefeller Foundation, and asked for the name of his tailor. The next performance found a proud Dorothy on the arm of her now properly attired good-looking son.

While they were in Paris, John contracted measles complicated by bronchopneumonia. French law mandated hospitalization, but Dorothy refused to allow her son to be admitted to the austere seventeenth-century Charité Hôpital and kept him (illegally) in their apartment under the care of a French physician.[334] At the end of spring semester at the University of Wisconsin, Charles joined them in Paris, eagerly looking forward to vacationing and going to concerts. But Dorothy had already decided that John needed to recuperate in the sun, so once again Charles sacrificed his own pleasures and accompanied them to Saint-Jean-de-Luz, a resort near the Spanish frontier.

Whenever Dorothy was separated from her sons, she wrote them every week and expected them to do likewise; not surprisingly, she was frequently disappointed. She signed her letters "your loving Mother, Dorothy Reed Mendenhall" or more frequently just "Dorothy Reed Mendenhall." These letters typically opened with local news she thought would interest them. A lecture on self-improvement followed, and she would close with a final admonition. She wrote to Tom at Le Rosey, "Working with my brain is the most fun of anything I do, but I would rather do it when I can have a hug from John and you three times a day."[335] Writing from Madison, she worried whether he would fulfill the requirements for Yale, as she had counted six misspellings in his last letter.[336] She announced that his father was looking for a new automobile but did not mention that after he bought it, he spent several sleepless nights worrying about the expense. After receiving only one letter in the past month, she warned Tom that unless he wrote regularly, he would not be coming home for Christmas.[337] On another occasion she penned a homily on the need for maturity before entering college: "Balance and poise come from experience," she wrote, adding that she would prefer him to achieve this before entering Yale, as "without a strong purpose one blows too easily off the path." She admitted that "this sounds like a sermon" and asked, "Do you ever go to church?"[338] At Thanksgiving, she missed her older son: "You and John are my life [*sic*] work and I shall be a Nobel Prize mother if you turn out to be the man you ought to be."[339]

Tom generally had little news to relate, which made letter writing all the more difficult. In an exception he reported, "A great calamity has arrived, I was kicked off the rowing team."[340] Apparently the eight failed to meet expectations and he was dropped, although he claimed it was not all his fault. He continued to row and subsequently earned the right to wear the Rosey Rowing Club cap with crossed oars and the citation "R.R.C. 1926"—the beginning of a lifelong infatuation with the sport.

That same year, the Rockefeller Institute commissioned Charles to survey European physics laboratories. Dorothy and Charles journeyed to Madrid to begin an odyssey that took them across Europe to Asia Minor. While Charles visited labs, Dorothy devoted herself to sightseeing. In Athens, she explored the Parthenon, rating it the most wonderful site in the world; in Turkey, she visited mosques and bazaars and sailed across the Bosporus in a yacht. After a dreadful crossing of the Black Sea to Constanta (Charles was horribly seasick), they continued on up the Danube to Romania, Czechoslovakia, and Austria; avoiding Poland because of civil strife, they headed north to Denmark, where business awaited them both.

Earlier in the year, Grace Abbott, the new director of the Children's Bureau, had discussed with Dorothy the persistent high maternal mortality rate in the United States. They concluded that a major factor was poor obstetric training in medical schools; Whitridge Williams, head of obstetrics at Johns Hopkins, agreed. One female physician summarized her obstetric education: "Reading text books, listening to lectures dealing chiefly with abnormalities, delivering a manikin, and the witnessing from the amphitheater the delivery of a few cases."[341] After passing an examination, she received a certificate to practice obstetrics. Organized medicine refused to believe the statistics; unwilling to look critically at themselves, they remained convinced that midwives were to blame.[342]

When Miss Abbott learned Dorothy was planning to visit Denmark, she asked her to discover why that country's maternal mortality rate was one-quarter of that in the United States. On her arrival in Copenhagen, Dorothy called at the board of health, where she was directed to a deaf elderly gentleman. Her heart sank; how could she possibly make him understand her needs? As it turned out, he sent her to all the right people. She met Dr. Gammeltoft, professor of obstetrics at the Danish National Medical School, where all the midwives trained. After greeting her, he came straight to the point: "It's easy to see what is the cause of your maternal mortality—you interfere, operate too much." He was referring to the American physician's readiness to use forceps to expedite delivery (cesarean section was still infrequent). The professor, who lived in a house adjacent to the hospital, had decreed that forceps could *not* be used unless he was present.[343]

In Denmark, Dorothy, for the first time, saw a woman delivered without anesthetic by a pupil midwife under supervision. She discovered that midwives delivered 85 percent of all women and handled all normal deliveries without forceps or anesthetics. Danish physicians, in contrast to their American counterparts, would willingly come in to take over abnormal or complicated cases. She stayed to lunch with the professor's wife, who told her that midwives had delivered all four of her children.

This visit formed the basis of Dorothy's important paper "Midwifery in Denmark," delivered at the Fifth Annual Conference of State Directors in Charge of the Local Administration of the Maternity and Infancy Act.[344] The main thrust of her report was *not* that midwives were better than physicians but that in rural areas, with few doctors and even fewer competent ones, a trained midwife was better than no physician or a poorly trained or a disinterested one.

Their business trip wound down in Holland. After Charles filed his report with the Rockefeller office in Paris, their sons joined them for a vacation in Brittany. The boys had enjoyed their European schools, and Tom asked if he could remain at Le Rosey and take his college boards from there. Charles, who had led a studious, fun-deprived childhood, found the thought of his son enjoying skiing and skating in winter, rowing in summer, and spending his vacations in the company of young women almost more than he could stomach. But he knew that if the boy wanted it and his mother approved, resistance was futile. Dorothy, concerned about Tom's level of emotional maturity, made him spend a year at Phillips Andover Academy before entering Yale and subsequently had John do the same before beginning Harvard. Charles opposed her choice of eastern universities and thought the Andover years a waste of time.

Leaving Tom behind, the family returned home via Montreal, Canada, where Charles had his usual problems with customs. He had compiled a long, detailed list of all his purchases, which totaled more than the duty-free allowance. The customs inspector looked at Dorothy and asked, "Is not this gentleman with you?" She nodded. "Since you are under, I will just add his excess to yours."[345] Charles, his Quaker soul mortified, suppressed an urge to make a voluntary donation to the Canadian government. As they entered the United States, nobody bothered to open their bags; when Charles proffered a half-full bottle of scotch, the US customs official said, "Keep it, Sonny." Subsequently, Dorothy took Charles to a furrier and, with the money he had set aside for customs duty, made him buy her an expensive fox fur that could have been bought much cheaper in Denmark.[346]

Gradually Dorothy became increasingly dissatisfied with the substantial early Victorian mansion on "Big Bug Hill," which had been their home for fifteen years. The expansion of the university, and particularly the conversion of a house across the street into the Delta Gamma sorority house, had created a noise problem. With their new inheritance, they could afford to move, so she began searching for a suitable place. An imposing, large three-story frame house perched on top of a hill caught her eye. Situated on three lots in University Heights, it was within walking distance of Charles's lab. Initially she considered it too big and too expensive, but as her search continued, she realized that it would be close to ideal. Eventually she obtained it in exchange for their house on Carroll Street plus $15,000 in cash. The addition of a porch, a new roof, a remodeled kitchen, and a new coat of paint cost an additional $15,000.

Today the house at 205 Prospect Avenue looks much as it did when the Mendenhalls lived there, except for the addition of a garage. A central porch capped by a high gable with a big circular window dominates the facade. On either side are two large windows with broken pediments. Dormer windows light the third-floor rooms. The bright and airy entrance hall with a ten-foot ceiling and cherry crown molding leads to a huge drawing room with a big stone fireplace that in Dorothy's time held a grand piano. Charles used the smaller, cozier room behind as his study. Beyond the hall lies a large library with another stone fireplace and big windows looking over the backyard. To the right is the dining room, which still houses the huge dresser from the Old Stone House in Talcottville and a dining table from the Kimball mansion in Columbus that seats sixteen on antique lyre-backed chairs brought by Adaline from Talcottville when she married Hannibal H. Kimball.[347]

The beautiful oriental rugs, vases, paintings, and a wonderful ancient sculptured head that TC brought back from Japan gave the house a distinctive character. Dorothy consigned the accompanying swords and armor to the attic. She loved her garden, and in the summer she would sit and write on the wide covered porch overlooking the flower beds on the north side of the house. Occasionally she would get up early and, still wearing her nightgown, go into the garden and deadhead flowers. As she never took regular exercise, she would return hot and sweaty and immediately flop down at the breakfast table—something she would never have permitted anyone else to do.[348]

Normally she breakfasted in bed and afterward discussed the plans for the day with her housekeeper. As she went about her business in town, she often encountered women whose children she had helped; they would greet her with evident affection and admiration and tell her the latest news of their "babies." After lunch, Dorothy rested. She spent a large part of the day in her room writing letters, then the principal form of communication. She, not Charles, handled the family affairs, paid the household bills, and made the decisions about the home, travel, and much else; in addition, she read *Barrons* and actively (and successfully) managed her investments. Most of her professional writing she did at home; she never learned to type. If her memoirs are any guide, she was able to write many pages in longhand with only an occasional erasure or correction.

Dorothy was open to most people if they were interesting and had good manners; she tolerated no less. She coped with people from backgrounds other than her own, which on occasion required a real effort for someone brought up with the rigid social code of upper-class Victorian America. If people met her standards, rank or the lack of it was never an issue. Professional women were her soul mates; her attitude toward those who were merely wives and mothers was all too frequently patronizing. She much preferred male company. "Her attitude toward men," as her cousin Edmund Wilson put it, "is alternately challenging and charming. After snubbing and telling them what's what, she compliments and smiles sweetly at them."[349]

She enjoyed taunting Charles Bardeen, the misogynistic dean at the University of Wisconsin Medical School, over his role in recruiting her into medicine, perhaps as a way to retaliate for her lack of an honorary faculty position.

As a couple, Charles and Dorothy led an active social life. They counted the university president as well as a majority of the senior faculty as their friends. Dorothy's work in the department of home economics and with the Attic Angels put her in contact with a different segment of the community. She became a founder-member of the Walrus Club, composed of a dozen Madison women with an extraordinary range of accomplishments who met monthly for lunch. In order to promote serious discussion, the customary frivolous topics of dress, domestics, and disease were banned. Afterward the members took turns in presenting learned papers. Dorothy's topics included the Italian Renaissance; artists Jan Vermeer, Peter Brueghel, and Vincent van Gogh; writers Herman Melville, T. S. Eliot, and Rudyard Kipling; medical men William Osler (her mentor at Hopkins) and Ronald Ross (the discoverer of the malaria-carrying mosquito); and her work on infant welfare at the Children's Bureau.[350]

The Mendenhalls met frequently with their closest friends, Judge Rosenberry of the Wisconsin supreme court and his wife, Lois, and Judge Burr Jones and his wife, Katherine, to dine and play bridge. Dorothy saw Pat Long regularly, traveled with Sophia Bigelow, and stayed in touch with the Seven from Smith. Mrs. Delmar Woodburn, the widow of a former professor, then in her late nineties and still living next door to the Mendenhalls' old house on Prospect Avenue, remembered Mrs. Mendenhall as a "good neighbor."[351] As was the fashion of the time, only a select few called Dorothy by her first name; to most people she remained "Mrs. Mendenhall."

Dorothy took her duties as wife of the departmental chairman seriously. She held regular Sunday teas for the faculty and their wives, and each year she gave a luncheon or dinner for newcomers.

She always made a special effort to help young faculty with children who were having medical problems or other difficulties. She delighted in entertaining the many distinguished European physicists who visited Charles's laboratory, and her dinner parties achieved a measure of international renown.

These elaborate affairs required weeks of preparation. Dorothy liked to take charge of the planning, have Cousin Louisa stage-manage the details, and let others do the work. Leaving her cook to prepare the food, Dorothy would travel all over town in search of the right ingredients in prime condition. The boys were enlisted to spruce up the yard, always with a nonoptional request. The house was brought up to inspection standard, the silver cleaned, the flowers arranged, and extra help brought in. On these occasions, the women wore long dinner gowns (Dorothy always looked her best in these), and the men wore tuxedos.

When she first arrived in Madison, formal dinners consisted of six courses—soup, fish, salad, and a main course of meat or poultry, followed by dessert, fruit, and cheese.[352] By the twenties, the fish was omitted, although the now fashionable cocktails and hors d'oeuvres preceded the meal. In accordance with local custom, wine was not served at the table, and the women did not leave the men at the end of the meal. Coffee and cordials followed in the drawing room. Charles was a wonderful host, genuinely interested in his guests. He could be relied on for engaging and stimulating conversation enlivened by his quiet sense of humor.

High moral values and intense loyalty to her friends characterized Dorothy's personality. Extreme emotional reactions, such as her response to Dr. Mackenzie's lecture, her decision to leave Hopkins, and her break with AJ, illustrate a rarely seen but recurrent facet of her makeup. With Dorothy, one acquired a friend (or an enemy) for life; she could never forgive a breach of trust.

Max Mason, a full professor in Charles's department, had for many years occupied the office next to Charles's, and they had published papers together. A man of great personal charm and gaiety, he was a brilliant mathematician and physicist as well as a gifted teacher. He had married his high-school sweetheart, Mary Louise Freedman, who became Dorothy's good friend. Dorothy's opinion of Max was ambivalent. She greatly enjoyed his quick-witted conversation and thought him the most interesting and most ambitious man she had ever known. At the same time, she found him completely egocentric and quite ruthless.

In 1925, Max left Madison and became president of the University of Chicago. The position suited his talents and outgoing personality; he flourished meeting and impressing people. His wife, however, felt uncomfortable with her new social responsibilities, and her husband criticized her repeatedly for letting him down. Never a strong character, she missed the support her Madison friends had provided. Severe emotional problems developed. Several years after the move, Max drove up to Madison to see Dorothy and enthusiastically announced his intention of divorcing Mary and marrying the wife of a physician on the faculty at the University of Wisconsin. Dorothy was stunned. She told Charles later, "I was speechless for the first time in my life."[353] She had visited Mary in Chicago a few times and sensed that she was unhappy but had failed to realize the cause and extent of the problem. She found the notion that Max, the head of a preeminent university, could throw over his wife of twenty-five years and the mother of their three children incomprehensible. When she told her husband, he agreed. Outraged, Dorothy took up the cause of her friend and traveled to Chicago to express to Max her anger over his behavior and the way he was flaunting social conventions. He said he was proud of himself and claimed that the circumstances justified his actions. After an acrimonious discussion, he agreed to allow Dorothy to meet his wife's psychiatrist who she discovered had not seen his patient recently, as she was "resting" in Virginia. Frustrated, Dorothy continued south to Staunton, where she found poor Mary, and brought her back to stay with her in Madison. Brokenhearted and depressed, Mary could talk of little else but her failed marriage. A month later, she developed pneumonia and died. At the end of this tragic, sordid episode—brought about, in Dorothy's opinion, by Max's unbridled ambition—she wrote "my nature was envenomed by hate."[354]

That summer, Dorothy too became very depressed; she kept Charles and the boys away from the house: "[I] wanted no human contact. My soul was gone sour."[355] Subsequently, Max was forced to resign the presidency of the University of Chicago. He married his friend and moved to the Rockefeller Institute and later became chairman of the Observatory Council at the California Institute of Technology. On hearing this Dorothy declared, "The wages of sin ought to be death but the punishment for the crime seems to have been delayed in this case."[356]

Dorothy always had faith in her sons' capabilities and did all she could to further their education and subsequent careers. After Tom's return from Europe, John, who was enjoying Madison Central High School, suddenly asked about *his* second year overseas. His mother was "thunderstruck," as she had not planned another European trip and felt she ought not to leave Charles alone again—at least not so soon. Besides, Cousin Louisa had returned to Tiffin and was unable to take charge of the household. After a series of "great discussions," it was decided that Dorothy would take John on a Mediterranean cruise. While much of the itinerary was old territory for her, she had never visited the Holy Land. When they docked in Palestine, as it was called in 1929, the ship's purser asked if he might put another passenger in the front seat of their car. Dorothy readily agreed but was surprised by the presence of a tall black man from second class, the self-educated minister of a large church in Jersey City. Dorothy found him "a simple, wise, consecrated person who (with his ency-clopedic knowledge of the Bible) did much to make our trip vivid and memorable."[357] They spent Easter in Jerusalem, which, apart from the great dome, reminded her of one of the walled cities of southern

Europe. After she returned home, she was surprised to find that her most vivid recollections were not of the ancient monuments or religious ceremonies but of the profusion of flowers on the bare hills.

They next visited Cairo and the Pyramids, where a mischievous cameleer placed her on his friskiest mount. Fortunately, an observant British sergeant saved her from a perilous ride. They returned leisurely to Geneva, Switzerland, where John took his college boards, and Charles and Tom joined them. While the menfolk took a walking tour in the Swiss Alps, Dorothy represented the Children's Bureau at a conference in London. On her return, they spent a month in the Black Forest, where Charles found some excellent fishing, Tom fell in love again, and John was just plain happy. At the end of their stay, nobody wanted to leave, but as she had already paid for opera tickets in Munich, they had to move on.

On their return to England, Charles was in trouble again; this time, he had forgotten to get a visa for the United Kingdom. As usual, he became very angry, more at himself for being so stupid than anyone else. Dorothy persuaded the authorities to let him in since he was part of the family. The next day, he went to the American embassy to learn that a visa could only be obtained outside the country. He paid the fee anyway and presumably felt better.

After Charles and the boys had returned to the United States, Dorothy joined a friend from Madison and spent a month touring Spain. She had hoped to stay longer, but since Charles had not written and told her to stay, she returned home for Thanksgiving. How characteristic of her selfish husband, she thought, to leave it to her to decide whether to stay or not. When she took him to task, he replied, "I didn't want you to be away. Couldn't say no, but I knew that you would stay if you wanted to."[358]

CHAPTER 13

Tribulation

Charles's Last Illness

Despite the Wall Street debacle of the previous year, the thirties opened with the promise of good things to come for the Mendenhalls. Charles was at the height of his career, Tom was in his final year at Yale, and John had entered Harvard. Dorothy, to her amazement, received an honorary DSc from her alma mater. With false modesty, she made light of it, saying the college had done so for no particular reason except it was her thirty-fifth class reunion. The citation read as follows:

> Dorothy Reed Mendenhall A.B. Smith 1895, M.D. Johns Hopkins 1900; Physician, teacher, writer; widely known as an authority on the feeding of children, an indefatigable worker in the cause of improving the physique of the rising generation.[359]

The night before the ceremony, she was the guest of honor at her class dinner, where something she ate made her very ill. The following morning, still feeling awful, she lay motionless in bed until some friends came to find her. Pulling an academic robe over her nightgown, they drove her to John M. Greene Hall and pushed her onto the platform in a wheelchair. Unwilling to have her friends see her as an invalid, she skipped the official photograph. When the boys failed to find her picture in the *New York Times*, they told her they saw no point in getting an honorary degree if one's picture did not make the papers. Their mother was not amused.

Tom enjoyed his time at Yale and graduated magna cum laude. The previous year, he had applied unsuccessfully for a Rhodes Scholarship to Oxford University and planned to try again from Wisconsin, as he thought his chances would be better away from the highly competitive East Coast.[360] Charles did not approve. He disliked the "eastern establishment" and felt that the snobbish English upper classes with their fondness for sport, drink, and high jinks made unsuitable companions for his older boy. Father and son, although close, differed sharply in temperament: one was frugal, retiring, and tightly constrained by his Quaker background while the other was friendly, fun-loving, extroverted, and extravagant. Both parents desperately wanted Tom to succeed. Charles thought he should take his PhD at the University of Wisconsin, which he believed, with some justification, to be as good a university as any, but Dorothy clearly recognized the social and political advantages offered by that ancient and romantic English seat of learning.

Tom's interview with the Rhodes committee took place in Milwaukee. His mother met the New Haven train and, after leaving him at the interview, spent the day shopping and praying for his success. Privately she thought his chances slim and planned a "bang-up dinner" to cheer him up. It was nearly six o'clock before the phone rang.

"Mother, I got it."

"Bully for you—hurry to the hotel and we can catch the last train back to Madison."[361]

Charles met them in Madison with mixed emotions—pride in Tom's success coupled with doubts about the value of an English university education. This did not surprise Dorothy, as her husband, a natural conservative, treated anything new with considerable skepticism. After a wonderful family Christmas, the boys returned to their respective universities. Back in 1918, TC, after congratulating Charles on his election to the National Academy of Sciences, had turned to John and said, "Young man, if you or Tom become members and there are three Mendenhalls in—we would be the only family to have this distinction."[362] Since Tom had neither an interest in nor an aptitude for the sciences, the onus fell on John. When he entered Harvard, his father wrote to the chairman of physics, suggesting he place his younger son in an advanced freshman physics course. Unfortunately, John shared his brother's enthusiasm for rowing, with the result that at the end of the year, Charles received this reply:

[Dear] Mendenhall, I passed your son in my course. Any other boy I should have flunked.[363]

Mortified, Charles said nothing. Not so Brother Tom, who rather disagreeably pointed out that while it might be hard to enter college, any fool ought to be able to keep up with the classes. The well-informed, quick-witted Tom invariably scored highly in exams (in Dorothy's view, better than he sometimes deserved) in contrast to his less facile, more deliberate brother, who often did worse than expected.

At the beginning of 1933, the Great Depression gripped the nation; many Madison businesses failed, and university salaries were reduced by one-third.[364] Dorothy was glad to teach in the home-economics department "for filthy lucre" to pay the boys' tuition. Her entrepreneurial spirit emerged: she took in a student lodger, served on the Food Committee of County Relief, helped form a welfare committee to assist young faculty, and opened a clothing exchange in her attic to enable graduate students to dress their ever-growing children.

The big news, Dorothy wrote Tom, was "Your old Ma is going into politics."[365] Disgusted by the incompetence and extravagance of the men running the city, the Civics Club resolved to field its own slate of female candidates at the forthcoming elections. Since Dorothy was sick and unable to attend the meeting, they voted her election chair. The give-and-take of politics did not suit her authoritarian approach; after a group of unemployed workers heckled one of her speeches, she wrote Tom, "Politics is the very devil. Keep out of it."[366] None of the female candidates was victorious, and Dorothy's political career abruptly ended.

Despite the hard times, Charles and Dorothy gave a big dinner party for their twenty-seventh wedding anniversary, where everybody had a grand time. Afterward she sent Tom (now back at Yale) an account of the festivities, commenting, "Poor dear [Charles], think how long he has had to stand me."[367] In late March she told Tom of the heaviest snowfall she could remember and proudly announced that Smith College had nominated her for the Phi Beta Kappa honor society. "Now both your parents are members of the intellectual aristocracy," she wrote, and "your children will be the fourth generation."[368]

She worried about Tom's weakness for the opposite sex. Always suspicious of her sons' girlfriends, she inquired in one letter, "Who is Clara Tyman?"[369] She feared her plans for the boys—a senior academic or administrative position—would be brought to an abrupt halt by any premature and inappropriate sexual entanglements. When she learned that Rhodes Scholars were prohibited from marrying, she felt greatly relieved. Every time one of her sons became seriously interested in a young woman, she would hightail off to check out the prospect. She warned Tom that some women think of men as nothing but potential fathers of their children:

> You want a mate of equal intelligence who subordinates and sublimates her emotions to the desire to be someone and to do something worthwhile in the world. Who will wait until she has met a man of congenial tastes, right standards and

whom she can not only love but trust before she lets go of herself and plays with passion. [Obviously, Dorothy had a selective memory.] I am hoping that both you and John meet the right girl and in your marriages have true happiness and understanding, which is the most worthwhile experience in life.[370]

She then launched into a diatribe about modern morality, citing some drunken engagement party and ending with the admonition, "Do control yourself, for your own good." Instead of the usual "Dorothy Reed Mendenhall," she closed with "Love, Mother."[371]

In her next letter, she wondered what had happened, as she had not heard from either boy for ten days. Delighted to learn that Yale had appointed her newly graduated son an instructor, she wanted to hear all about his first lecture. She was sorry to say that John, rowing happily on the Charles River, appeared content to go through life a D student. Her husband was away on his annual junket with that well-known chowder and marching society—the National Academy of Sciences. While he was gone, friends invited her out every night; everywhere the Depression dominated conversation.

In her last letter to her son at Yale, she told him how much they'd enjoyed their first picnic of the year at Middleton Quarry and that she was now busy planning a birthday party for Charles to which she planned to ask the Reeves because Niels Bohr, a Nobel laureate from Copenhagen, would be staying with them. Bohr later escaped from Nazi-occupied Europe by submarine and helped build the first atom bomb. "Dad," she added, "just like him—gave up teaching summer school because his salary divided could help out *two* younger men—I am mad but admiring."[372]

In September, Dorothy saw Tom off to England and continued on to New York, where she dined with Florence Sabin at the Cosmopolitan Club. Dorothy considered her "one [of], if not the greatest medical woman."[373] Florence Sabin was the first woman to become a full member of the Rockefeller Institute (equivalent to full professor). She was also the first woman to be elected to the National Academy of Sciences and to the presidency of the Society of America Association of Anatomists.[374] Like most successful women of the period, she never married. Undoubtedly this meeting, possibly the first since Dorothy's marriage, led Dorothy to ponder her own life and what it might have been like if she had stayed in pathology at Hopkins. What if AJ had not been such a self-centered cad? Both their lives would have been changed immeasurably.

Not one to dwell on the past, she told Tom, "I reviewed my life and feel that in my sixtieth year I am more content and more nearly satisfied than I have ever been before. If you boys find yourselves and are happy in your chosen fields, I have nothing more to ask."[375] She announced her completion of a course on Spanish art and was busy preparing a talk on Velázquez for the Walrus Club, as well as two medical presentations.

She continued her work with the Madison Health Centers, which now numbered four, although she attended clinics at only two. Unfortunately, one of her nurses (Lena K. Schmidt) was killed in an automobile accident. Called upon to identify the body, Dorothy had to visit the morgue. This upset her more than she expected; she never enjoyed her clinic work in quite the same way again. In October she attended a conference on malnutrition in Washington, DC, where she heard Mrs. Roosevelt speak and witnessed the unveiling of a statue of labor leader Samuel Gompers. On the way home, she stopped in Chicago, where she visited the Art Institute (twice) and Charles took her to *Dinner at Eight*. In a note appended to one of her letters to Tom, her husband added, "She had a grand time in the East. I never knew her so enthusiastic."[376]

In the same postscript, Charles, still unhappy about Tom's entry into Balliol College, Oxford, as part of the select group of Rhodes Scholars, continued, "I haven't much sympathy with the ironclad conservatism which I think characterizes a good many Oxford people."

While this may have been true of his acquaintances at the professorial level, it was certainly not true of the undergraduates, many of whom were ardent left-wingers. In 1933, students at an Oxford Union Society debate voted their support for the shameful Joad resolution: "That this house will in no circumstances fight for its King and Country."[377] The notorious Communist spies Guy Burgess, Donald Maclean, and Kim Philby were all at Cambridge University about this time.

Oxford has always welcomed Americans. Tom, with his outgoing personality and charm, quickly made many friends at his college—Balliol and elsewhere in the university. Rowing, or crew, was a major sport at Oxford and Cambridge. Tom's tremendous enthusiasm and the skills he had acquired at Le Rosey afforded him easy entry into the college's rowing club. The eight-man shells practiced three or four afternoons a week; in the period preceding the intercollegiate races, training became even more demanding. This, coupled with Tom's natural tendency toward procrastination and the many diversionary temptations all too readily available at Oxford, seriously threatened his academic career. Some Rhodes Scholars, such as former President Bill Clinton, become so involved in Oxford life that they never graduate. Dorothy was not going to let this happen to her son. She resumed her weekly letters, which capture the essence of their relationship and provide a contemporary account of her activities and concerns.

In her first letter to England, she told Tom how pleased she felt about his entry into Oxford and encouraged him to do his best. Understandably, she could hardly wait to get his first impressions. Meanwhile, she had visited John, who was now off probation at Harvard, and had taken him to see Professor Henry A. Christian—the man who had left Hopkins for Harvard after Dorothy outranked him for a medical internship.

Delighted by Tom's first letter from England and news of his safe arrival, she replied in an upbeat and generous mood: "I think of you butting around delightful London, having a gorgeous time; squeeze every drop of pleasure and profit from your experiences."[378] Worried about her son crossing the open quad to get to the bathhouse clad in his pajamas, she told him to buy a heavy bathrobe. She also suggested he order special milk from London or dry milk imported from Paris and asked him to get a heavy blanket as a present from her, adding she would send him his heavy sheepskin coat.[379] Unable to restrain herself, she exhorted, "I have always told you—there is plenty of room at the top."[380]

A recent talk on Australian Aborigines at the year-end meeting of the Walrus Club led her to remark on the diversity of pursuits of the university community where they lived. John was home for the holiday; even so, "Christmas is a lonely day," she wrote. "As you grow older ever present memories make you sad." Both she and Charles were feeling tired and off color; she underwent some tests, but they revealed nothing wrong.

In her first letter of the New Year (1934), Dorothy chided her son about his irregular letters, due undoubtedly to the good time he was having skiing in Switzerland. After he returned to Oxford, she told him about the large number of iceboats racing on Lake Mendota and concluded,

> Now get down to work—save money for your next fling and show the stuff that's in you. You have had a grand time and it will be easier to pay for it by real concentration in your field. As ever, old emerald,
> Dorothy Reed Mendenhall.[381]

Tom wrote her about the Torpids, as the spring boat races were called, adding that he was short of money. His failure to concentrate on his studies alarmed his mother, who suggested an intensive "reading period" before the year was over. Although she owed the bank $1,500, she agreed to send him an additional $750, commenting, "I honestly think an extra thousand a year to your Rhodes stipend is all an American in your position and achievement has any right to."[382]

Tom doubtless attended the annual Oxford and Cambridge boat race held on the Thames in London. The associated consumption of malt and other beverages always resulted in a great deal of high-spirited behavior on the part of the undergrads (and others), necessitating the mobilization of police reserves and the construction of a protective barrier around the statue of Eros, which in those days stood in the center of Piccadilly Circus. By late spring, rowing was in high gear in preparation for the final races of the university year, and Tom was gratified to be in his college's first boat. "Your rowing must be great fun," Dorothy wrote. "I am glad you are having such a chance to know English ways from the inside."[383]

On hearing of a friend's inappropriate marriage, she wrote Tom, "I want you to marry as soon as you have a job and meet the unknown goddess." She asked about his vacation plans (the English academic year ended in early June), pointing out, "A little work would probably be a change and might not come amiss."[384]

Dorothy had been busy in Madison. The Walrus Club had met at her house, and she'd had to provide lunch; she had gone to two lunches and a bridge dinner, and as a result she felt quite exhausted. She told her son of a dear friend's sad death; fortunately he had taken out a large life-insurance policy that enabled the family to continue living in their home. Shortly afterward, Charles passed a physical and took out a $10,000 policy on his own life. Tom must have asked for more money, because she felt like a "dirty dog," telling him, "I do want you to have all you have had; my only regret is that I have not more to give you."[385]

In April Dorothy and Charles traveled east so he could attend the meeting of the National Academy of Sciences as well as the banquet of the ancient and distinguished Philosophical Society of Philadelphia. Dorothy also attended the meetings of the Public

Health Society and the Academy of Pediatrics. Shortly afterward, the American Society of Arts and Sciences elected Charles a member. She let Charles go alone to the seven-course banquet that followed graduation exercises at the University of Wisconsin, as she thought the president's wife "the silliest, most pretentious person [she] had ever met" and, at this stage in her life, was not about to do anything she did not enjoy.[386] Apart from Charles's annual fishing trip to the Dakotas, they stayed home all summer.

John, on vacation, was happily sailing their C Scow *Pretzel* in the local regattas and reading, with some gratification, in the Madison press of his successes. Away from Tom's domination, he had found himself; he was off probation, making good grades, and planning a career in medicine. He wanted to stay on at Harvard, but his father, always suspicious of the East, thought he would do just fine at the University of Wisconsin; neither Dorothy nor John agreed. John, concerned about his early poor performance and thinking it prudent to have a fallback position, asked his mother if "some of her buddies at Baltimore might be able to help him in entering Hopkins." Dorothy's blood boiled. She made it perfectly clear that she "would not use pull to get a good student into the Medical School, much less [her] own son with his poor record."[387] She told him his grades were not good enough for medicine and suggested he try the B-school. As it turned out, he graduated cum laude, causing his father to "wonder how Harvard marks," and was accepted into Harvard Medical School.[388] She wrote Tom, perhaps ominously, "I have never been so happy before in my life—since I feel that you are the on the road for a career and John is booked for medicine. I have just told your father, 'We are lucky.'"[389]

Later that summer, Dorothy noticed Charles was looking drawn and tired; when she questioned him, he admitted he had not been feeling well. At her insistence, he saw his physician, who found an enlarged, hard prostate and performed a transurethral resection, which revealed cancer. The diagnosis floored Dorothy—at his insurance physical a year earlier her husband had received a clean bill of health. "Charles's condition is far more serious than he realizes," she wrote Tom, "but his physician counseled me to make light of it… Deceiving him or anybody else isn't easy for me."[390] Even though John was home for the summer, his mother, under the stress of Charles's illness, missed Tom terribly. With his cheerful and forthright personality, she found him easier to discuss things with. Actually, he was in Germany having a good time and probably not thinking much about Madison. She worried about his academic career and told him he ought to devote part of the summer to hard work. In August she wrote him:

> We have to face the certainty that Charles, in all probability, will not live many years, and I do want him to have as much happiness in the time remaining as possible…I have recovered my poise…It's a great life if you don't weaken, and I am going to make every day count. Love as ever, Dorothy Reed Mendenhall.[391]

In those days England was really very far away. Travel was almost exclusively by boat and generally took one to two weeks. Telephones were not very common. It was practically unheard of for students to have one in their rooms. Most likely, there was only one pay phone for student use in the college. In addition, transatlantic calls were very expensive, and the reception was terrible.

Two weeks after her previous letter, Dorothy reaffirmed her devotion to her husband: "As long as he lives, I shall not be separated from him again by more than a few hours."[392] In September, the couple returned to their favorite vacation spot, Deadwood, South Dakota, where Dorothy spent much of the time taking long walks over the Black Hills. Charles, following the extraction of an abscessed tooth and a little fishing, felt better. Encouraged, she thought they should consider surgery and sent his chart, x-rays, and pathology report to

Dr. Hugh Hampton Young, the chief of urology at Hopkins. He thought the cancer far advanced and the prognosis poor but offered to attempt a radical prostatectomy if Charles wished it. This posed a real dilemma, as his physician, following the customary practice of the time, had told him neither the diagnosis nor the prognosis. Dorothy hated this duplicity, as she and Charles had always been totally honest with each other. After much soul-searching, she concluded that she must tell him the truth. But how? She decided to write out what she wanted to say; then, sitting at her desk with her back to Charles, she read her words aloud. For what seemed like an eternity, Charles stood silent, looking out the window. Finally he said, "I will talk it over with Sisk." After meeting with his physician, he told her, "Sisk thinks the operation would be useless, and I have decided not to go to Baltimore."[393]

During the remaining ten months of his life, Charles, with his characteristic reticence, never mentioned the subject again. Since no effective treatment existed, Dorothy was compelled to watch, powerless, the gradual, inevitable decline of her brave, stoic, and adoring husband. Miraculously, his spirit remained unbroken. He went regularly to his laboratory until the effort became too much; then his staff and devoted graduate students brought work to his home. He embarked (with two collaborators) on a textbook, *College Physics*, continuing to write almost to the end, as he believed (correctly) his wife would need the royalties.[394] Beside herself with worry, Dorothy found solace in bridge; had it been possible, she would have played all day.

Tom became her principal confidant. "How I wish we were not so far apart," she wrote. "I certainly should like to talk over many things with you." Understandably, she worried about the expense of Charles's illness (health insurance was not widespread then) and urged her son to economize and to work hard: "From now on, I think that you should make every hour tell toward finishing your examination creditably...you have [had] all the time for *wanderjahre* a man is entitled to—now produce." She continued, "It seems only just to ask for a return commensurate with the capital outlay neces-sary." Feeling perhaps that she had been too harsh, she added, "I didn't mean to write so at length on finance, but since my girlhood, I have had to scheme and manage to keep the wolf from the door, or thought I did and it became a habit."[395]

After an abrupt mood swing, she wrote Tom, "Saturday I am sixty—old enough to die if I had sense." Charles, feeling a little bet-ter, took her out for a birthday dinner. In that same letter, she contin-ued with an account of her annual luncheon for the faculty wives and her dinner for the new man in Charles's department. She concluded,

> Whatever comes or does not, the children of men must not be afraid. I love you and think of you constantly.
> Love,
> Dorothy Reed Mendenhall.[396]

Not surprisingly, she thought more and more about spiritual matters:

> Prayer or a gesture of the mind begins with meditation and recollection, the second stage is complete detachment and then formal prayer petition—best formalized—answer com-ing when connection has been made with the effective forces in the universe.[397]

That fall, Dorothy learned that Tom, while in Europe, had had an affair with a married woman. Thunderstruck, she foresaw her worst nightmares coming true: a forced marriage to a divorced woman (a big stigma in those days) and the premature burden of a child. All her hopes for his career were destroyed. She vented her feelings over ten closely written pages. Here is an excerpt:

> You have been thoughtless and indiscreet in what you have done together...You are *emerald;* you have to shine clear...

There is no time for either philandering or dissipation however harmless or pleasant—but the time has come for you to prove your intellectual mettle and fit yourself to contribute… map out a program…ambition may not seem very alluring but there is nothing that would lighten my heavy heart as having you make the most of yourself. Happiness is in the lap of the gods, but it is in our power to play the part assigned to us well…[398]

John, she continued, had just started medical school. This opened old wounds: "A man can be an excellent surgeon," she wrote, "and be quite a shit," adding, "[medicine] is a great world if you happen to be a man, but no place for a woman." With this off her chest, she felt better. "I have my courage back again. My motto: 'By tomorrow, today will be yesterday.'" She advised Tom to live in the present, but at the end of the letter, despair overtook her: "How I wish there was no future."[399]

Tom had returned to Oxford after his European fling. His mother, understandably, was still upset over his affair. "Although there may be great compensation in caring for such a fine woman," she wrote, "I cannot help fearing for you the strain of continued pain…"[400]

Although her world was now focused on her husband, she did not abrogate her other responsibilities. She took in a new student lodger and remained as active as ever with the Civics Club, the bridge club, the clothing exchange in her attic, the Walrus Club, the university theater, the Madison Literary Club, and the College Club. She continued as medical director of the Madison Health Clinics and found time to participate in clinical studies on hemoglobin levels in infant blood and the effects of iron and copper therapy.[401] Dorothy had enjoyed a visit with one of the first female members of the British Parliament. She was expecting a visit from Auntie Pat (Margaret Long) and later Gertrude Stein (speculating maliciously on whether Charles and Alice B. Toklas would hit it off). Afterward she told

Tom that Gertrude's lecture "gave a vital panorama of the centuries. She is absolutely sincere but crazy."[402]

Tom was expected for Christmas. "I am still in a trance over your coming home," she replied. "It seems too good to be true." She thought about him all day and included him in her prayers for those in peril on the sea. She even considered driving east to meet him off the ship. By now, she had come to terms with life. "[Charles and I] are both on even keels now," she told her son, "and prepared to view everything that happens in a rosy light. After you accept the worst, you can have a lot of fun out of life."[403]

With the family all together, Christmas passed joyously and all too quickly. Everyone was sad to see Tom leave. On his way back to Oxford, he stopped in New Haven to firm up a position at Yale for when he returned. The New Year found Charles decidedly weaker, which Dorothy attributed to the excitement and activity of the holidays. He began radiation therapy, but after each treatment he seemed even more exhausted. She thought about taking him to Los Angeles, where there was the most powerful x-ray machine in the world, but she did not: she recognized that while doing so would make *her* feel better, it would probably not help her husband, who looked ghastly. Miraculously, Charles kept his spirits up and even managed to do a little work.

On their twenty-ninth wedding anniversary, they omitted the usual celebratory dinner, as the sight of food nauseated him, but friends sent flowers, which cheered them both. Dorothy now found anniversaries so painful that she wondered if it would not be better never to observe them. "Life," she wrote Tom, "is a queer mixture of joy and sorrow so that it is often hard to tell what feeling predominates."[404] Charles, in a postscript to one of her letters, wrote, "I am horrid a lot of the time."[405] Solicitous as ever of Dorothy's well-being, he added to another letter, "My continued illness is a great strain on your mother, who worries a good deal about expenses now and in the future."[406]

Charles's relentless decline continued, but he plodded doggedly on with his textbook. Just picking at his food, he grew progressively thinner and feebler. Jaundice developed due, Dorothy feared, to metastatic cancer. After she took him to hear a lecture at the club, he returned home in a state of collapse. His doctor began a course of insulin injections, which made him feel better. "At times my self-control slips," Dorothy admitted, "and it is the greatest thing that I can do to keep an even optimistic attitude."[407] The strain took its toll on them both. She wrote Tom:

> Your father seems to resent that the doctors can do nothing for him. They practically leave his medications to me on the grounds that if it is malignant, it is hopeless and, if not, time will take care of it. I am sorry now that I did not take him to Mayo's in January. They would have suggested a laparotomy, I am sure, and I am dead against it in cases of probable cancer as it can only increase the discomfort...and, never as in your father's case, give a ghost of a chance at a cure. He is wonderfully patient and gentle and apparently feels some hope that he may recover. All the men at the hospital think we have done the wisest thing but perhaps I gave up without trying everything. The diagnosis last summer settled the nature of the trouble and it would be expected that the liver condition was due to a similar involvement in the pancreas...I am sorry that at some time in the past nine months we did not try another place. I should not write so as to depress you, but your father may linger for months or the end may come quickly at any time. God grant that he may not suffer. Except for weakness and itching he has no pain and his mind and judgment are [sharper] than usual.[408]

Dorothy now regretted that John had not gone to medical school in Madison. "I would like him to be home to break the ghastly loneliness that I dare not contemplate, but I have always been able to meet things when they come up."[409] Tom's usual letter had failed to arrive, depressing her even more; she reminded him that "getting a letter is like talking to a person, even if you are far apart."[410] When it finally arrived, it told of Tom's purchase of an automobile, which placed him among a select and affluent few at Oxford. Understandably, this wanton, unnecessary extravagance annoyed his father. With final examinations coming up, his mother counseled him, "Be sensible and try to work as early as possible and by daylight as much as you can."[411] She even sent him some tablets containing one-sixtieth of a grain (one milligram) of strychnine in case he felt sleepy during the actual tests.

One of Dorothy's young cousins had returned from college with an infected cut on his lip and died six days later. This tragedy upset her more than anything had since Richard's death; she shared her feelings with Tom:

> The one unbearable thought is to feel that one we love is gone, forgotten, blotted out and that nobody cares. Their tragedy combined with your Father's serious condition floored me and on Sunday and Monday I was a gibbering weakling.[412]

Inexplicably, Charles rallied, and Dorothy's spirits improved. She listened on the radio to the Oxford and Cambridge boat race and saw the movie *The Lives of a Bengal Lancer* with Gary Cooper, which she enjoyed and recommended to Tom. She felt more optimistic about her husband—he had gained weight and the jaundice had faded—but she recognized that "the menace of the more serious prostrate [*sic*] condition still hangs over him."[413] At a dinner with her niece Dorothy Sharp and her husband, she learned of a friend's death from appendicitis and wrote immediately to warn Tom: "The horror of it touched me especially as I have always worried about your appendix. Do consult a good surgeon early if you get a tummy ache." A month later, she was encouraging Tom in his rowing: "I want to give you endurance and do your best the entire way through. It's the end of the race that counts having the staying power."[414]

When John returned home from Harvard, the change in his father's condition shocked him; he could scarcely bear the sight of his father's frail, enfeebled body. Now a fine young man, he helped his mother enormously during that difficult summer. On the first day of August, Charles's physician found a tumor blocking the outflow of urine from his bladder. After a sad birthday party, Charles's sixty-third, they took him to Madison General Hospital, where his urologist carried out a limited transurethral resection. The procedure was performed without anesthetic, as the doctor feared Charles might not survive one. In excruciating pain and with beads of sweat on his brow, Charles crushed Dorothy's hands in his until she thought that *she* would cry out—he never uttered a sound. After it was all over, the surgeon took her aside and gave her a large whiskey.

The next two weeks passed as if in a dream; Charles still tried to work, correcting proofs and seeing people from his department. One morning she found him looking "radiant." Somebody from the department had told him he was to continue on as chairman. Buoyed up, he ordered his first real meal in a long time, saying it was "to get [his] strength back."[415] Despite this fleeting ray of hope, Charles's clinical state remained unchanged. He survived only with the aid of injections and blood transfusions. Initially these helped, but when one unit induced a serious reaction, Dorothy stopped it. Searching out his physician, she was surprised to find that he was annoyed with her for interfering, arguing that it was his duty to prolong life. She responded angrily, "Your Hippocratic oath did not specify that a physician was to prolong suffering. If you can tell me that you can save Charles's life, or even prolong it more than a matter of days, I will acquiesce." The physician admitted that her husband had only a week or two to live and stopped the transfusions.[416]

Tom's arrival from England delighted Charles, who, despite continual pain, enjoyed long talks with his son. After one conversation, he remarked to Dorothy,

He is a fine man. He is turning out just as I hoped he would...
I didn't see eye to eye with you on your plans for the boys—
Europe, prep schools, Eastern Universities—you were right
and I was wrong. *You did it.*[417]

After dinner on the seventeenth of August, Dorothy visited the hospital to find Charles with his face distorted in agony and Tom on his knees at his bedside. She asked the nurse to give him morphine, but there were no orders, so Dorothy went off in search of the house officer. Once Charles was sedated and she had assured Tom that his father's suffering had passed, they drove home. After everybody was in bed, she slipped quietly out of the house and returned to the hospital, where she found Charles lying comatose. She remained by his side to the end.

Since her husband was an agnostic, Dorothy arranged for the funeral to be held in their home; she specified no flowers and told the Episcopal clergyman "no remarks." The house was full of mourners, many of whom sent flowers, and the rector, much to the family's annoyance, read Edgar Guest's poem "Good Man." When asked about an autopsy, Dorothy's pathology training came out, and she readily agreed; it revealed two quite distinct primary cancers, one in the prostate and the other in the pancreas. Charles, from the onset, had been doomed.

Dorothy took his epitaph from *The Meditations of Marcus Aurelius*:

He is better bred and a gentleman that takes leave of the world without a blot on his scutcheon, and has nothing of falsehood and dissimulation, of luxury or pride, to tarnish his character.[418]

Tributes flowed in. The faculty of the University of Wisconsin passed a special motion of appreciation. A colleague wrote,

He has been an outstanding member of our group of distinguished professors. A scholar and a gentleman of straightforwardness, reasonableness and judgment, taste, and gentleness, unselfishness and charm.[419]

A graduate student commented,

He was universally respected, admired and indeed loved by all of us who worked with him.[420]

Cousin Louisa expressed her grief:

[I] go over and over in my mind the glimpses I have had of you together each time endearing me still more to that gentle honorable and loyal soul.[421]

The underlying moral fiber that guided all Charles's actions was made clear in a final note by his wife:

He was not a cipher.[422]

Now, he was gone forever.

Epilogue

Revelation

A Faustian Bargain

DOROTHY, DESPITE HER RATHER FORMIDABLE appearance and talk of toughness, felt Charles's death deeply. She attended to the depressing business of responding to what seemed innumerable expressions of sympathy and began to settle Charles's affairs.

Reflecting on nearly thirty years of marriage, she felt it had turned out better than she might have expected. "If Charles hadn't married me," she wrote, "I don't think that his life would have been as varied as it was, nor that he would have been as happy as he was in his silent, undemonstrative way in his family."[423] Charles loved her from the outset; she was thankful for this and recognized how much he had contributed to her life. For her part, despite her passionate letters at the time of their engagement, her attachment and devotion to him developed slowly over the years. She recognized the impact on both their lives of the deaths of their two children, Margareta and Richard, and the burden these deaths imposed on Charles. "I would have suffered less," she wrote, "but it is through suffering that one develops. The effort I had to make the first ten years to go on at all hardened me and gave me an unpleasant drive that must have been hard to live with."[424] Her adoring husband bore the brunt of all this together with her egocentricity, her loud and, on occasion, domineering manner, as well as her prolonged absences, without a murmur. Despite his forbearance, she still complained that he was difficult to live with because he had been so repressed as a child. "He always loved me," she wrote, "but we had few interests in common other than a real joy in outdoors." His work always came first, "yet he was never satisfied with what he accomplished nor did what he was capable of."[425] She thought lack of imagination had prevented him from achieving great distinction. While Charles had enjoyed life, his pleasures were limited to his graduate students, fly-fishing, and music; he regarded his wife as a "cheerful pessimist" and considered himself a "gloomy optimist."[426]

Dorothy's sons became the focus of her life:

> Both Thomas and John are men that I am proud of—four-square and true. They have never given me a sleepless night [another example of her selective memory], and I feel have made the most of their capabilities. Charles was proud of them too—and satisfied. Perhaps our two sons are the best answer to was our marriage a success.[427]

That September, she drove the boys east. With Charles gone, the wrench of seeing Tom off was greater than ever; England seemed so very far away. Afterward she took John back to Cambridge, where he insisted she accompany him to a meeting with the dean of Harvard Medical School, where, to his mother's surprise, he told the dean of his father's death and said he would like to apply for a scholarship.

In the spring of 1936, Dorothy gave up the directorship of the Madison Health Centers, clearing the way for her promised visit to Oxford. Easter found her aboard the USS *Pennland*, crossing the Atlantic for the thirteenth time. Tom met the ship, and after a brief stop in London, they took the train to Oxford, where she stayed two months. Dorothy was looking forward to "Eights Week." Miserably cold weather and the failure of the Balliol crew—captained by

Tom—to dislodge New College from its position as Head of the River marred the festivities. She watched from the Senate House gallery as her son, in a ceremony conducted exclusively in Latin, received his BA. His failure to obtain first-class honors (he took a second) always irritated and disappointed his mother, as she was quite sure such lay within his powers had he made the effort. Subsequently he earned a B. Litt. for a thesis entitled "The Shrewsbury Drapers and the Welsh Wool Trade in the XVI and XVII Centuries," which was so hastily written the examiner remarked that his spelling was "Elizabethan."[428] Ten years later, when it remained unpublished, his mother wrote, "This still hurts and is inexplicable to me. I should have finished and published original research I had started or died in the attempt."[429] It finally appeared in print in 1953.

Dorothy bought a car, obtained an English driving permit, and, accompanied by an old friend from Smith, set out to explore England's historic treasures. They toured the Cotswolds and saw Shakespeare's *King Lear* in Stratford-on-Avon before continuing on to Devon and Cornwall. While driving down a very narrow lane in Shropshire in search of Clun, one of Housman's "quietist paces,"[430] she saw a youth riding a bicycle, carrying a sickle in one hand and a scythe in the other, and talking with somebody on the far side of a hedge. He pedaled into the side of her car, sending the scythe flying overhead. She yelled at him for not looking where he was going, but his broad country dialect rendered his reply unintelligible. Once assured he was unharmed, she drove on. When they reached their destination, a horrified Dorothy discovered his scythe, with its long, wickedly curved blade, lying on the backseat of her car.[431] Once again she had confirmed Jack Yates's prediction that she was born to hang.

After her companion returned to the United States, Tom joined her, and together they drove north, visiting Ripon and Hadrian's Wall on their way to Scotland. Beyond Edinburgh, they stayed in a small hotel on Loch Leven, where the talk of fishing made her wish that Charles could have been there to enjoy it.[432] At Loch Ness she met a friend from Madison. While they visited the Isle of Sky, Tom returned to Oxford to pack his belongings. When Dorothy rejoined him at his lodgings, she encountered an enormous pile of luggage; even so, she had to visit the open air market to buy an extra tin trunk. As they were about to depart, Tom discovered another closet full of clothes and had to run out and buy yet another trunk; they required two cabs to transport his thirty pieces of luggage to the train station.

With a day to spare before their ship left Southampton, Tom took his mother to visit the family of his best friend at Balliol, who, prior to Oxford, had been head boy at Eton College, arguably the best and certainly the most expensive school in England. Dorothy found the man's mother a frightful hypocrite and snob, which reinforced her impression that there was little to admire in the English upper classes, who, she thought, placed social status above achievement.[433]

Immediately after their return to Madison, Tom departed for Detroit to attend a friend's wedding. As an usher, he was paired with the tallest bridesmaid, Cornelia Isabel Baker. On his return home, he told his mother, "I have met my wife."[434] Nellie, as everyone except Dorothy called her, lived with her parents in New York City, and as soon as Dorothy decently could, she visited them. In the cab after they had left the Baker apartment on Park Avenue, Dorothy remarked, "Cornelia, I like your parents, good stock."[435] Their marriage took place in New York City in June 1938; unfortunately illness prevented Dorothy from attending. The couple subsequently had three daughters. Nellie thought Dorothy a model grandmother: she never interfered but always knew what was going on; if asked she gave very good advice and very appropriate presents. To the grandchildren she remained a formidable, distant figure. When Dorothy went to see her first grandchild, a nurse barred her way, saying it was inconvenient. In a quiet and authoritative tone, she replied, "I am Dr. Mendenhall; I would like to see my grandchild now." The nurse took her straight in.[436] Years later, when Dorothy was staying with Tom's family, Nellie discovered, to her horror, that her mother-in-law traveled with a handgun, which she placed in a drawer in the nightstand.[437]

John Mendenhall graduated from Harvard Medical School in 1939. Following an internship at Boston City Hospital, he took a year of pathology at Johns Hopkins because, as he put it, "Dr. MacCallum [chairman of the pathology department] was a friend of mother's."[438] John's duties included teaching pathology to the medical students, one of whom was Sally Cornell. After the pathology classes were over, the pair began dating. When Dorothy asked John if it was serious, he replied, "I like her a lot."[439] Immediately his mother began making plans to visit Baltimore. Shortly after their marriage in New York City on December 12, 1942, John enlisted in the United States Navy. He took part in the landings in North Africa and Sicily; on D-day, July 6, 1944, his mother's heart stood still as he landed in the second wave on Utah Beach, where he remained for two months.

After John finished his pathology fellowship at Hopkins, this letter reached his mother:

Dear Dorothy,
Please forgive me if I address you like this instead of formal Mrs. Mendenhall. It is so I remember you. I sent you a picture today that I took from memory too and hope it will take you back some years.
But I want to tell you what a splendid boy you have sent me. He is my assistant in teaching; the students and I have the greatest admiration for his whole character.
I hope that everything is happy with you and that you are quite well and interested in things. Do write to me some day and tell me about yourself. I treasure the memories of you and you are a heroine in pathology.
As ever yours
Will MacCallum
Nov. 17, 1941.[440]

Dorothy's own photograph of William MacCallum.
On the back of this she has written a series of dates,
the significance of which remains unclear.

> *MEDITATIONS.*   25
>
> for books, cast away your thirst after them, that you
> may not die complaining, but go off in good-humour,
> and heartily thank the gods for what you have had.
>   4. Remember how often you have postponed mind-
> ing your interest, and let slip those opportunities

Dorothy's notation on the death of William MacCallum on
page 25 of her copy of *The Meditations of Marcus Aurelius.*
The stain down the left hand side of the page was produced
by the clipping of MacCallum's obituary from the New York
Times that had lain there for more than fifty years.

The tone of this letter suggests a more than casual relationship in the past. Could Will MacCallum have been the love of Dorothy's life? In 1901, MacCallum, like AJ, had just returned from a trip to Germany. Among Dorothy's memorabilia is his photograph in a black cardboard mount. Written in pencil on the back and only visible in oblique light is a series of dates starting with New Year's Day 1901, the day she first met AJ. However, there is insufficient information to match other dates with their meetings.

Less than three years after the receipt of this letter, Dorothy inadvertently and indisputably resolved for posterity the riddle of AJ's identity. One morning in late February 1944, she clipped William MacCallum's obituary from the *New York Times* and inserted it between pages 24 and 25 of her copy of *The Meditations of Marcus Aurelius*, and wrote in the margin, "AJ 1944."[441] The clipping remained hidden until the author, while visiting with Tom's widow, Nellie Mendenhall, found it in Dorothy's copy of the *Mediations*, just as she had left it. As an epitaph for her old lover, Dorothy underlined the phrase "Go off in good humor, and heartily thank the gods for what you have had."[442]

It is easy to understand why Dorothy wished to keep her affair and the name of her lover a secret, but why did she always refer to him as AJ? There is no obvious connection between the initials AJ and anything at Hopkins or in MacCallum's private life. Perhaps Dorothy was a fan of detective stories and she was referring to A. J. Raffles (called AJ by his sidekick, Bunny Manders), a popular figure in late Victorian fiction, created by the Englishman E. W. Hornung, the brother-in-law of the creator of Sherlock Holmes, Arthur Conan Doyle.[443] Raffles, a distinguished cricketer, amateur cracksman, and skilled thief, was, in the parlance of the time, "a complete cad"—smug, self-satisfied, overbearing, and totally amoral. He possessed an extraordinary power to compel people to follow his lead in illegal activities they normally would never think of doing. Obviously MacCallum was not a crook, but he did display some of these qualities. In the eyes of a woman whose heart has been broken, an ex-lover possesses few redeeming qualities.

What sort of a man was MacCallum? While extremely bright, he was also smug and self-satisfied. A man of strong moods, at times he could be likable and charming, and at others a ready and penetrating critic. Over the years he is said to have had a series of high-profile women friends, but he never married. Even as a youth, MacCallum was a keen naturalist and biologist. In the summer after he graduated from medical school, he discovered that the flagellated form of the malaria parasite represented the male gamete, a discovery that led to the elucidation of the life cycle of the parasite. He did groundbreaking research in a number of other areas, including the anatomy of the lymphatic system, the relationship between calcium metabolism and the parathyroid gland, and diabetes.[444]

MacCallum played a key role in achieving international recognition for Dorothy's work on Hodgkin's disease, which otherwise might have languished in obscurity between the covers of the Hopkins house journal. In 1916, he published his widely read *Textbook of Pathology*.[445] This remarkable work represented the first attempt to classify diseases on a basis of their etiology instead of following the usual systematic organ-by-organ approach. The book remained the standard work for medical students until after the end of World War II. In his copiously illustrated six-page section on Hodgkin's disease, MacCallum cites Dorothy's work extensively with references such as, "In the smaller nodes the beginning of the process, as Dr. Reed pointed out, consists in a proliferation of lymphoid cells" and "Dr. Reed made much of the presence of [these large cells]." These references were probably responsible for the subsequent worldwide recognition of her name and the designation of "Reed cells" for the large cells mentioned by MacCallum. Dorothy would have us think that he gave her this exposure to prevent others from taking credit for her work, but it seems more likely it had to do with affairs of the heart rather than research on diseases of the lymph glands.

Dorothy carried a torch for MacCallum all her life. She admitted to seeing her old lover a few times, and after Charles's death, she fantasized that they could pick up where they had left off. Later when she reread this dream in her memoirs, she wrote in the margin, "Poppycock!"[446] Together they would have been an unstoppable but probably highly inflammable couple. Their contribution to pathology would have been gargantuan.

In the early forties, when Harvard was once again considering admitting women to its medical school, Alice Hamilton told Dorothy that during the faculty's long deliberations on the subject, her career—or rather the Harvard faculty's perception of a lack of one—was cited as an argument against admitting female medical students.[447] Alice, in 1919, was the first woman to receive a faculty appointment there but had to agree not to use the Faculty Club and not to apply for football tickets. Every year Alice's invitation to commencement carried the handwritten warning that women were not permitted to sit on the platform.[448] Dorothy would have rejected such humiliation outright.

The gall of the Harvard medical faculty infuriated her, particularly as she felt certain she had done more good for more people than anybody there. While many professors were probably aware of her paper on Hodgkin's disease, her work in the field of maternal and child health would have counted for little in topflight medical circles, although it subsequently formed the basis for the highly successful federal Healthy Start program. Her appointment as part-time lecturer in the department of home economics at a midwestern state university would have cut no ice in Harvard Yard.

Considering her circumstances and the standards of the time, Dorothy's writings were impressive: besides the three scientific papers she published at Hopkins, she coauthored, in the thirties, three more on infantile anemia; she wrote ten papers on infant health and nutrition, presented at least three papers to the Association for Study and Prevention of Infant Mortality, and wrote or edited a dozen pamphlets for the Children's Bureau. The number of lives she saved can be estimated. In 1915, when she opened the first Attic Angels Health Center, infant mortality in Wisconsin was approximately one hundred per one thousand live births. In 1937 Madison received an award for having one of the lowest infant mortality rates in the nation (thirty per one thousand live births), largely due to Dorothy's activities.[449] Since approximately one thousand children were born annually in Madison,[450] she was responsible for preserving seventy infant lives yearly, not to mention the lives saved indirectly through the Madison Health Clinics and as a result of her writings. No wonder she was mad at Harvard.

Home again in Madison after her English trip, Dorothy resumed her work in the department of home economics, taught summer school at the University of Chicago, and held a visiting professorship at the University of Utah in Provo. She remained active socially and involved with the Walrus Club. Travel became her principal interest; she visited the West and Southwest, Jamaica, and Mexico. She thought Guatemala the most beautiful place she had ever seen and found Central American art and textiles fascinating. She was busy planning another trip to Europe when Hitler invaded Poland in August 1939 and World War II erupted. Following the Japanese attack on Pearl Harbor, she resumed the directorship of the Madison Health Centers.

Dorothy found the war years very hard. As she grew older, she felt the long, harsh midwestern winters more and more. In 1943, she joined a number of friends who escaped the cold by fleeing to Tryon, North Carolina—the start of a regular winter pilgrimage. When the Allies crossed the Rhine River in March of 1945, a wave of profound depression and introspection swept over her. "I am only waiting to die," she cried. "My life is over—a complete failure."[451]

After the war, John, Sally, and their rapidly growing family returned to live with Dorothy in the big, old family house in Madison. As is so often the case, the arrangement was not particularly harmonious. A major burden fell on Dorothy when John contracted pulmonary tuberculosis, necessitating two major operations and a year-long stay in a sanitarium. Eventually John moved his family to a house farther down the street, and she sold up and decamped to a small apartment in Tryon. There she led an active and reasonably happy life, driving around the countryside, eating out, and playing bridge. Gradually old age took its toll; she gave up driving but was able to hire a chauffeur. She grew heavy and less and less mobile; as her friends passed on, her social circle contracted. She suffered recurring depressions; ten years before her death, she spoke of her demise as though it were imminent. In those last years of her life, without the solace of creative work, she felt lonelier than ever before. She reflected,

> I have often thought of the weeks and months of loneliness that my mother must have endured, and I have regretted many times that I had not shown her more affection and lightened her burden.[452]

When Dorothy learned of her son Tom's appointment to the presidency of Smith College, she remarked that he had better do well the first year; otherwise the college would fire him. When a newspaper reporter asked Tom why he thought he was named president, he replied, "I'd like to think it was due to my firm conviction that education for women may be even more important than for men."[453] Truly he was his mother's son. Dorothy must have felt very proud when she attended his installation.

She made one last visit to the Old Stone House in Talcottville, which her cousin Edmond Wilson, the author and critic, had inherited. He described her, at eighty-one, as dumpy and with much of her old magisterial dignity gone. She continued to wear her hair, which remained dark, piled on top of her head, but her face showed her age. Periodically something she said or the way she smiled would produce a glimpse of the old presence. At five thirty every afternoon, she enjoyed one stiff bourbon on the rocks and frowned visibly on those who arrived late to the party or felt the need for a second or third drink. When she saw on the sideboard Orazio Andreoni's bust of her as a young girl, which she had had workmen dump in the millpond many years before, she threatened to throw it back again into the water.

Dorothy was always a formidable backseat driver. As Edmund and her niece, Dorothy Sharp, drove her round the countryside, she remembered everything. When a storm engulfed them and incessant lightning ripped the sky and thunder rent the air, the old lady was the only person who was not afraid.

Dorothy Reed Mendenhall died in her ninetieth year.[454]

NOTES

My prime source is Dorothy Reed Mendenhall's handwritten autobiography at Smith College, Northampton, Massachusetts, supplemented by visits with her son John T. Mendenhall, her daughter-in-law Cornelia (Nellie) Mendenhall, and other family members. Dorothy's archives are housed in the Sophia Smith Collection at Smith College, Northampton, Massachusetts. I have made multiple visits to Northampton and Martha's Vineyard, Massachusetts, where Mrs. TC Mendenhall lived, as well as to Madison and the University of Wisconsin; Johns Hopkins Medical School and the Chesney Archives; Talcottville, New York; Berlin, New Hampshire; and the National Archives. I have consulted biographies and obituaries of all the principal subjects.

Jill Ker Conway has published extracts from Dorothy Reed Mendenhall's unpublished memoir in *Written by Herself*, and parts of Dorothy's story appeared in "Whatever Happened to Dorothy Reed?" my 2003 article in *Annals of Diagnostic Pathology*.

PROLOGUE

1. Dorothy Reed Mendenhall Papers, Sophia Smith Collection, Smith College, Northampton, Massachusetts. Box 1, Folder 13, Section E, 8.
2. Mendenhall Papers, Box 1, Folder 13, Section E, 9.

CHAPTER ONE

3. "Reed Family History," accessed February 15, 2005, www.rootsweb.ancestry. com.
4. Correspondence: William Pratt Reed and Adeline Grace Reed, DRM Papers, Box 10, Folders 6 and 7.
5. Franklin County Probate Court Record #18-3-3-2 (filed January 7, 1881).
6. Mendenhall Papers, Box 1, Folder 4, Section A, 21.
7. Obituary notice of William Pratt Reed, *Columbus Dispatch*, November 11, 1880; see also *Daily Ohio State Journal*, November 12, 1880.

8. William Pratt Reed, "Rules for the Guidance of My Father," DRM Papers, Box 10, Folder 7, and Mendenhall Papers, Box 1, Folder 4, Section A, Insert following p. 23.
9. Mendenhall Papers, Box 1, Folder 4, Section A, 21.
10. Franklin County Probate Court Record #18-4711 (filed November 21, 1880) and Record 22-229 (completed July 5, 1883). The best estimate of Reed's net worth is Reed and Jones (one-half interest), \$361,055.04; personal property, \$2,261.75; life insurance, \$1,942.86 plus \$5,000; real estate; four properties and five lots in Columbus and 1,200 acres in Iowa, Kansas, and Minnesota; and an unspecified interest in the firm of Steinberger and Hensel.
11. Mendenhall Papers, Box 1, Folder 4, Section A, 14.
12. Leonard A. Morrison and Stephen P. Sharples, *History of the Kimball Family in America from 1634–1897* (Boston: Damrell and Upham, 1897). In her autobiography, Dorothy mistakenly places Rattlesden near Norwich, England.
13. Mendenhall Papers, Box 1, Folder 6, Section B, 18.
14. Mendenhall Papers, Box 1, Folder 6, Section B, 4.
15. Mendenhall Papers, Box 1, Folder 4, Section A, 14.
16. Mendenhall Papers, Box 1, Folder 6, Section B, 7.

Chapter Two

17. Edmund Wilson, *Upstate: Records and Recollections of Northern New York* (New York: Farrar, Straus and Giroux, 1971), 49–51. Wilson states that the county records show that Baker acquired the house in 1832 from Jesse Talcott. This is hard to reconcile with Baker's marriage to Saphronia, which he dates at March 10, 1851.
18. Edmund Wilson, *The Fifties* (New York: Farrar, Straus and Giroux, 1986), 40 and Wilson, *Upstate*, 87.
19. Mendenhall Papers, Box 1, Folder 4, Section A, 20.
20. Wilson, *Upstate*, 88.
21. Mendenhall Papers, Box 1, Folder 6, Section B, 20.
21. Mendenhall Papers, Box 1, Folder 6, Section B, 29.
22. Mendenhall Papers, Box 1, Folder 6, Section B, 29.
23. Mendenhall Papers, Box 1, Folder 6, Section B, 35.

24. Mendenhall Papers, Box 1, Folder 6, Section B, 20.

CHAPTER THREE
25. Mendenhall Papers, Box 1, Folder 6, Section B, 38.
26. John M. Greene, "Historical Addresses: The Origin of Smith College," in *Celebration of the Quarter Centenary of Smith College* (Cambridge: Riverside Press, 1900), 90.
27. Constance Morrow Morgan, *A Distant Moment* (Northampton: Smith College, 1978), and Harriet Seelye Rhees. *Laurenus Clark Seelye: First President of Smith College* (Boston and New York: Houghton Mifflin, 1929), 131.
28. Kate Sanborn, "Social Life at Smith College." *Demorest's Monthly Magazine,* 19 (July 1883), 539, cited by Helen L. Horowitz, *Alma Mater.* (Amherst: University of Massachusetts Press, 1984), 80, ref. 41.
29. Mendenhall Papers, Box 1, Folder 10, Section D, 3.
30. Grace (Rickey) Landon, *Recollections of Smith College, Class of 1893.* History Class of 1893 Records, Grace Landon Biographical File, Box 1472, Sophia Smith Collection, Smith College.
31. Morgan, 63.
32. Mendenhall Papers, Box 1, Folder 10, Section D, 7.
33. Mendenhall Papers, Box 1, Folder 10, Section D, 13.
34. DRM. to Margaret Long, Mendenhall Papers, Box 17, Folder 11 and Mendenhall Papers, Box 1.
35. Mendenhall Papers, Box 1, Folder 10, Section D, 21.
36. Newspaper clipping, November 1892, Mendenhall Papers, Box 9, Folder 3.
37. Mendenhall Papers, Box 1, Folder 10, Section D, 15.
38. Confusion exists here. Dorothy in her autobiography gives the figure of $500, but in the letter in her archives cited in the text, whose date corresponds with that of the incident, Will asks for $1,200.
39. Mendenhall Papers, Box 1, Folder 10, Section D, 16. This incident occurred in the fall of Dorothy's senior year; she graduated in 1895. Bessie's oldest child, Willard Hart Furbish, was born in 1895. Contrary to what Dorothy says, her niece, also called Dorothy, was not born until 1896.

40. *The Meditations of Marcus Aurelius*, trans. Jeremy Collier (New York: F. A Stokes, 1889).

41. Mendenhall Papers, Box 1, Folder 10, Section D, 19.

42. Mendenhall Papers, Box 1, Folder 10, Section D, 19.

43. Mendenhall Papers, Box 1, Folder 13, Section E, 2.

44. Mendenhall Papers, Box 1, Folder 13, Section E, 1.

45. Mendenhall Papers, Box 1, Folder 10, Section D, 25.

46. Mendenhall Papers, Box 1, Folder 13, Section E, 7.

47. Mendenhall Papers, Box 1, Folder 13, Section E, 7.

48. Mendenhall Papers, Box 1, Folder 13, Section E, 6.

CHAPTER FOUR

49. Susan B. Anthony and Ida Harper, eds., *The History of Woman's Suffrage*, vol. 4, (New York: Arno and the New York Times, 1969), 453–8.

50. Carolyn Spieler, ed., *Women in Medicine, 1976* (New York: Josiah Macy Foundation, 1977), 11.

51. Several land grant colleges in western states accepted small numbers of women; the first was the University of Michigan in 1870.

52. Alan M. Chesney, *The Johns Hopkins Hospital and The Johns Hopkins University School of Medicine: A Chronicle, vol. 1, Early Years 1867–1893* (Baltimore: The Johns Hopkins Press, 1943), 13–17, 153.

53. John Shaw Billings, *Johns Hopkins Hospital: Reports and Papers Relating to Construction and Organization, No. 1* (privately printed), quoted by Chesney, vol. 1, 30.

54. Billings, quoted by Chesney, vol. 1, 30.

55. Billings, quoted by Chesney, vol. 1, 65.

56. Edith Finch, *Carey Thomas of Bryn Mawr* (New York: Harper, 1947), 244.

57. Kathleen Waters Sander, *Mary Elizabeth Garrett: Society and Philanthropy in the Gilded Age* (Baltimore: The Johns Hopkins Press, 2008), 111.

58. Simon Flexner and James T. Flexner, *William Welch and the Heroic Age of American Medicine* (New York: Viking Press, 1941) 216–217.

59. *Medical School Fund*, Johns Hopkins Hospital Bulletin, 1 (1890), 103–4.

60. *Medical School Fund*, Johns Hopkins Hospital Bulletin, 1 (1890), 103–4.

61. *Baltimore News American*, November 15, 1890.

62. Cardinal James Gibbons, *On the Opening of the Johns Hopkins School to Women.* Open Letter, *Century Magazine* (February 1891), 632–3.

63. Chesney, vol. 1, 202

64. Chesney, vol. 1, 202.

65. Resolution adopted by Board of Trustees October 28, 1890, cited by Chesney, vol. 1, 197.

66. Flexner, 217.

67. Flexner, 217.

68. "The Conditions of Miss Garrett's Gift to the Medical School of Johns Hopkins University," *Boston Medical and Surgical Journal* 128 (1898), 71–72.

69. Chesney, vol. 1, 204.

70. Daniel Coit Gilman, *The Launching of a University* (New York: Garret Press, 1969), 123.

71. Harvey Cushing, *The Life of Sir William Osler* (London: Oxford University Press, 1940), 388.

72. Chesney, vol. 1, 220.

73. Alan M. Chesney, *The Johns Hopkins Hospital and The Johns Hopkins University School of Medicine: vol. 2, A Chronicle, 1893–1905* (Baltimore: The Johns Hopkins University Press, 1958), 46.

74. Chesney, vol. 2, 47.

Chapter Five

75. Michael Bliss, *William Osler: A Life in Medicine* (Oxford: Oxford University Press, 1999), 205.

76. Mendenhall Papers, Box 1, Folder 13, Section E, 11.

77. Mendenhall Papers, Box 1, Folder 13, Section E, 12.

78. Bertram M. Bernheim, *The Story of The Johns Hopkins* (New York: McGraw-Hill, 1948), 53–59.

79. William H. Howell, ed., *An American Text-book of Physiology* (Philadelphia: Saunders, 1903).

80. Mendenhall Papers, Box 1, Folder 13, Section E, 15.

81. D. R. Reed to Grace Reed, February 1897, Mendenhall Papers, Box 1, Folder 13, Section E, following p. 15.

82. Mendenhall Papers, Box 1, Folder 13, Section E, 28.

83. Bliss. 211.
84. Dorothy M. Reed, "The Bacillus Pseudo-tuberculosis Murium; Its Streptothrix Forms and its Pathogenic Action," *The Johns Hopkins Hospital Reports* 9 (1901), 525–541.
85. Mendenhall Papers, Box 1, Folder 13, Section E, 20.
86. Mendenhall Papers, Box 2, Folder 2, Section H, 1.
87. Mendenhall Papers, Box 2, Folder 2, Section H, 3.
88. John N. Mackenzie, "The Physiological and Pathological Relations between the Nose and Sexual Apparatus of Man," *Bulletin of the Johns Hopkins Hospital* 9 (1898): 10–17.
89. Mendenhall Papers, Box 1, Folder 13, Section E, 21.
90. Mendenhall Papers, Box 1, Folder 13, Section E, 22.
91. Mendenhall Papers, Box 1, Folder 14, Section F, 3.
92. Surgeon General, US Navy to DRM, July 28, 1898, DRM Archives, Box 18, Folder 2.

CHAPTER SIX

93. Lilian Welsh, *Reminiscences of Thirty Years in Baltimore* (Baltimore: The Norman Remington Press, 1925), 44. According to Bliss, 234, this is the only documentation for Osler's remark.
94. Bliss. 231.
95. Bernheim, 33.
96. Mendenhall Papers, Box 1, Folder 1, Section E, 23.
97. Bliss, 237.
98. W. Osler, *On the Opening of the Johns Hopkins Medical School to Women*. Open Letter, *Century* (February 1891), 632–3.
99. Henry A. Christian, "Osler: Recollections of an Undergraduate Medical Student at Johns Hopkins," *Archives of Internal Medicine* 84 (1949): 77–83.
100. W. Osler, *Aequanimitas* (Philadelphia: P. Blakiston's Son and Co., 1904), 33.
101. W. Osler, *Principles and Practice of Medicine* (New York: Appleton and Company, 1898).
102. Mendenhall Papers, Box 1, Folder 13, Section E, 24.
103. Mendenhall Papers, Box 1, Folder 13, Section E, 34.

104. William Osler, "The Inner History of the Johns Hopkins Hospital," in Donald G. Bates and Edward H. Bensley, eds., *Bulletin of the Johns Hopkins Hospital* 125 (1969), 184–194, and Thomas B. Turner, *Heritage of Excellence: The Johns Hopkins Hospital Medical Institutions 1914–1947* (Baltimore and London: The Johns Hopkins University Press, 1974), 110.

105. William G. MacCallum. "Biographical Memoir of William Stewart Halsted, 1852–1922," *National Academy of Sciences Biographical Memoir* 17 (1937): 151–170.

106. Bernheim, 144–145.

107. Mendenhall Papers, Box 1, Folder 13, Section E, 37.

108. Mendenhall Papers, Box 1, Folder 13, Section E, 37.

109. Payton Rous to Elizabeth D. Robinton, March 3, 1967, Mendenhall Papers, Box 1, Folder 13, Section E, 26. Peyton Rous in his letter to Professor Robinton describes the technique Sabin used and the animosity between her and Gertrude Stein.

110. Gertrude Stein, *The Autobiography of Alice B. Toklas* (New York: Modern Library, 1980), 81–83.

111. Mendenhall Papers, Box 1, Folder 13, Section E, 40.

112. Mendenhall Papers, Box 1, Folder 13, Section E, 43.

113. Mendenhall Papers, Box 1, Folder 13, Section E, 43.

114. E. M. Lawton, unpublished, Sophia Smith Archives, Smith College.

115. Mendenhall Papers, Box 1, Folder 13, Section E, 53.

116. Mendenhall Papers, Box 1, Folder 13, Section E, 51.

117. Mendenhall Papers, Box 1, Folder 13, Section E, 57–58.

118. Mendenhall Papers, Box 1, Folder 13, Section E, 61.

119. Mendenhall Papers, Box 1, Folder 13, Section E, 59.

120. Mendenhall Papers, Box 1, Folder 13, Section E, 60.

121. Mendenhall Papers, Box 1, Folder 13, Section E, 63.

122. Mendenhall Papers, Box 1, Folder 13, Section E, 62.

123. Mendenhall Papers, Box 1, Folder 13, Section E, 63.

CHAPTER SEVEN

124. Handwritten sheets (part of diary that Dorothy subsequently buried), September 1, 1900, Mendenhall Papers, Box 3, Folder 12.

125. Mendenhall Papers, Box 1, Folder 16, Section F pt. 1, 2.

126. Mendenhall Papers, Box 1, Folder 16, Section F pt. 2, 2.

127. Mendenhall Papers, Box 1, Folder 16, Section F pt. 1, 3.

128. Mendenhall Papers, Box 1, Folder 16, Section F pt. 1, 3.

129. Mendenhall Papers, Box 1, Folder 16, Section F pt. 1, 3.

130. Mendenhall Papers, Box 1, Folder 16, Section F pt. 1, 3.

131. Mendenhall Papers, Box 1, Folder 16, Section F pt. 1, 5.

132. Mendenhall Papers, Box 1, Folder 16, Section F pt. 1, 7.

133. Mendenhall Papers, Box 1, Folder 16, Section F pt. 1, 5.

134. Mendenhall Papers, Box 1, Folder 16, Section F pt. 1, 5.

135. Mendenhall Papers, Box 1, Folder 16, Section F pt. 1, 6.

136. Bliss, 222.

137. Warfield T. Longcope, "Random Recollections of William Osler 1899–1918," *Archives of Internal Medicine* 84 (1949): 93–103.

138. Mendenhall Papers, Box 1, Folder 13, Section E, 52.

139. Mendenhall Papers, Box 1, Folder 13, Section F pt. 1, 16.

140. Mendenhall Papers, Box 1, Folder 13, Section F pt. 1, 16.

141. Mendenhall Papers, Box 1, Folder 13, Section F pt. 1, 17.

142. Mendenhall Papers, Box 1, Folder 13, Section F pt. 1, 9.

143. Mendenhall Papers, Box 1, Folder 13, Section F pt. 1, 10.

144. William Osler, *Principles and Practice of Medicine* (New York: Appleton and Company, 1898). McCrae subsequently became professor of medicine at Jefferson Medical College, Philadelphia.

145. Mendenhall Papers, Box 1, Folder 13, Section F pt. 1, 13.

146. Mendenhall Papers, Box 1, Folder 13, Section F pt. 1, 12.

147. Mendenhall Papers, Box 1, Folder 13, Section F pt. 1, 10.

148. Mendenhall Papers, Box 1, Folder 13, Section F pt. 1, 10.

149. Mendenhall Papers, Box 1, Folder 13, Section F pt. 1, 23.

150. Mendenhall Papers, Box 1, Folder 13, Section F pt. 1, 22.

151. Mendenhall Papers, Box 1, Folder 13, Section F pt. 1, 18.

152. Mendenhall Papers, Box 1, Folder 13, Section F pt. 1, 25.

153. Mendenhall Papers, Box 1, Folder 13, Section F pt. 3, 2.

154. Mendenhall Papers, Box 1, Folder 4, 18, and Folder 13, Section F pt. 3, 1.

155. Mendenhall Papers, Box 1, Folder 13, Section F pt. 3, 2.

CHAPTER EIGHT

156. Dorothy claimed his mill burned down, but I could find no evidence of this at the Berlin Historical Society. It seems more likely that Willard's lack of interest and absence of business skills led to its failure.

157. Mendenhall Papers, Box 1, Folder 16, Section F pt. 2, 2.

158. Mendenhall Papers, Box 1, Folder 16, Section F pt. 2, 3.

159. Mendenhall Papers, Box 1, Folder 16, Section F pt. 2, 2.

160. Payton Rous to Elizabeth D. Robinton, March 3, 1967, Faculty Biographical Files, Elizabeth D. Robinton, "Correspondence and Research Material on Florence Sabin, 1966–1967," File Box 988, Smith College Archives.

161. Carl Sternberg, "Über eine einenartige unter dem Bilde der Pseudoleukämie verlaufende Tuberculose des lymphatischen Apparates," *Zeitschrift für Heilkunde* 19 (1898): 21–91.

162. Thomas Hodgkin, "On Some Morbid Appearances of the Absorbent Glands and Spleen," *Proceedings of the Medical and Chirurgical Society of London* 17 (1832): 68–114. The author rediscovered the original illustrations Hodgkin used to illustrate his talk in 1832; Peter J. Dawson, "The Original Illustrations of Hodgkin's Disease," *Archives of Internal Medicine* 121 (1968): 288–290.

163. Samuel Wilks, "Cases of Lardaceous Disease and Some Allied Afflictions, with Remarks," *Guy's Hospital Reports* 2 (1856): 103–132, and "Cases of Enlargement of the Lymphatic Glands and Spleen (or, Hodgkin's Disease), with Remarks," *Guy's Hospital Reports* 11 (1865): 56–67.

164. Carl Sternberg. "Über eine einenartige unter dem Bilde der Pseudoleukämie verlaufende Tuberculose des lymphatischen Apparates," *Zeitschrift für Heilkunde* 19 (1898): 21–91.

164. William Osler to DRM, November 14, 1901, DRM Papers, Box 17.

165. Dorothy M. Reed, "On the Pathological Changes in Hodgkin's Disease, with Especial Reference to its Relation to Tuberculosis," *Johns Hopkins Hospital Reports* 10 (1902): 133–196.

166. Reed, 151–2.

167. F. Parker, H. Jackson, G. Fitz Hugh, and T.D. Spies. "Studies of Diseases of Lymphoid and Myeloid Tissue, IV: Skin Reactions to Human and Avian Tuberculin," *Journal of Immunology* 22 (1932): 277–282.

168. S. A. Rosenberg and H. S. Kaplan, "Evidence for an Orderly Progression in the Spread of Hodgkin's Disease," *Cancer Research* 26 (1966): 1225–1231.

169. Dorothy M. Reed, "A Case of Acute Leukaemia without Enlargement of the Lymphatic Glands," *The American Journal of the Medical Sciences* 124 (1902): 653–669.

170. Edward T. James, ed., *Notable American Women* (Cambridge, Massachusetts and London: Belknap Press of Harvard University, 1971), s.v. "Wald, Lillian D." by Robert H. Bremner.

171. Mendenhall Papers, Box 1, Folder 16, Section F pt. 2, 10.

172. Cary Thomas to DRM, January 25, 1901, Mendenhall Papers, Box 17, Folder 17.

173. Mendenhall Papers, Box 1, Folder 16, Section F pt. 2, 11.

174. Mendenhall Papers, Box 1, Folder 16, Section F pt. 2, 13.

175. Mendenhall Papers, Box 1, Folder 16, Section F pt. 2, 13.

176. A. McGehee Harvey, Gert H. Brieger, Susan L. Abrams, and Victor A. McKusick, *A Model of Its Kind*, vol. 1, *A Centennial History of Medicine at Johns Hopkins* (Baltimore: The Johns Hopkins Press, 1989), 155.

177. Bernheim, 63–71.

178. Katherine A. Downes and William R. Hart, "History of Gynecological Pathology, VII. Dr. Elizabeth Hurdon," *International Journal of Gynecological Pathology* 19 (2000), 85–93. Following the outbreak of World War I, Hurdon returned to Britain to serve in the Royal Army Medical Corps. After the war she was appointed surgeon to the Marie Curie Hospital in London. She became an expert in radiation therapy for gynecologic cancer.

179. Mendenhall Papers, Box 1, Folder 16, Section F pt. 3, 5.

180. L. Emmett Holt to DRM, May 21, 1902, Box 17, Folder 18, and "Correspondence Friends and Associates, William Welch 1900–1903," Box 17, Folder 18.

181. Mendenhall Papers, Box 1, Folder 16, Section F pt. 2, 15.

182. Mendenhall Papers, Box 1, Folder 16, Section F pt. 2, 15.

Chapter Nine

183. Mendenhall Papers, Box 1, Folder 18, Section G pt. 1, 7.

184. Mendenhall Papers, Box 1, Folder 18, Section G pt. 2, 1.

185. Mendenhall Papers, Box 1, Folder 18, Section G pt. 2, 9.

186. George W. Corner, *A History of the Rockefeller Institute 1901–1953* (New York: Rockefeller Institute Press, 1964), appendix III.

187. Wilson, *Upstate*, 60–61.

188. Peter M. Dunn, "Dr. Emmett Holt (1855–1924) and the Foundation of North American Pediatrics," *Papers of Diseases in Childhood: Fetal and Neonatal Edition* 83 (2000): 221–223.

189. Emmett L. Holt, *The Care and Feeding of Children* (New York: D. Appleton & Company, 1894), 66.

190. "Books That Influenced America." *The New York Times Book Review*, April 21, 1946.

191. Holt, 24–25.

192. Mendenhall Papers, Box 1, Folder 18, Section G pt. 2, 9.

193. Mendenhall Papers, Box 1, Folder 18, Section G pt. 2, 43.

194. Babies Hospital. *Annual Report* 1903–04, 27–33.

195. Mendenhall Papers, Box 1, Folder 18, Section G pt. 2, 44.

196. Mendenhall Papers, Box 1, Folder 18, Section G pt. 2, 36.

197. Mendenhall Papers, Box 1, Folder 18, Section G pt. 2, 14.

198. Mendenhall Papers, Box 1, Folder 18, Section G pt. 2, 16, and Reuel B. Kimball, "Gonorrhea in Infants, with a Report of Eight Cases of Pyemia," *Medical Record* 20 (1903): 761–66.

199. Mendenhall Papers, Box 1, Folder 18, Section G pt. 2, 11.

200. Mendenhall Papers, Box 1, Folder 18, Section G pt. 2, 11.

201. Mendenhall Papers, Box 1, Folder 18, Section G pt. 2, 11, and A. Commire, ed., *Women in World History: A Biographical Encyclopedia* (Detroit: Yorkin Publications, 2002), 703.

202. Mendenhall Papers, Box 1, Folder 18, Section G pt. 2, 58.

203. Mendenhall Papers, Box 1, Folder 18, Section G pt. 2, 60.

204. Wilson, *The Fifties* 322.

205. Mendenhall Papers, Box 1, Folder 18, Section G pt. 2, 21.

206. Dorothy asserts the mill burned down, but there is no record of this at the Berlin Historical Society, Berlin, New Hampshire.

207. Elizabeth (Bessie) Reed Furbish died on August 18, 1903.

208. Mendenhall Papers, Box 1, Folder 18, Section G pt. 2, 23.

209. Mendenhall Papers, Box 1, Folder 18, Section G pt. 2, 24.

210. CEM to DMR, August 8, 1901, Mendenhall Papers, Box 11, Folder 3.

211. CEM to DMR, August 7 (this letter lacks the year but was probably written in 1902), DRM Papers, Box 11, Folder 3.

212. Mendenhall Papers, Box 1, Folder 18, Section G pt. 2, 25.

213. Mendenhall Papers, Box 1, Folder 18, Section G pt. 2, 25.

214. DRM to CEM, undated, Mendenhall Papers, Box 11, Folder 3.

215. Mendenhall Papers, Box 1, Folder 18, Section G pt. 2, 11.

216. Mendenhall Papers, Box 1, Folder 18, Section G pt. 2, 29.

217. Mendenhall Papers, Box 1, Folder 18, Section G pt. 2, 26.

218. Mendenhall Papers, Box 1, Folder 18, Section G pt. 2, 26.

219. Mendenhall Papers, Box 1, Folder 18, Section G pt. 2, 27.

220. "W." (probably William G. MacCallum) to DRM, undated, Mendenhall Papers, Box 17, Folder 12.

221. DMR to CEM, August, 1904, Mendenhall Papers, Box 11, Folder 3.

222. Mendenhall Papers, Box 1, Folder 18, Section G pt. 2, 34.

223. Mendenhall Papers, Box 1, Folder 18, Section G pt. 2, 35.

224. DMR to CEM, undated (probably 1905), Mendenhall Papers, Box 11, Folder 3.

225. Mendenhall Papers, Box 1, Folder 18, Section G pt. 2, 64.

CHAPTER TEN

226. Merwin Kimball Hart (1881–1962), born in Utica, New York, and educated at Harvard, was a soldier, lawyer, and businessman, who in later life became violently pro-Fascist, anti-Communist, and anti-Semitic. He strongly opposed the entry of the United States into World War II. There is no evidence that Dorothy shared any of these extreme views.

227. Consultation with Laura McLaurin. Dress in possession of Mrs. Thomas Mendenhall.

228. Henry Crew, "Thomas Corwin Mendenhall 1841-1924," *National Academy of Sciences of the United States: Biographical Memoirs* 16 (1936): 331–335.

229. Mendenhall Papers, Box 2, Folder 2, Section H pt. 1, 1.

230. Mendenhall Papers, Box 1, Folder 2, Section H pt. 2, 65.

231. Mendenhall Papers, Box 2, Folder 2, Section H pt. 1, 1.

232. Mendenhall Papers, Box 2, Folder 2, Section H pt. 2, 7.

233. Wilson, *The Fifties* 311–12 and 324.

234. Conversation with Mrs. TC (Nellie) Mendenhall.

235. Christopher Hibbert, *Rome: Biography of a City* (New York: Penguin, 1987), 276.

236. Gertrude Slaughter, *Only the Past Is Ours: The Life Story of Gertrude Slaughter* (New York: Exposition Press, 1963), 107.

237. Slaughter, 111.

238. Mendenhall Papers, Box 2, Folder 2, Section H pt. 2, 10.

239. Mendenhall Papers, Box 2, Folder 2, Section H pt. 2, 11.

240. Mendenhall Papers, Box 2, Folder 2, Section H pt. 2, 13.

241. Mendenhall Papers, Box 2, Folder 2, Section H pt. 2, 13.

242. Mendenhall Papers, Box 2, Folder 2, Section H, pt. 2, insert following p. 13.

243. Mendenhall Papers, Box 2, Folder 2, Section H pt. 2, 14.

244. Photo of Dorothy, Mendenhall Papers, Box 2, Folder 2.

245. Mendenhall Papers, Box 2, Folder 2, Section H pt. 2, 10.

246. Mendenhall Papers, Box 2, Folder 2, Section H pt. 2, 17.

247. Mendenhall Papers, Box 2, Folder 2, Section H pt. 2, 16.

248. Mendenhall Papers, Box 2, Folder 2, Section H pt. 2, 18–19.

249. Mendenhall Papers, Box 2, Folder 2, Section H pt. 2, 10.

250. Mendenhall Papers, Box 2, Folder 2, Section H pt. 2, 19.

251. William K. Reed to DRM, August 18, 1909, Mendenhall Papers, Box 16, Folder 3.

252. Clara K. Reed to Grace Reed, January 4, 1911, Mendenhall Papers, Box 10, Folder 8.

253. Jamie M. Gesen to DRM, January 10, 1911, Mendenhall Papers, Box 16, Folder 3.

254. Mendenhall Papers, Box 2, Folder 2, Section H pt. 2, 19.

255. A preparation containing five milligrams of codeine, to which some people are allergic.

256. Mendenhall Papers, Box 2, Folder 4, Section J, pt. 2, 3.

257. Mendenhall Papers, Box 2, Folder 2, Section H p. 2, 24.

258. Mendenhall Papers, Box 1, Folder 18, Section G pt. 2, 24.

259. Mendenhall Papers, Box 2, Folder 4, Section I pt. 2, 5.

260. Mendenhall Papers, Box 2, Folder 4, Section I pt. 2, 4.

261. Mendenhall Papers, Box 2, Folder 4, Section I pt. 2, 5.

262. Mendenhall Papers, Box 1, Folder 6, Section B, 17.

265. Later this function was transferred to the Department of Agriculture, with its network of county agents and access to local Farmers' Institutes.

263. Mendenhall Papers, Box 1, Folder 6, Section B, 17.

264. Mendenhall Papers, Box 2, Folder 4, Section I pt. 1, 9.

265. Mendenhall Papers, Box 2, Folder 4, Section I pt. 1, 10.

266. Molly Ladd-Taylor, *Raising a Baby the Government Way: Mothers' Letters to the Children's Bureau 1915–1932* (New Brunswick, NJ: Rutgers University Press, 1986), 49, and National Archives, US Children's Bureau, October 19, 1916, 4-3-0-3.

267. Susan H. S. Doane, *The Attic Angel Association: 1889–1949* (Madison: Democrat Printing Company, 1949).

268. Doane, According to Philip Van Inge (p. 290), privately maintained infant welfare stations existed in 92 cities in 1915. "Recent Progress in Infant Welfare Work," *American Journal of Diseases of Children* 10 (1915): 212–221.

269. Mendenhall Papers, Box 2, Folder 4, Section I pt. 2, 7.

270. Mendenhall Papers, Box 2, Folder 4, Section I pt. 2, 16.

271. J. Whitridge Williams, "The Limitations and Possibilities of Prenatal Care," *Journal of the American Medical Association* 64 (1915): 95–101.

272. Dorothy R. Mendenhall, "Report on Obstetrical Conditions in Country Communities," *Fifth Annual Meeting American Association for Study and Prevention of Infant Mortality* 5 (1914): 233–4.

273. Dorothy R. Mendenhall, "Prenatal and Natal Conditions in Wisconsin," *Wisconsin Medical Journal* 15 (1917): 351–365.

274. Mendenhall, 361. She does not reference her statement that the mortality of soldiers in the Franco-Prussian war was about three-quarters of one percent, about the same as that of women in childbirth in 1917.

275. Mendenhall, 355.

276. John M. Beffel, in discussion of Mendenhall, 368.

CHAPTER ELEVEN

277. Mendenhall Papers, Box 2, Folder 4, Section I pt.1, 6.

278. H. Garrison Fielding, "History of Pediatrics," in *Pediatrics*, Isaac A. Abt, ed. (Philadelphia and London: W.B. Saunders and Company, 1923), vol. 1, 153.

279. Molly Ladd-Taylor, *Raising a Baby the Government Way: Mothers' Letters to the Children's Bureau 1915–1932* (New Brunswick, NJ: Rutgers University Press, 1986), 6.

280. *Congressional Record*, 60th Congress, vol. 43 (February 22, 1909), 3rd. sess., 2897–98, cited by Kriste Lindenmeyer, *A Right to Childhood: The U.S. Children's Bureau and Child Welfare, 1912–1946* (Urbana and Chicago: University of Illinois Press, 1997), 23.

281. Lindenmeyer, 44.

282. Lindenmeyer, 43.

283. Emma Duke, *Infant Mortality: Results of a Field Study in Johnston, Pa.*, *Children's Bureau Publication*, *No. 9* (Washington, DC: US Government Printing Office, 1915). and Beatrice Shields Duncan and Emma Duke, *Infant mortality: Results of a Field Study in Manchester, N.H. Based on Births in One Year*, Children's Bureau Publication, No. 20 (Washington, DC: US Government Printing Office, 1917).

284. Grace L. Meigs, *Maternal Mortality from All Conditions Connected with Childbirth in the United States and Certain other Countries, Children's Bureau Publication, No. 19* (Washington, DC: US Government Printing Office, 1917), 22.

285. Marian F. MacDorman, Donna L. Hoyert, Joyce A. Martin, Martha L. Munson, and Brady E. Hamilton, "Fetal and Perinatal Mortality, United States, 2003," *National Vital Statistics Reports* 55 (2007): 1–9.

286. Mrs. Max (Mary) West, *Prenatal Care, Children's Bureau Publication, No. 4* (Washington, DC: US Government Printing Office, 1914) and *Infant Care, Children's Bureau Publication, No. 8* (Washington, DC: US Government Printing Office, 1915), and Ladd-Taylor, 2.

287. Mendenhall Papers, Box 2, Folder 4, Section I pt. 3, 9.

288. B. A., Kentucky to Children's Bureau, May 26, 1918, Children's Bureau Archives, Box 47, 4-16-4-1.

289. DRM response to above letter, November 6, 1918, Children's Bureau Archives, Box 47, 4-16-4-1. Dorothy's correspondence at the National Archives totals more than one thousand pages.

290. DRM's response, April 26, 1919, Children's Bureau Archives Box, 95, 8-6-2-2-3.

291. DRM's response October 10, 1919, Children's Bureau Archives, Box 95, 8-6-2-2-3.

292. Dorothy R. Mendenhall, "Child Welfare and the Milk Problem." *The Child (London)* 9 (1918): 54–56.

293. Dorothy Reed Mendenhall, *Milk: The Indispensable Food for Children*, Children's Bureau Publication No. 35 (Washington, DC: US Government Printing Office, 1918), 6.

294. Mendenhall, 6.

295. Mendenhall Papers, Box 2, Folder 4, Section I pt. 3, 11.

296. Mendenhall Papers, Box 2, Folder 4, Section I pt. 3, 18.

297. Mendenhall Papers, Box 2, Folder 4, Section I pt. 3, 14.

298. Dorothy Reed Mendenhall, "Work of the Extension Department in Educating the Mother along the Lines of Prenatal Care and Infant Hygiene Report on Obstetrical Conditions in Country Communities," *Transactions of the Seventh Annual Meeting of the American Association for Study of Infant Mortality* 7 (1916), 217–220.

299. Dorothy Reed Mendenhall, "Nutrition Problems in War Times," *Transactions of the Ninth Annual Meeting of the American Association for Study of Infant Mortality* 9 (1918): 172–177.

300. Dorothy R. Mendenhall, "Conservation of Mothers," *The Survey* (New York: Funk and Wagnalls, August 19, 1916).

301. L. Fischer, *The Health Care of the Growing Child* (New York and London: Funk and Wagnalls, 1916), and C. H. Davis, *Painless Childbirth* (Chicago: Forbes Publishing Company, 1916).

302. Mendenhall, August 19, 1916.

303. Mendenhall Papers, Box 2, Folder 4, Section I pt. 3, 21.

304. Mendenhall Papers, Box 2, Folder 4, Section I pt. 3, 22.

305. Mendenhall Papers, Box 2, Folder 4, Section I pt. 3, 23.

306. Mendenhall Papers, Box 2, Folder 4, Section I pt. 3, 32.

307. Mendenhall Papers, Box 2, Folder 4, Section I pt. 2, 7.

308. Children's Bureau, *Child Care and Child Welfare: Outlines for Study*, Publication No, 90, (Washington, DC: US Government Printing Office, 1921). Dorothy also wrote Outlines 2, 3, 4, and 5 of Section II, "Development, General and Feeding of the Child," as well as part of Outline 5 of Section III, "Safeguarding the Health of the Child."

309. *Children's Bureau, Minimum Standards of Prenatal Care, Folder No. 1* (Washington, DC: US Government Printing Office, 1923).

310. Dorothy Reed Mendenhall. *What Is Happening to Mothers and Babies in the District of Columbia?* (Washington, DC: US Government Printing Office, 1928).

311. Grace L. Meigs, "*Maternal Mortality from All Conditions Connected with Childbirth in the United States and Certain other Countries, Children's Bureau Publication, No. 17* (Washington, DC: US Government Printing Office, 1917).

312. Lindenmeyer, 77; and Committee on Labor Hearings on *The Hygiene of Maternity and Infancy*, House of Representatives, 65th Cong., 3rd. sess., H. R. 12834 (Washington, DC: US Government Printing Office, 1919), 28–33.

313. Children's Bureau, *What Builds Babies.* Folder No. 4 (Washington, DC: US Government Printing Office, 1925).

Chapter Twelve

314. Mendenhall Papers, Box 1, Folder 6, Section B, 16.

315. Dorothy R. Mendenhall, Course 66 A: Child Care: Hygiene of Maternity and Infancy (Department of Home Economics, University of Wisconsin).

316. Dorothy R. Mendenhall, Course: Modern Parenthood (Home Economics Department, University of Wisconsin); also given at University of Chicago.

317. Dorothy Reed Mendenhall, Course 7, Assignment I, "The Prospective Mother" (Home Economics Department, University Extension Division,

University of Wisconsin) and Mendenhall Papers, Box 2, Section I, Folder 4 pt. 1, 12.

318. Mendenhall Papers, Box 2, Folder 4, Section I pt. 1, 7.

319. Dorothy Reed Mendenhall. *Minimum Standards for the Child Health Center.* Children's Bureau publication No. 90, (Washington, DC: US Government Printing Office, 1919), and Mendenhall Papers, Box 2, Folder 4, Section I pt. 2, 9.

320. Signé Cooper (registered nurse), personal communication.

321. Mendenhall Papers, Box 2, Folder 4, Section I pt. I, 11.

322. Mendenhall Papers, Box 2, Folder 4, Section I pt. 2, 12.

323. *Wisconsin State Journal* (December 12, 1916; December 20, 1916; December 23, 1916). *Madison Democrat* (December 20, 1916).

324. Dorothy Reed Mendenhall, "Madison and its Pre-School Day," *Child Health Magazine* (January 1925): 20–23.

325. Dorothy Reed Mendenhall, "Preventive Feeding for Mothers and Infants," *Journal of Home Economics* 16 (1924): 570–578.

326. J. H. Van Vleck, "Biographical Memoir of Charles Elwood Mendenhall 1872–1935," *National Academy of Sciences Biographical Memoirs* 18 (1937): 1–22.

327. Richard Unsworth, personal communication.

328. Mendenhall Papers, Box 2, Folder 6, Section J pt. 2, 6.

329. John Talcott Mendenhall, personal communication.

330. It is not clear from Dorothy's account whether TC paid the bill personally or if the money came from his trust fund.

331. Mendenhall Papers, Box 2, Folder 6, Section J pt. 2, 6.

332. Mendenhall Papers, Box 2, Folder 6, Section J pt. 2, 8.

333. "Louisa K. Fast," obituary notice, *Ohio Voter* (March/April 1980), published by League of Women Voters of Ohio. Class of 1898 records, Louisa K. Fast Biographical File, Box 1564, Smith College Archives.

334. The hospital, the second oldest in Paris, was the first to house patients individually in beds. Situated on Rue des Saints-Pères, it was demolished in 1935 to make way for the Faculté de Médecine.

335. DRM to Thomas C. Mendenhall, February 24, 1924.

336. DRM to Thomas C. Mendenhall, September 10 or 18, 1926.

337. DRM to Thomas C. Mendenhall, October 2, 1926.

338. DRM to Thomas C. Mendenhall, October 10, 1926.

339. DRM to Thomas C. Mendenhall, November 26, 1926.

340. Thomas C. Mendenhall, Rolle, Switzerland, to DRM, May 30, 1925, Mendenhall Papers, Box 12.

341. Florence Sherbon, in discussion of Grace L. Meigs, "Rural Obstetrics," *American Association for Study and Prevention of Infant Mortality* (Seventh Annual Meeting, 1917): 63.

342. Mendenhall Papers, Box 2, Folder 6, Section J pt. 2, 17.

343. Letter from DRM, Göttingen, Germany, June 7, 1926, to Miss Abbott, Children's Bureau, Washington, DC; Mendenhall Papers, Box 2, Folder 6, Section J pt. 2, *following* p. 18.

344. Dorothy Reed Mendenhall, *Midwifery in Denmark* (Washington, DC: US Government Printing Office, 1929).

345. Mendenhall Papers, Box 2, Folder 6, Section J pt. 2, 21.

346. Mendenhall Papers, Box 2, Folder 6, Section J pt. 2, 22.

347. Wilson. *Upstate* 115, and Mendenhall Papers, Box 1, Folder 13, Section E, 5.

348. Nellie Mendenhall, personal communication.

349. Wilson, *Upstate* 113.

350. Emily H. Earley, *Walrus Club History 1911–1991* (unpublished).

351. Delmar Woodburn, personal communication, 2003.

352. Gertrude Slaughter. *Only the Past Is Ours: The Life Story of Gertrude Slaughter* (New York: Exposition Press, 1963), 107.

353. Mendenhall Papers, Box 2, Folder 2, Section H, 37.

354. Mendenhall Papers, Box 2, Folder 2, Section H, 44.

355. Mendenhall Papers, Box 2, Folder 2, Section H, 45.

356. Mendenhall Papers, Box 2, Folder 2, Section H, 45.

357. Mendenhall Papers, Box 2, Folder 6, Section J pt. 2, 28.

358. Mendenhall Papers, Box 2, Folder 2, Section H, pt. 2, 52.

CHAPTER THIRTEEN

359. Honorary degree citation. *Smith Alumnae Quarterly* 21 (July 1930): 462.

360. Mendenhall Papers, Box 2, Folder 2, Section H pt. 2, 56.

361. Mendenhall Papers, Box 2, Folder 2, Section H pt. 2, 56.

362. Mendenhall Papers, Box 2, Folder 2, Section H pt. 2, 57.

363. Mendenhall Papers, Box 2, Folder 2, Section H pt. 2, 57–58.
364. DRM to Thomas C. Mendenhall, April 5, 1933. This and the following correspondence between Dorothy and Thomas Mendenhall were at the home of John Talcott Mendenhall, Middleton, Wisconsin, and are now with his daughter, Dory Blobner, in Waunakee, Wisconsin.
365. DRM to Thomas C. Mendenhall, January 3, 1933.
366. DRM to Thomas C. Mendenhall, February 6, 1933.
367. DRM to Thomas C. Mendenhall, February 13, 1933.
368. DRM to Thomas C. Mendenhall, March 23, 1933.
369. DRM to Thomas C. Mendenhall, April 13, 1933.
370. DRM to Thomas C. Mendenhall, March 23, 1933.
371. DRM to Thomas C. Mendenhall, March 23, 1933.
372. DRM to Thomas C. Mendenhall, March 23, 1933.
373. DRM to Thomas C. Mendenhall, September 27, 1933.
374. P. D. McMaster and M. Heidelberger. "Biographical Memoir of Florence Rena Sabin, 1871–1953," *National Academy of Sciences Biographical Memoirs* 34 (1960): 272–311.
375. DRM to Thomas C. Mendenhall, September 27, 1933.
376. DRM to Thomas C. Mendenhall, October 12, 1933.
377. Winston S. Churchill. *The Second World War*, 3rd ed., (London: Cassell Co., 1950), vol. l, *The Gathering Storm*, 77.
378. DRM to Thomas C. Mendenhall, October 2, 1933.
379. DRM to Thomas C. Mendenhall, October 25, 1933.
380. DRM to Thomas C. Mendenhall, November 21, 1933.
381. DRM to Thomas C. Mendenhall, January 22, 1934.
382. DRM to Thomas C. Mendenhall, February 28, 1934.
383. DRM to Thomas C. Mendenhall, March 30, 1934.
384. DRM to Thomas C. Mendenhall, March 7, 1934.
385. DRM to Thomas C. Mendenhall, April 11, 1934.
386. DRM to Thomas C. Mendenhall, June 11, 1934.
387. Mendenhall Papers, Box 2, Folder 2, Section H pt. 2, 59.
388. Mendenhall Papers, Box 2, Folder 2, Section H pt. 2, 63.
389. DRM to Thomas C. Mendenhall, April 11, 1934.

390. DRM to Thomas C. Mendenhall, July 22, 1934.

391. DRM to Thomas C. Mendenhall, August 7, 1934.

392. DRM to Thomas C. Mendenhall, August 28, 1934.

393. Mendenhall Papers, Box 2, Folder 2, Section H pt. 2, 61.

394. Charles E. Mendenhall, Arthur S. Eve and David A. Keys. *College Physics* (New York: D. C. Heath, 1935).

395. DRM to Thomas C. Mendenhall, September 20, 1934.

396. DRM to Thomas C. Mendenhall, September 20, 1934.

397. Mary Austin. *Can Prayer Be Answered?* (New York: Farrar and Reinhardt, 1934, chapter 2), quoted in DRM to TCM, September 27, 1934 [This is a summary of Reinhardt's views rather than a direct quotation].

398. DRM to Thomas C. Mendenhall, October 4, 1934.

399. DRM to Thomas C. Mendenhall, October 4, 1934.

400. DRM to Thomas C. Mendenhall October 15, 1934.

401. C. A. Elvehjem, W. H. Petersen and Dorothy Reed Mendenhall, "Hemoglobin Content of the Blood of Infants," *American Journal of Diseases of Children* 46 (1933): 105-112; C. A. Elvehjem, Arlyle Siemers and Dorothy Reed Mendenhall, "Effect of Iron and Copper Therapy on the Hemoglobin Content of Blood of Infants," *American Journal of Diseases of Children* 50 (1935): 28-35; C.A. Elvehjem, Dorothy Duckles and Dorothy. Reed Mendenhall, "Iron Versus Iron and Copper in the Treatment of Anemia in Infants," *American Journal of Diseases of Children* 53 (1937): 785-793.

402. DRM to Thomas C. Mendenhall, November 23, 1934.

403. DRM to Thomas C. Mendenhall, November, 1934 (day omitted from letter).

404. DRM to Thomas C. Mendenhall, February 21, 1935.

405. DRM to Thomas C. Mendenhall, February 21, 1935.

406. March 14. DRM to Thomas C. Mendenhall, February 21, 1935.

407. DRM to Thomas C. Mendenhall, March 27, 1935.

408. DRM to Thomas C. Mendenhall, March 21, 1935.

409. DRM to Thomas C. Mendenhall, March 21, 1935.

410. DRM to Thomas C. Mendenhall, March 27, 1935.

411. DRM to Thomas C. Mendenhall, March 27, 1935.

412. DRM to Thomas C. Mendenhall, June 4, 1935.

413. DRM to Thomas C. Mendenhall, April 28, 1935.
414. DRM to Thomas C. Mendenhall, May 26, 1935.
415. Mendenhall Papers, Box 2, Folder 2, Section H pt. 2, 65.
416. Mendenhall Papers, Box 2, Folder 2, Section H pt. 2, 66.
417. Mendenhall Papers, Box 2, Folder 2, Section H pt. 2, 66.
418. *The Meditations of Marcus Aurelius*, trans. Jeremy Collier (New York: F. A Stokes, 1889), Book IX, 145.
419. Mendenhall Papers at the home of John T. Mendenhall.
420. S. R., Ingersoll. Mendenhall Papers at the home of John T. Mendenhall.
421. Louisa K. Fast to D.R. Mendenhall, August 20, 1935, Mendenhall Papers at the home of John T. Mendenhall.
422. D. R. Mendenhall, undated, Mendenhall Papers at the home of John T. Mendenhall. For biographical details of Charles Mendenhall, see: J.H. Van Vleck, "Charles Elwood Mendenhall 1872-1935," *National Academy of Sciences of the United States: Biographical Memoirs* 18 (1937): 1-22.

EPILOGUE

423. Mendenhall Papers, Box 2, Folder 2, Section H pt. 2, 70.
424. Mendenhall Papers. Box 2, Folder 2, Section H pt. 2, 70.
425. Mendenhall Papers, Box 2, Folder 2, Section H pt. 2, 70.
426. Mendenhall Papers, Box 2, Folder 2, Section H pt. 2, 7.
427. Mendenhall Papers, Box 2, Folder 2, Section H pt. 2, 71.
428. Mendenhall Papers, Box 2, Folder 10, Section K, 2
429. Mendenhall Papers, Box 2, Folder 10, Section K, 2.
430. A.E. Housman. "A Shropshire Lad," in *The Collected Poems of A. E. Housman* (New York: Henry Holt, 1945): 74.
431. Mendenhall Papers, Box 2, Folder 7, Section J pt. 1, 11.
432. Mendenhall Papers, Box 2, Folder 7, Section J pt. 1, 13.
433. Mendenhall Papers, Box 2, Folder 7, Section J pt. 1, 15.
434. Mendenhall Papers, Box 2, Folder 7, Section J pt. 1, 16.
435. Nellie Mendenhall, personal communication.
436. Nellie Mendenhall, personal communication.
437. Nellie Mendenhall and daughter Nealy Small, personal communications.
438. John T. Mendenhall, MD, personal communication.

439. Mendenhall Papers, Box 2, Folder 10, Section K, 1.

440. William G. MacCallum, MD, to DRM, Nov. 17, 1941.

441. William G. MacCallum,. Obituary. *New York Times.* 4 February 1944. For the author's discovery in 2001of this clipping, see Peter J. Dawson, "Whatever Happened to Dorothy Reed?" *Annals of Diagnostic Pathology* 7 (2003): 195–203. Prior to this time, Kate Weigand and other staff members of the Sophia Smith Collection suspected AJ's identity but could not prove it.

442. Jeremy Collier translated from the Latin, *Meditations of Marcus Aurelius.* Book 2, paragraphs 3, 25.

443. E. W. Horning. *The Complete Short Stories of Raffles—The Amateur Cracksman* (New York: St. Martin's, 1984), 475. Dorothy omitted the periods between the initials except in her posthumous comment.

444. Arnold R. Rich, MacCallum's successor at Hopkins, has written a sympathetic appreciation of his former chief: "William George MacCallum, M.D. 1974," *Archives of Pathology* 38 (1944): 182–185. Reprinted with some additions in *Bulletin of The Johns Hopkins Hospital* 75 (1944): 73–80, and Wiley D. Forbus, "William George MacCallum 1874–1944," *Journal of Pathology and Bacteriology* 56 (1944): 603–607.

445. William G. MacCallum. *A Textbook of Pathology* (Philadelphia: Saunders, 1916), 791–796, and 7th ed. (1941), 922–929.

446. D. R. Mendenhall Memoirs, Box 2, Folder 10, Section K, 7.

447. D. R. Mendenhall Memoirs, Box 2, Folder 4, Section I, pt. 1.

448. Alice Hamilton. *Exploring the Dangerous Trades* (Boston: Little Brown & Co., 1943), 253.

449. Betty Cass. "Madison Day by Day," *Wisconsin State Journal* (undated).

450. D. R. Mendenhall. "Madison and Its Pre-School Day," *Child Health Magazine* (January 1925): 20–23.

451. Mendenhall Papers, Box 2, Folder 10, Section K, 6.

452. Mendenhall Papers, Box 1, Folder 18, Section G, 19.

453. Mary Cremmen. "Women's Education More Vital than Men's, Says Smith Head," *Boston Globe* (November 4, 1959).

454. Dorothy Reed Mendenhall died in Chester, Connecticut, on July 31, 1964.

Index